Voice of Dissent

THEOPHILUS GOULD STEWARD
(1843-1924) AND BLACK AMERICA

William Seraile

CARLSON
Publishing Inc

BROOKLYN, NEW YORK, 1991

Copyright © 1991 by William Seraile

Library of Congress Cataloging-in-Publication Data
Seraile, William, 1941-
  Voice of dissent : Theophilus Gould Steward (1843-1924) and Black
America / William Seraile.
        p.   cm.
  Includes bibliographical references and index.
  ISBN 0-926019-58-9
  1. Steward, T. G. (Theophilus Gould), 1843-1924 or 5. 2. Afro-
Americans—Biography. 3. African Methodist Episcopal Church-
-Clergy—Biography. 4. Wilberforce College—Biography.
I. Title.
E185.97.S83S47   1991
973.8'092—dc20
[B]   91-38540

Typographic design: Julian Waters

Typeface: Bitstream ITC Galliard

Case design: Alison Lew

Index prepared by Scholars Editorial Services, Inc., Madison, Wisconsin, using NL
Cindex, a scholarly indexing program from the Newberry Library.

Printed on acid-free, 250-year-life paper.

Manufactured in the United States of America.

Contents

List of Illustrations vii
Acknowledgments xi
Preface xiii
Theophilus Steward Family Genealogy xv

I.   The Early Years in New Jersey 1
II.   Missionary to South Carolina 9
III.   Georgia: The Making of a Leader 25
IV.   Delaware and Haiti 43
V.   Brooklyn, 1874-1879 59
VI.   Pennsylvania and Delaware: Time of
        Personal Crisis, 1877-1883 69
VII.   Return to Pennsylvania, 1883-1886 81
VIII. Washington, Baltimore, and the End
        of Itineracy, 1886-1891 93
IX.   Fort Missoula, 1891-1898 111
X.   Spanish-American War and Philippine Pacification 129
XI.   Fort Niobrara and the End of Chaplaincy 147
XII.   Educator and Traveler 157
XIII. The Last Years 175

Notes 183
Bibliography 219
Index 237

List of Illustrations

1. Theophilus Gould Steward, ca. 1891 114

2. Elizabeth Gadsden Steward, ca. 1890 115

3. Susan Smith Steward, ca. 1870 121

4. Theophilus Gould Steward, ca. 1900 140

5. Theophilus Gould Steward, ca. 1920 171

6. The Theophilus Steward Family, 1922 178

To the memory of my mother, Marguerite,
and two brothers, Calvin and Dick

and

To the memory of Garfield W. Steward,
who embodied the activist spirit of T. G. Steward

Acknowledgments

The research and writing of this book covered a period of five years. Numerous people provided assistance. I wish to thank Joan Maynard, Romana Lowe, Anna Steward Bishop, Winona Steward, Gary Steward, Eulalie Steward, Mollie Steward, Frank and Louise Steward, Vincent Terrell, Robert Swan, Robert Morris, David W. Wills, Albert Miller, Louis R. Harlan, and Dale Harger.

I wish to thank the staffs of the Library of Congress, the National Archives, the Brooklyn Historical Society, the Amistad Research Center, the Veterans Administration Office in New York City, the Moorland-Spingarn Research Center, the Schomburg Center for Research in Black Culture, Boston University Mugar Memorial Library, and the Cumberland County Court House in Bridgeton, New Jersey. I am indebted to Boston University for permission to quote from the Monroe Trotter/Guardian Papers and to Harvard University for permission to quote from David W. Wills's "Aspects of Social Thought in the African Methodist Episcopal Church, 1884-1910." Portions of Chapter 5 previously appeared in *Afro-Americans in New York Life & History*.

My good friend Henry Gilfond, a gifted writer, provided me with many enjoyable hours of conversation. He taught me much about writing. I wish to thank Cynthia Merman for copyediting.

The preparation of this book took valuable time away from my family. My wife Janette was there to share the joy of major research finds. Her support during the trying days of research, writing, and editing proved uplifting. My children Garnet and Aden missed opportunities to be with their father. Thank you, children, for your patience. To my son's frequent query, "Dad, is your book finished yet?," the answer, son, is yes.

Finally, I profoundly acknowledge the guiding spirit of Theophilus Gould Steward.

Preface

My interest in Theophilus Gould Steward developed in 1981 when I was researching the life of his second wife, Dr. Susan McKinney-Steward, the first African-American female physician in New York State and the third in the nation.

Theophilus Gould Steward was a major figure in the African Methodist Episcopal Church. He served the itineracy as a pioneer missionary in South Carolina and Georgia during the stormy days of Reconstruction. He pastored churches in Delaware, Philadelphia, Brooklyn, and Washington, D.C., including several years as minister of Metropolitan AME Church in Washington. Steward also visited Haiti in 1873 to revive African Methodism in that troubled land. From 1891 to early 1907, he served his nation and race as a chaplain in Montana, Nebraska, Texas, and with the Twenty-Fifth United States Colored Infantry in the Philippines. The remaining years of his life were devoted to Wilberforce University, where he was a key member of the faculty.

His involvement in the church, the military, and university teaching placed him in the leadership of African Americans. His concern for the development of his race was evident in his numerous published articles and his active membership in the American Negro Academy. Steward was more a creator of ideas than a leader of men. He wrote extensively for the *Christian Recorder* and the *AME Church Review*, organs of the African Methodist Episcopal Church, and was also the author of eight books. He oftentimes engaged in arguments, which earned him a reputation for controversy. It was his argumentative manner that may have cost him the presidency of Wilberforce University in 1884 and a bishopric in 1888.

Steward was well known during his life, particularly in the nineteenth century. But since his death in 1924, he has been relegated to footnotes in the historical account of the rise of African Methodism, despite his major role in the AME itineracy from 1864 to 1891.

In 1985, I published an article on Steward. I thought about writing a book on his life, but was hesitant; it was not known whether his personal correspondence or diaries existed. Fortunately, in early 1987, Ramona Lowe, a Harlem resident interested in Theophilus Steward, suggested that I contact Anna Steward Bishop, the granddaughter of Theophilus. Not only did Mrs. Bishop express enthusiasm for my project, she invited me to go through three large boxes of journals, diaries, and family letters.

The Steward papers are rich in theological history, but shed very little light on his personal relationships. His diaries, letters, and journals, while illuminating, cover only portions of his life. Some of his papers were destroyed in a house fire. His published autobiography, *From 1864 to 1914: Fifty Years in the Gospel*, ignored many important personal and professional incidents and events. For these reasons, I chose to write a general biography.

Steward's contributions to the church, the military, and his race have been obscured for too long. The purpose of this book is to bring him back to a prominence that he richly deserves.

Theophilus Steward Family Genealogy

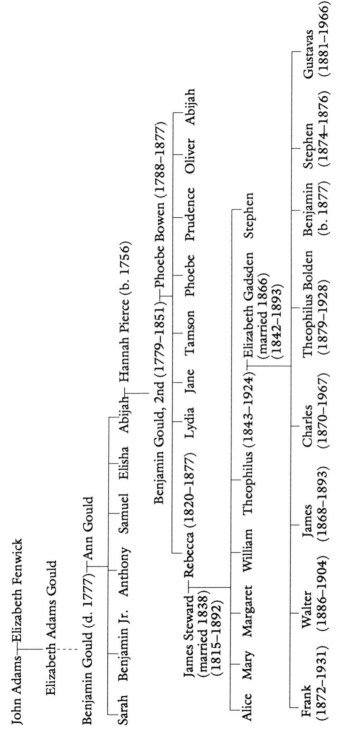

Voice of Dissent

ONE

The Early Years
in New Jersey

The Gouldtown cemetery in South New Jersey resembles most small-town graveyards, with its tombstones predating this nation's independence. Here the progeny of Elizabeth Adams, the white granddaughter of Lord John Fenwick, and Benjamin Gould, an African, rest.

Fenwick, who served in Oliver Cromwell's army, arrived in the colony in 1675 accompanied by three daughters, their husbands, and three grandchildren. Eight years later nineteen-year-old Elizabeth expressed her love for Gould. Fenwick was outraged: "He hath been ye ruin." For not renouncing her love for "that black," Elizabeth was denied in her grandfather's will five hundred acres of land in Cumberland County, New Jersey. At least racial bigotry had not yet evolved to the point where it was legal to castrate any slave who attempted to or had sexual intercourse with a white woman.[1]

Family tradition has it that Elizabeth eventually received her inheritance. On this marshy, sandy land, until 1908, would live nine generations or twelve hundred direct descendants of the daring couple. Among them was Theophilus Gould Steward, who throughout his life struggled with the issues of color and race.[2]

For a century the descendants of Elizabeth and Benjamin kept to themselves on the Gouldtown property near the city of Bridgeton (then named Bridgetown). Like biblical figures they begat among themselves. Some offspring died in infancy and others, the subject of whispers about "bad blood," died of strange maladies. Yet many lived for fourscore years or more. Around 1800, two mulattoes, John and Peter Pierce, arrived from the Caribbean and soon after married two Dutch women. They founded the settlement of Piercetown, located on the other side of the tracks from Gouldtown. Over the years the Goulds and Pierces intermarried. Occasionally someone would marry a white person and remain in the Gouldtown

1

settlement; others would intermarry and leave the area to pass into white society. These marriages and the wedding of a Gould to a Pierce, Murray, Lee, or Cuff kept the settlement populated by fair-skinned and nearly white looking yeomen.[3]

Although Gouldtown was the best known of the black New Jersey settlements, it was not the only one. Other settlements had names mindful of the residents' African heritage: Guineatown in Camden County, Timbuctoo in Burlington County, Skunk Hollow, Saddletown, Springtown, and Snowhill (known as Lawnside after 1887). Unlike Gouldtown, Springtown and Snowhill were established by a mixture of runaway and manumitted slaves. The residents were darker in complexion than their counterparts at Gouldtown, and as former fugitives they willingly accepted migrants from Delaware, Maryland, Virginia, the Carolinas, Georgia, and Florida who came in search of a better economic life. Similar conditions led to the development of an all-black community in Westchester County, New York, known as "the Hills." This settlement, established in the late colonial period, lasted until the early twentieth century, when economic conditions dispersed the inhabitants. During the 1820s North Carolina Quaker slaveholders, compelled by religious orders to manumit their slaves, relocated the freedmen to Indiana and Ohio, where over the years runaways via the Underground Railroad added to their numbers.[4]

Numerous strangers from the South passed through Cumberland County, but few received a welcome reception in Gouldtown. Word soon circulated that those high yellow people did not care for dark-skinned travelers. The distance between Gouldtown and Springtown was about ten miles, but a "tacitly drawn color line . . . separated the social life of the two communities."[5]

Isolating themselves, the Gouldtown residents turned to church and family for spiritual and emotional support. The sandy land didn't provide them with much, but they were rich in nonmaterial ways. They were honest people who prized physical and moral strength. The Goulds believed that luck might provide men with material comforts, but life's ultimate rewards came from fearing God. They encouraged their children to live according to the Ten Commandments. Their homes were cold, their food plain, and sanitation was almost nonexistent. Family historians stressed the residents' love of literature. They were familiar with English history, Robert Burns's poetry, Milton, Shakespeare, *Pilgrim's Progress*, and *Robinson Crusoe*. Highly prized was Baxter's *Saints' Rest*.[6] Why were these poor people so attracted to the books usually found in the elegant libraries of the gentry? Their poverty was due to geographical bad luck, not to any laziness. It was not a sin to be a victim of circumstance. God rewarded men of faith, but man's mind was a gift from Him that needed to be developed to its utmost.

This is the legacy that Theophilus Gould Steward inherited when he was born on April 17, 1843. His parents, James Steward and Rebecca Gould Steward, would produce six children—Stephen, William, Alice, Margaret, Mary, and Theophilus. Neither parent was a practicing Christian at the time of their marriage in December 1838. His parents joined the Gouldtown African Methodist Episcopal Church on October 12, 1846.[7]

The Stewards provided their children with a rich legacy of righteous living that shaped their characters. James Steward was born in New Jersey in 1815. His mother and father emigrated to Haiti in 1824 and were never heard from again. Young James, an orphan, became a bound boy, indentured to a man who treated him so severely that he ran away almost immediately. Elijah Gould and his family took pity on him and brought him into their home. At age fifteen, he was apprenticed to a blacksmith. His early harsh life taught James to be determined. His will, according to Theophilus, was iron. James, a typical stoic nineteenth-century father, tolerated neither laziness nor complaints about hard work.

In 1858, fifteen-year-old Theophilus was sent by his father to work in what the boy called "the swamp." His chore was to cut the marshland grass that was used as animal bedding or as a protective nighttime cover for strawberries. Young Theophilus complained that the biting insects made the task too hard. Some fathers would have thrashed their sons for this impudence, but James secured for Theophilus the job of waiter aboard a coastal steamer. The unfamiliar chores, the constant supervision, and the lack of free time made the job unbearable. Six days after departing Gouldtown, Theophilus returned home with the wisdom that marshland grass was greener. "I never got a cent for my time on the boat," he wrote over sixty years later.[8]

His father taught him the ways of men: how to till the land, hunt in the woods, and provide for a family. It was Rebecca Steward who tempered James' sternness with affection. She encouraged Theophilus to be inquisitive, to challenge the "established truths," and to keep the "love of learning briskly burning all the time." Rebecca, daughter of Benjamin and Phoebe (Bowen) Gould, acquired her love of reading from her father, who believed that girls should be just as educated as boys. Poor like her neighbors, Rebecca attended school for only a few months a year, the rest of the time working in the fields and cleaning and cooking for others. The family home was crowded—one room shared by all eleven family members. Like James, she "learned quite early the stern realities of life."[9]

Despite this humble background, Rebecca was a voracious reader of Milton, Shakespeare, and the Greek philosophers. Her knowledge of the Bible was thorough, but filled with a healthy skepticism. This set her apart from many others in Gouldtown. Rebecca encouraged her children, especially Theophilus, who she considered was given to the Lord from birth, to question the meaning of orthodox religion and its relationship to the faithful. She did not cater to irrelevant religious observances, a practice that her son would adopt. Theophilus recalled in 1877, after his mother's death, that "religion, not even in its forms, was forced upon the children but on the contrary it was so attractive, that the children . . . would crowd around [her] . . . and tease her to tell a story." Usually, he noted, it was a biblical story. In her spare time, Rebecca wrote penetrating analyses of theology, which caused a minister to declare, "her writing will give her a rank in the future that scarcely one minister . . . in a thousand will get."[10]

Not all the children in Gouldtown had mothers who could regale them with theological lessons, but many parents provided their offspring with biblical stories to supplement their formal religious instruction. And in addition to teaching morality, the Sunday school provided the rudiments of writing and reading.

Throughout the North, Sunday schools were important places of learning for both children and adults. Poverty and lack of free time prevented many from attending day school. In addition, black children couldn't attend the white public schools. Finally white philanthropists cooperated with African-American charity societies to establish private schools for black youth. This led in the District of Columbia, for example, to the establishment of forty private schools between 1807 and 1862, when Congress enacted a law for the formation of public schools for Negroes.[11]

Despite the assertion of *Freedom's Journal* in 1827 that its readers "awake from this lethargy . . . and make a concentrated effort for the education of our youth," poor funding, white hostility, and small concentrated urban populations made it difficult to establish high schools for the race. A notable exception was Philadelphia's Institute for Colored Youth. Established in 1852 by Quakers and led by the spirit of Fanny Jackson Coppin, ICY offered a solid academic base in science, the classics, Latin, and higher mathematics. Over the years, hundreds of teachers trained by the school spread their knowledge throughout the nation. Of course, many children did not attend high school.

But they could still learn from the educational forums established by benevolent, fraternal, political, and literary societies.[12]

This variety of institutions underscored the African Americans' interest in controlling the entire business of education, from teacher hiring to curriculum development. This led some to reject the integrated schools provided by state law. Power and control meant much to people whose color and race denied them access to nearly every facet of American society. As educational historian Vincent P. Franklin declared, "the general belief of . . . white[s] . . . in the innate inferiority of blacks determined not only the social status of Africans in American society, but also the amount and type of schooling made available to blacks at public expense."[13]

For Theophilus and the other children of rural Gouldtown, schooling was pragmatic. Their teachers were mainly white men hired without examination or license to "keep school" by three trustees who had little knowledge of pedagogy. School was a place to occupy children when they were not needed in the fields or homes. Steward attended school in Bridgeton for less than six months a year, with most of his classmates his thirty-two cousins. The boys learned reading, writing, and mathematics, including geometry and trigonometry. Both Theophilus and Stephen kept workbook solutions to trigonometry problems. Girls learned, in addition, botany and philosophy. Although a friend described his education as "a good English education," and Steward believed that "upon the whole we attended a good public school," the Gouldtown children were not challenged to contemplate life or man's conduct and character. Steward complained that students were not inspired "to advance materially or even intellectually." To fill this void, Theophilus turned to the Gouldtown Literary and Moral Improvement Society for lectures on literature, politics, and philosophy. Steward was a bright boy but sometimes bored with his lessons. He argued with his classmates and occasionally had difficulty with the teachers as he heeded his mother's advice to challenge "established rules."[14]

Neither school nor field occupied all of the children's time. They learned how to butcher hogs and cows, salt pork, corn beef, store apples in the ground, spin cotton, make quilts, set traps in the woods, and a host of other essential skills. This was fine for the majority, who would marry a cousin, raise a family, and live out their lives in this insular land. But it was not enough for young Theophilus.

An incisive mind like Steward's needed to grow. He had no interest in farming. Staying in Gouldtown as a teacher was a possibility, but it would not have satisfied him intellectually. Even as a boy he was easily excited by tales of travel. Once again, his mother encouraged his fantasies. During the Mexican War Steward's maternal grandfather brought home the newspapers and said to his daughter, "come, Becky, come read me the news; let us see what old Santa Anna is doing." Rebecca told Theo about the exploits of soldiers in Mexico and the telling whetted his appetite to travel to that land. He fulfilled this dream in 1906. Another dream was to visit Haiti, the land where his paternal grandmother emigrated to in 1824. He would accomplish that in 1873.[15]

Religion had a major influence on Steward. His mother frequently told him that God chose him at birth to praise his name. She urged him not to approach God halfway, but to *come unto Him and be saved or stay away and be lost.*[16] This powerful message had a profound impact on Theophilus; he was taught to fear the "bad man." The boy never heard the names of God or devil uttered. "They were names too high and awful for us yet to speak," recalled brother William in 1917.[17]

Their father's example of hard work, good manners, and wise selection of friends kept the Steward children from developing bad habits, but it does not fully explain why Theophilus chose the ministry. Several answers were provided by Theophilus, and others can be surmised. Steward revealed in his autobiographical *My First Four Years in the Itineracy* (written in 1868, but not published until 1876), that in December 1860, at age seventeen, he "embraced religion" and joined the AME church. He was informed by a vision to preach. "For nine months I hesitated, until the necessity was laid upon me, and I felt the salvation of my own soul depending upon complying." His anxiety was poignant. "I felt truly the words, 'woe is me if I preach not the Gospel.' " He shared his feelings with his church leader Abijah Gould, who warned him that a minister's life was one of scorn.[18]

A different version of his calling appeared in his 1921 autobiography, *From 1864 to 1914, Fifty Years in the Gospel Ministry.* He revealed that the Rev. Joseph H. Smith helped to lead him to the ministry. After reading Baxter's *Saints' Rest,* he felt "chosen. The clear light of pardon and acceptance came to me on a bright moonlight night as I was walking home from the [church] meeting. . . . I knew then that God owned me as His child." The next day, however, he got into a fight. The incident left him "chagrined, sorry and in spiritual darkness." His mother convinced him that God forgave him and that he could still pursue a ministerial course. "I was saved," he joyously exclaimed.[19]

Other factors contributed to his decision to join the ministry. Prejudice limited opportunities for intelligent black men in the mid-nineteenth century. Few could become attorneys or physicians or own businesses. The ministry, while attracting some mediocre men and, in some instances, incompetent ones, was an avenue that some of the most intelligent and dedicated men of the race traveled. Steward was not unmindful of the crusading spirit of evangelical abolitionists who were seeking to separate the slave from his chains. Finally, Steward, like Alexander Crummell, Henry Highland Garnet, and Bishop Daniel A. Payne, believed it was his duty to uplift the race from ignorance. For Theophilus, laboring on behalf of his race and Christ was a mission that would guide him throughout his life.

Steward was licensed to exhort in April 1862, and he received his preaching license on September 26, 1863. The following year, on June 4, after the Philadelphia Annual Conference examined him on doctrine, discipline, and general information, he became an AME minister on probation. He immediately expressed a desire to go to the South, but he was advised against it because of the Civil War. Instead he was appointed to Macedonia AME Church in South Camden, New Jersey. Steward was hesitant, fearing failure. But the Rev. William Moore provided him with assistance. "I may say," he wrote, "he bore me up by his strong arm as a broad chested experienced swimmer would hold up a child. I shall never repay the debt of gratitude I owe to that great and good man." Steward managed to conduct the church business efficiently, and even added six souls to the church.[20]

The young minister with limited formal education sought to improve himself by embarking on an ambitious but undisciplined daily program: 7-9 a.m., ancient history; 9-10, theology; 10-11, homiletics; 11-12, Fletcher's appeal, etc.; 3-4, composition; 4-5, reading. "No one but a 'boy' unschooled could have conceived a day of seven hours or more spent on books," Steward admitted.[21] With the exception of later formal divinity studies in Philadelphia, Steward's knowledge was achieved through self-study.

Steward's brief assignment at Macedonia was a proving ground. It gave him an opportunity to develop his ministerial and interpersonal skills, which would be honed throughout his many assignments in the AME itineracy. In retrospect, it was lucky that Steward's first assignment was in South Camden, and not the South. Macedonia Church was close enough to Gouldtown that Steward could return home for kind words, love, and emotional support. Now, in early 1865, he was preparing to leave this nurturing environment.

Barely twenty-two years old, he was going to South Carolina to labor for the freedmen and Christ.

TWO

Missionary to South Carolina

The decisive military victories of Union commanders under the leadership of General Ulysses S. Grant led to the defeat of the Confederacy in early 1865. The bloody conflict that pitted brother against brother and slave against master cost this nation 618,000 lives. The addition of the Thirteenth Amendment to the Constitution in December 1865 legally terminated the "peculiar institution," but it was the combined forces of white and colored soldiers that toppled the short-lived Confederate States of America.

Abolitionists rejoiced over their answered prayers. The walls had fallen, but the destruction of the southern infrastructure left the former slaves without homes, food, or work. Farms and plantations were abandoned as slaves sought employment with Union troops or followed the destructive path of generals to the cities that were incapable of providing assistance. A missionary poignantly pleaded to the American Missionary Association for help, "for God is opening a wide door through which millions are soon to go free!"[1]

The response to the plight of the freedmen came from about fifty organizations, secular and religious, black and white. Many freedmen's aid societies sent teachers to the South. They represented a coalition of Boston-based churches that combined transcendentalism with a liberal theology or else they were connected with the American Missionary Association, which was the leader of the evangelical wing. The nonsectarian AMA commissioned only teachers who were members of some evangelical church. Financial support for evangelical Protestant sects benefitted the African Methodist Episcopal Church, two of whose bishops, Daniel A. Payne and Jabez P. Campbell, were AMA trustees.[2]

By the end of 1862, the AMA had several schools in Virginia and at the Sea Islands off the coast of South Carolina.[3] The close friendship of Payne and George Whipple, secretary of the AMA's executive board, proved fortunate for

9

the African Methodists' missionary work in the former confederacy. The AMA sent south any evangelical Protestant who was "dedicated to providing freedmen with both academic instructions and religious training." The AME Church, which was forced to leave South Carolina in 1822 because some of its members were implicated in the Denmark Vesey conspiracy, was happy to have sponsorship for its mission work. On April 27, 1863, the Reverend C. C. Leigh, financial officer of the National Freedmen Aid Association and agent for the Freedmen's Commission, attended the Baltimore Annual Conference of the AME Church. His graphic description of the deplorable condition of fugitive slaves moved the delegates. Urged by Leigh to send two missionaries to Charleston, South Carolina, Bishop Payne, presiding officer of the conference, chose James Lynch and John Hall. In 1864 the AMA proposed to the AME General Conference that if they would furnish buildings for schools and board for teachers, their organization would assist with salaries. Bishop Payne urged the membership to accept the offer and to send to their southern brethren educated ministers who were "thoroughly sanctified unto God." Enthusiastic about the possibility of reestablishing African Methodism in South Carolina, the delegates agreed. The war made it impossible for mission work to begin until April 1865. On May 9, 1865, Payne wrote to the AMA executive committee requesting that they pay one-half of the salaries of AME missionaries. The AMA agreed. Clara De Boer argues that the AMA's dedication to brotherhood created a climate that attracted more black teachers than any other white organization. The AMA allowed all evangelical Christians to send through them their own teachers, ministers, and missionaries to teach and develop churches "according to their own denominational forms and doctrinal belief."[4] The AME church aggressively capitalized on the fairness of the American Missionary Association.

Bishop Payne had the awesome decision of selecting missionaries for the important trip to South Carolina. They had to be men of strong moral character, good health, and a willingness to endure hardship. Payne chose James A. Handy, James H. A. Johnson, and Theophilus Gould Steward. Two of Steward's brothers-in-law had been killed in the war. Perhaps he wanted to go south to labor among the freedmen to sanctify their sacrifice. Steward's family were abolitionists who fought hard for equal rights; his brother and two other relatives would soon found the New Jersey Equal Rights League while he was in South Carolina. He was taught to be of service to his fellow man. What greater service could a man provide than to work among those so desperately in need of uplifting? On May 9, from New York City, the four men boarded the government transport *Arago* bound for Hilton Head, South Carolina.[5]

Serving the Lord inspired many others to labor among the former slaves. This was particularly true of African Americans, who believed that religious faith destroyed slavery and that a just Holy Father would through their instrumentality lift the veil of ignorance from their southern brethren. Clara Duncan stated in her application to the AMA that she was prepared to give up everything, "even life for the good of the cause, and count it not a hardship but an honor." Nathan T. Condol, a student at Oberlin College, traveled to Mississippi as an AMA teacher. He declared in his application, "I am called upon by the Supreme Being working within, to go immediately South and work in His vineyard."[6] Hundreds of others expressed similar sentiments.

Doing God's work excited the quartet as the sight of Charleston appeared before them on May 13. None was more thrilled than Payne, who had been banished from that city thirty years earlier for teaching his people to read.[7] Charleston was ravished by war. Emotions were raw, as many whites resented the occupying presence of the Fifty-fifth Massachusetts Colored U.S. Regiment. The city was a place of little business; grass was growing in the streets. Steward observed, "what a scourge war is. Who can number or estimate its evil?" Several months later, a visitor described Charleston as "full of country negroes" who faced acute poverty.[8]

The missionaries started their first full day in the city with a sunrise prayer meeting followed by a 10:00 a.m. service in which Steward delivered the sermon. A huge hollow cone was suspended over the pulpit, reminding Steward of a " 'dead fall' to entrap the preacher." Later that same day he witnessed Richard H. Cain administer the Lord's Supper at Old Bethel Church. The act astonished the congregation—"never had a Negro dared to do a deed so glaringly defiant."[9]

Cain's action was a signal that the old associate membership whereby slaves sat in the rear or the balcony, known as Nigger Heaven, was no longer acceptable. The freedmen left the white churches in droves. To its credit, the Methodist Episcopal Church, South, recognizing in August 1865 that the exodus was irreversible, told its ministers, "if they elect to leave us, let them go with the assurance that we . . . continue to be their friend." The effect was monumental. On the eve of the war, 42,000 black Methodists worshiped in South Carolina's biracial churches; only 600 remained a decade later. In 1859 there were 4,246 blacks in Charleston's four Methodist Episcopal churches;

not one was in attendance in 1866. Throughout the South, approximately 240,000 would leave to join the AME church.[10]

The African Methodists benefitted tremendously from the assistance of the Church, South. The southern Methodists opposed the efforts of the Church, North's to proselytize among former slaves. This opposition was rooted in the 1844 schism between the two branches over the slavery issue. Secretary of the Army Edwin C. Stanton's wartime decision permitting northern Methodists to take over "disloyal" churches in Union-occupied areas led to bitter property disputes between the two factions. The AME allied itself with the Church, South to undermine northern Methodism. For a while the African Methodists hoped to obtain title to slave-built churches under Church, South control. That hope was shattered in 1870, when the titles were transferred to the newly organized Colored Methodist Episcopal Church. Angered, the AME church sought alliance with the northern Methodists to stop the "machinations" of the Church, South.[11]

Having eliminated competition from both branches of Methodism, the African Methodists now found their stiffest competition for the freedmen coming from black Baptists who were decentralized and more democratic in structure than their rival. Baptist preachers heard the "calling" to take the pulpit; the emotionality of their services appealed to the Africanness of many. Nevertheless, the African Methodists were able to expand rapidly. From May 15 to May 22, 1865, fewer than a dozen men attended the first Annual South Carolina Conference at Zion Presbyterian Church in Charleston. Within months the conference would embrace four thousand souls in South Carolina, North Carolina, and the coastal islands of Georgia.[12]

Both the Baptists and the African Methodists attracted the freedmen. As the Reverend Benjamin T. Tanner noted, *"blood is always more potent than money."* The freedmen were able to find in the black church "an asylum from the blasphemous and degrading spirit of caste."[13]

The AME missionaries were successful because they made extraordinary efforts to recruit their brethren. The secret to their success was due in part to the church's willingness to promote young ministers. On May 16, 1865, three days after arriving in South Carolina, Steward and James H. A. Johnson were examined for both deacon's orders and elders' orders. Two days later they were ordained to the diaconate. As Johnson recalled in 1889, "there was no time for experiments, or for the observances of the technical forms of [church] law. The delicate work . . . could not be entrusted to disqualified hands or restricted licentiates."[14]

The handful of missionaries prayed for success and then departed for their assignments to bring lightness where darkness prevailed. Steward was assigned to the Beaufort River circuit, which included Beaufort City, Halfway House, Ladies' Island, and St. Helena Island. He and his colleagues departed Charleston on May 26 aboard the *Loyalist* for Hilton Head.[15] Theophilus Steward arrived in Beaufort on May 27, eager to bring freedmen into civilization and a loftier Christianity.

Recent studies of the factors motivating teachers have challenged earlier views of northern teachers as arrogant meddlers, misguided zealots, or crazy abolitionists or the recent description of them as "soldiers of light and love." Linda Perkins's examination of black female AMA teachers suggests that white upper- and middle-class women ventured south to escape cultural oppression that defined femininity as devotion to family and home. In contrast, her examination of the hundreds of applications submitted to the AMA by African-American women revealed that many stressed racial uplift as their reason for wanting to work in a hostile South. Ronald Butchart's study of African-American teachers in the southern schools indicates that white teachers from New York rarely harbored abolitionist sentiments. Instead, many were guilty of practicing accommodationism and paternalism. Fourteen percent of black teachers from New York were abolitionists, a figure that far surpassed that of white teachers. The African-American teachers attended abolitionist meetings, contributed financially to abolitionist causes, or submitted antislavery essays to abolitionist journals. While Butchart's study is a preliminary one, it clearly indicates that blacks did not go to the South for the same reasons that attracted whites.[16]

On June 18 Steward commenced his pastoral work. He chose for his first sermon "I seek my brethren," because it had been used successfully by Bishop Alexander W. Wayman. He told the congregation that they were *all* bound together by slavery; the slaveholder's prejudice was no different from the bias of northern bigots. In a voice pregnant with hope, he implored, "will you receive me . . ., or, will you like Joseph's brethren sell me to the Ishmaelites? Will you stand by me . . . or will you flee from me and say, 'we desire no knowledge of your ways.' I'm at your mercy. You can support me or starve me. But I trust you. I believe you will not leave nor forsake me while I shall be able to present you an upright character."[17] This plaintive plea was one that few white missionaries could exclaim. The sharing of pain and humiliation contributed to the bonding of former slaves and freemen from the North.

Black teachers were a disadvantaged group. Their salaries were less than those of whites, and women received less pay than men. The American Freedmen's Union Commission paid teachers between $20 and $30 a month. The AMA paid $15 to $25, depending on gender. Others paid similarly. African-American teachers, even experienced ones, went south despite the financial hardship. Matilda C. Anderson, a resident of Brooklyn, New York, wrote to the AMA in 1864, "if my circumstances should allow me to do so, I would heartily engage in this work without compensation. But being poor . . . I regret that I cannot serve from motives of pure benevolence." She requested an adequate salary. Edmonia G. Highgate, an experienced teacher, wrote to the AMA, "I am willingly making some sacrafice [sic] by leaving a situation that yields me twice the salary which I hope for my new field." Hazikiah Hunter stressed the duty of the race in his 1865 application: "I believe we that are competent owe it to *our* people to teach them as our specialty."[18]

Steward's reference to starvation was more than rhetorical—food supplies in the immediate postwar years were inadequate. Letters poured in to the AMA and the Freedmen's Bureau requesting aid. Brevet Major General R. K. Scott, assistant commissioner of the bureau, indicated in an 1867 report that more educated freedmen would teach if meals were provided. He described how a native African, fluent in ten languages, the Greek Testament, and the Koran, was laboring as a field hand and teaching in the evening. He would teach full time to eighty children if his food were guaranteed.[19]

Others wanted adequate and *regular* salary to have the wherewithal to purchase their own food. H. H. Hunter, a South Carolina teacher, wrote the AMA in desperation: "Sir, you will please be so kind as to forward . . . some money by next steamer as we are about moneyless." W. T. Richardson informed George Whipple, corresponding secretary of the AMA executive committee, that teachers came out to South Carolina without knowing what their salaries would be. "They are anxious to know the am[ount] they are to receive this season. *Please inform them*," he implored. Mary Still, a teacher in Beaufort, South Carolina, had a schedule that included household duties until 2:00 p.m. and teaching until 9:00 p.m. She complained, "I am allowing myself three dollars a week for board; as low as I can get along with. I do wish my salary raised."[20]

The AME teachers/missionaries fared no better. Although the AMA promised to pay one-half of the salaries of teachers sent out by the AME church, funds still had not arrived after several months. On July 6, 1865,

Bishop Payne requested from George Whipple funds for eleven missionaries. He asked for $700 annually for those stationed in Charleston, Savannah, Beaufort, Hilton Head, and the North Carolina cities of Wilmington and Raleigh. "The others," like Steward, "who are on circuit which covers many plantations will need about $500 each for support." Evidently Payne was asking for both salary and board because Thomas Cardoza, superintendent of AMA schools in Charleston, received at this time $492 plus board.[21]

The AMA was severely challenged to provide funds. There were seventy-six teachers (twenty-four of them black) in South Carolina by the end of 1865 who were on the AMA payroll. By June 1, 1866, the number had increased to 148. It cost $72,000 to operate the state's seventy-five schools. The AMA hoped in late 1865 to raise $250,000 from Congregational churches, the major religious group supporting the organization, to assist the freedmen. They managed to raise $225,000. In South Carolina, from June 30, 1865 to June 30, 1866, the AMA spent nearly $73,000 to educate 9,017 pupils, with another $71,000 allocated for teachers' salaries. This was similar to the nearly $158,000 spent on goods and cash disbursed to the freedmen in southern areas under AMA's auspices from September 30, 1864 to September 30, 1865.[22]

Steward was troubled by his financial uncertainty. He wrote in July 1865 to Whipple, indicating that he came to South Carolina with Payne and that even though his salary was not stated, he believed that one-half was due from the AMA. Whipple responded on July 25, "you are right in the part we assume of your support. We shall remember you with interest as we see you toiling." Although he was listed as one of the teacher/missionaries in South Carolina in the AMA executive committee's report for 1865, Steward never received any funding from them. His name was not in the 1866 report.[23]

Adding to Steward's pain of being insolvent was the indifference shown to him by the AME church. On July 28, 1865, he left for New Jersey, a victim of what fellow missionary Mary Still described as "the two great heats, the sun and the fire." Weakened by fever, he arrived in New York City "greatly emaciated and shaken with chills." Desperately ill and in need of money, he wrote on August 1 from Camden, New Jersey, to George Whipple, "I have had but little except my daily bread since I left home. I am really *poor*." Despite Whipple's July 25 letter to Steward, someone endorsed this letter, "I find this letter in my file at this late date with no explanation. I do not know in what capacity he went South, whether with any agreement from us (I can find none) nor how long, and with what he labored there."[24]

15

Steward took to his bed for fifteen days. His concerned mother roused him from a stupor and asked him if he was dying. "I remember now," he wrote fifty years later, "the full consciousness and full assurance with which I answered: my work is not done."[25] This profound faith was shared by others who ventured forth to assist the freedmen. They believed that they were God's instrument to bring civilization and the Scriptures to those who had been chained to ignorance for so long.

On September 1, weakened but determined to return to his station, Steward traveled to Washington to secure military permission for reentry into South Carolina. He also hoped to obtain funds from the AME missionary society, as he had received only $13 since May. In Washington, Steward and Reverend A. L. Stanford preached in various churches and raised $200 for the mission field. None of this money went toward Steward's salary. Instead, it was used to pay the traveling expenses of the society's membership. "I was mystified, mortified, and worst of all," complained the missionary, "I had no money." Bishop Payne gave Stanford a letter to take to the missionary society's leader in Baltimore. Coincidentally, Steward was at the minister's home when Stanford arrived. Asked to decipher Payne's nearly illegible writing, Steward gleefully "read in his ear . . . a peremptory order to honor our claims at once."[26]

In early November Steward departed from New York aboard the *Empire City*. Not certain of continued funding, he wrote to Whipple on November 10 asking if he was to receive anything from them. Despite his money worries, he lent some money to a soldier aboard ship. This act of charity left him nearly insolvent and he arrived in Charleston on November 13 with only one dollar to pay to "get my trunk up to my stopping place." He had no prospects of funding, but his faith was rewarded when he received a fee for conducting a wedding.[27]

Steward was assigned to Summerville, twenty-two miles north of Charleston in pine tree country. The poor community had only fifty houses, four stores, and three churches. He was in a strange community, recently recovered from a debilitating fever, and minister to a congregation that was "one day's rations ahead of starvation." He was dejected. He rejected free boarding with a married teacher because he did not want to accept her charity. He pleaded with the readership of the *Christian Recorder* to support the southern missionaries.[28]

Five weeks after arriving in Summerville, he pawned his watch and committed "the heinous offence of abandoning [his] work." Steward returned to Charleston, where there was neither work nor money. At this point he could have quit and begged for funds to return to New Jersey. Instead he decided to marry Elizabeth Gadsden, whom he had known for only six weeks. He was impressed with this grocery store cashier, a year his senior, whose "neatness of dress, reposeful countenance and ease of manners gave assurance . . . of genuine womanhood." The Reverend Richard H. Cain married them on January 1, 1866, in the home of his wife's mother. Years later, looking back on his times in South Carolina, he declared that the trying experience was well repaid by his marriage to a woman whose "heart and mind [gave] to [their] sons . . . elements of character."[29]

Steward's motto was "pick up the pieces" and go forward. He could not return to New Jersey believing that he failed in South Carolina. Instead he took the risk of taking a wife without any means of supporting her. Even he knew that this action would "call forth . . . censure." It appears that the couple lived off her modest income for several months until he received assistance from the Reverend B. F. Whittenmore, an army chaplain and a superintendent of education, who represented the New England branch of the Freedmen's Aid Society. Both Stewards were appointed teachers on April 2, 1866, to Marion, South Carolina, under the auspices of the American Freedmen's Aid Commission Eastern Department.[30]

Steward was able to obtain assistance because in addition to his own outstanding credentials, the intense competition between the various freedmen's aid societies created teaching jobs. But this competition also invoked a cooperative effort to lift the veil of ignorance that flourished during slavery. Regardless of the secular or religious nature of these organizations, they all believed that the freedmen needed black role models. For example, the Unitarians were not popular with the freedmen in South Carolina, but they cooperated with the African Methodists by establishing freedmen's libraries throughout the state to assist the AME teachers. It was important that the black teachers were intellectually prepared, for as William Steward, Theophilus's brother and an AMA teacher in Americus, Georgia, noted, only the "truly good and educated of ourselves" can bring the freedmen "into the light of higher civilization and a loftier Christianity."[31]

Theophilus Steward found Marion a comfortable station that allowed him to prosper in a good church. He had good relationships with whites, two of whom even donated land and lumber for a church. This was significant; other whites had burned down the previous church. Some whites, thinking that he was a Catholic priest, asked him to exorcise a house supposedly haunted by the recent gunshot death of a man. A white woman asked him to teach her to read the Bible. A white convict waiting for execution requested that Steward pray with him.[32] Similar interracial experiences were commented on by William Steward, who said that the whites in Americus treated him kindly and with "utmost equality. In no case among them have I been treated as a colored man." These positive encounters do not suggest that racial bias was nonexistent. One woman in Americus called William Steward a "low down Yankee" who was "passing off for a Negro."[33] The Stewards' light complexion gave them advantage with both races. Whites generally considered fair-skinned blacks more intelligent than full-featured Africans. Fair complexion helped to identify the social elite in the African-American communities of Charleston, New Orleans, Savannah, and other southern cities.[34]

Whites justified slavery, in part, by insisting that white was the badge of freedom and black was the badge of inferiority. The Civil War did not eradicate this sentiment. Clara De Boer has stated that the AMA was color-blind in its treatment of teachers. This view has been challenged by Linda Perkins's study of five black female teachers who went to Virginia in 1863 and 1864. They were housed separately from white teachers. Clara Duncan, a light-skinned woman, was refused meal service en route to Virginia in 1864 and was referred to as a "nigger wench" and relegated to a separate compartment aboard the steamer. It is clear from teachers' reports from South Carolina and Georgia that the AMA teachers were segregated in school assignments: white and black teachers taught black students, but white northerners did not teach white southerners, and white and black teachers did not teach together in the same schools.[35] All of the African-American teachers who labored in the South, despite any friendships with individual whites, had to be cautious. Whites used physical and psychological intimidation against them. Throughout Reconstruction, beatings, burning of schoolhouses, and verbal threats made it difficult for many northerners to live free from fear. The commitment of these teachers and ministers who spent three or more years in the South was a testament to their devotion to helping the former slaves.

Despite the potential of violence to his body or spirit, Steward worked hard to educate the freedmen of Marion. When he first opened his school to one hundred students, children and adults, only two, both servants of a military officer, knew the alphabet. Six months later nearly all could read and most could write.[36] The usual curriculum consisted of reading, writing, arithmetic, history, geography, and the practical subjects of civics, politics, home economics, and vocational training plus an inculcation of middle-class values.[37]

Some teachers, however, sought to expose students to a more rigorous offering. William Steward proposed that students in Americus study French, German, vocal music, and algebra in addition to the above mentioned.

Theophilus Steward was also making great strides in bringing African Methodism to Marion. In early 1866 Richard H. Cain informed the *Christian Recorder* that the church was making rapid progress in the South Carolina city "under Rev. Theophilus G. Steward, with a fine prospect of a large flourishing congregation." Theophilus worked hard to earn the respect of the people. He was, as his brother William declared, "lawyer, doctor, scribe, and general director, bookkeeper . . . moral adviser, Sabbath school teacher, and lecturer." William Steward's school in Americus, Georgia, had neither desks nor any school apparatus. A Beaufort teacher informed the AMA that "we are greatly annoyed . . . for want of books. The Boston society had not agreed to bear their share of the expense and let the New York society do the furnishing. It seems to us a pity that we teachers should be left without books for our schools while societies are bickering about such things."[38]

All these men and women who came to the south endured deprivations. Cain's call for missionaries who could point out to the freedmen "the duties of social life and family responsibilities" aptly described what Steward was achieving in Marion. The freedmen, only months out of bondage, had to be taught "how to *live like freemen*," declared Cain. Or, as William Steward suggested, missionaries and teachers were needed who had "true piety" and who wanted to make their leadership a necessity. If deprivations were a test of a race's moral fabric, then the South needed more "colored teachers . . . whose moral and religious reputation will bear any test," suggested Sallie Daffin, an AMA teacher in Arlington, Virginia.[39]

Testing determined one's mettle. Will one harden oneself to the challenge or will one quit? Shortly after arriving in South Carolina, Steward met a woman from his home state who would not cooperate with him because she felt he did not meet her standards for mission work. He resented her attitude and ignored her demands on his time. Having the ear of Payne, she created such a word imagery of Steward's petulance that Payne wrote a letter to Theophilus "surcharged with exhortations, pathetic enough to make one's flesh creep." The criticism unnerved Steward, who responded, "to be doing your best and at the same time receiving exhortations to do more by one who certainly cannot *know* what you are doing, is very trying." The problem, according to Steward, was the "abnormal mind of an ancient unmarried lady." The incident so disturbed him that he admitted that he was not adapted to the rough work of the ministry. Throughout his ministerial career he would be accused of being uncooperative, a "quitter," and a self-centered person who wanted always to be right. His response to this episode was to view himself as a martyr. He vowed to remain in the ministry and not to be defeated.[40]

For twenty-five years, Steward and Payne would often come to intellectual blows over theological questions. But it was Cain who clashed with Steward. Cain, southern born but northern raised, was nearly twenty years older than Steward. He was superintendent of the Southern Division with charge of the Charleston mission. The South Carolina Conference that met in Savannah from May 14 to 23, 1866, reassigned Steward from Marion to the Morris Street mission in Charleston. He was unhappy with the decision because he had brought two hundred members into his Marion church during one month alone. He believed that Cain had persuaded Payne to remove him from Marion. In his journal he wrote, "success attended me but my course gave offense to R.H.C. and I was removed." What was his offense? "I did not recognize two of his ladies which caused much trouble to them and much choler to him." He elaborated in his autobiography: "I was . . . moved, through the instigation of the irrepressible 'R.H.' " He complained that he was assigned to Charleston where Cain could keep him under control. Instead of taking immediate charge of the mission, he went home to New Jersey in the late spring, returning to Charleston on September 1.[41]

While he was home, the upset minister lashed out at the church for its nonsupport of the missionaries. He wrote the *Christian Recorder* on August 13 asking, "Has Our Church a Missionary Society?" He complained that he had to sell his watch and books and turn to the Freedmen's Aid Society for assistance because the church had turned its back on him. He intimated that he would probably have to "sell quack medicines and 'pin ballads' " to have money for his return trip. "All say, too," he wrote, "that I must educate myself, and buy books . . . yet I do not possess . . . a dictionary . . . nor the means to buy one." He urged the church to support the missionaries to help "the evangelization of a race."[42]

Steward's comments were brash, direct, and uncompromising. They stung the Reverend John M. Brown, corresponding secretary of the Parent Home and Foreign Missionary Society. He responded in the *Christian Recorder* with ammunition to humble the young missionary. He attacked Steward for not filing a report, without which Brown could not honor Steward's claim. But wanting to assist Steward, Brown put Steward's request before the executive committee. A member intimated that Steward was receiving $60 a month.

Since others were more destitute, there was no pressing need to act on his application. Questioning Steward's devotion to the ministry, Brown lectured the missionary: "I have worked my passage from Louisville to New Orleans on the boat because I had no money. I did not wait and complain," he emphasized. Adding more weight to his blows, Brown suggested that Steward and others emulate former missionary James Lynch, then editor of the *Christian Recorder*, and "work with their hands, plan with their heads, trust in God and go forward." Brown concluded his barrage of advice by urging readers to ignore fault-finders like Steward. Despite Brown's admonition, the AME church had a serious problem in financing the southern missionaries. Richard H. Cain, one of the pillars of the mission field, complained that unless they had funding the missionaries in the interior would starve, as the crops were poor. "Help! help! brethren," he pleaded, "or we suffer."[43]

Dissatisfied but not defeated, Steward returned to Charleston in early September 1866. Back in Cain country, Steward took charge of the Morris Street mission and circumstances forced Steward and Cain to share the parsonage. Ironically, Bishop Alexander W. Wayman visited the city and found the two "living comfortably together." "It made me think," he wrote, "of what David said: 'how pleasant it is for brethren to dwell together in unity.' " Steward's contact with Cain was probably limited to official church duties. He had his wife for social companionship. Typically, in this assignment and in later ones, Steward worked earnestly to build up the congregation. Wayman visited Steward's church on February 17, 1867, and described the early morning service's singing "like that of the Jews when returning to Zion." The afternoon service was described by the bishop as "fine" and "brother Steward has a pleasant field of labor."[44] This favorable comment would later take on significance when Cain denounced Steward's ministerial abilities.

Cain was a powerful early figure in the AME church. Later, that honor would be bestowed on Steward. But Cain during the mid-1860s was, as described by Wayman, "the great iron wheel in South Carolina" who built churches and an old folks' home. "He is indeed a great commander-in-chief," added Wayman. It was Cain's insistence that subordinates had to obey his decisions that deeply disturbed the sensitive Steward. He noted that he had to "bury my individuality and sacrifice my identity and content myself with clinging to R. H. [Cain] as the branch to the vine. This position is contrary to my *constitution*."[45]

Cain was so taken aback with Steward's insubordination that in late summer 1869, two years after Steward had left the state, the two publicly aired their differences. On August 14, an article appeared in the *Missionary Journal*, edited by Cain, claiming that Steward "refused to give his time and talents to the education of the youth . . . and for these causes the wisdom of the bishop removed him." Steward accused Cain of writing "vile slander." He warned his elder "that the least said about my sojourn in Charleston, the better, as I have the documents . . . to bring actions to light that are not creditable to men in high ecclesiastical position."[46]

Steward was like a wounded animal striking out to protect himself from further pain, but he had a formidable foe in Cain, who had been elected a bishop in 1868. Cain accused Steward of misstating the facts. He claimed that he wrote that Steward had "moved the school out of the church and *rented a room, and set up a school on his account.*" He attacked Steward for refusing "to give his time and *talents* to the education of the [church] youth . . . *unless it paid him better.*" He further insisted that Steward refused to teach school in the church because it was under Cain's control as presiding elder. Ripping into the younger man, Cain castigated Steward for being hardly the equal and certainly not the superior of any church official, but "he dare to crack his whip of insolence over our heads." He criticized Steward's "missionary work *as one of the most successful failures of all ministers of our church.*" Wanting to humiliate his nemesis, Cain added, "every man of Southern birth, has done better, and has been more successful than he has in raising congregations, and in building up our church."

The angry bishop was expressing both regional and color chauvinism. Cain was labeling Steward a carpetbagger who did not belong in the southern ministry. Cain was much darker in complexion; his features were very African. There is no evidence that Steward ever used his northern birth or fair color to lord it over others. But Cain's bitterness caused him to exaggerate Steward's shortcomings. He accused him of being a chronic complainer "because he did not receive large amounts of salary for his most imperfect work."[47] The scathing attack undoubtedly angered Steward, but any response is unknown (there are missing issues of the *Christian Recorder* for several weeks following Cain's accusations). Like many other unpleasant incidents in his life, Steward did not write about this fight in his autobiography. Ironically, years later, in 1887, the funeral service of Cain was held in Washington's Metropolitan AME Church. The pastor was Theophilus Gould Steward.

Cain correctly assessed Steward's obsession with money. This concern would cause him problems with church officials for several decades. But contrary to Cain's assertion, Steward was a diligent church worker who consistently built up congregations wherever he was assigned. His preaching and organizational skills were praised both by the *Christian Recorder* and fellow ministers. In 1867 the church paper commended him for ordering weekly twenty-five copies of the newspaper for sale to his congregation.[48] Steward felt that his revival at the Morris Street Church was successful. "The church," he wrote, "seems to be enveloped in a flame of divine love. Oh.! I cannot express how dearly I love the work in this field. The husbandman has only to thrust in the sickle and reap. Ah! the Lord is truly building up Zion again in these lands."[49] Others commented on Steward's abilities. Bishop Alexander W. Wayman described Steward's congregation as a large one.[50] A church historian described Steward as one of the "trailblazer[s]" who "penetrated the South Atlantic States, leaving . . . a burning torch to guide those who might follow in the same holy cause."[51] The Reverend Benjamin T. Tanner noted that *"they* [Cain and Steward] *are both doing great work."*[52]

Steward not only made contributions to the development of African Methodism in the South, but he also used his astute powers of observation to comment on the freedmen's baptism in freedom. In July 1865, only two months after arriving in South Carolina, Steward informed the *Christian Recorder* and the AMA that too many wanted to stereotype the former slaves as either lazy animals or paragons of morality. "They are," he wrote, "neither all intelligent, moral and religious nor all stupid, lazy and dishonest but are like any other community of men in this Christian country." He noticed that although slavery had degraded some, others, such as house servants, had a head start on the intellectual march. Steward had great expectations of the freedmen, in whom he recognized a burning hunger for education. His willingness to accept the freedmen as people, not stereotypes, made it easier for him to accept them as his brethren rather than objects to uplift. He accepted and appreciated much that the ex-slaves had to offer. The freedmen in South Carolina held on to African cultural traits, such as strong religious emotionalism. Steward had a powerful mental picture fifty years later of a woman singing in the woods, "ah, sinner! ain't you tired a sinnin'? Yes, my Lord. Gwine to join the hand with the angels. Dark clouds a rising! Thunder bolts a bustin'. Master Jesus comes a ridin' by with a rainbow on his shoulder."[53]

Steward did not dismiss this unique expression of God's acceptance. Instead, he openly accepted the power of this music, which helped him to understand and communicate with the victims of American greed and brutality. He identified with the freedmen's faith. Listening to a visiting preacher say, "trust the Lord and do good; so thou shalt dwell in the land; and verily thou shalt be fed," Steward indicated that the minister was "bringing the message of the Lord directly to me and my wife [who had] neither bread, money, nor home."[54]

It was the spring of 1867 and he had no funds. Disregarding his own advice to his congregation to avoid gambling, Steward had invested in a joint stock printing company, which went bust. He had no home after Cain criticized him at conference. Fortunately, the South Carolina Conference had organized new conferences in Florida and Georgia. It was to the conference in Georgia that Steward would go, strengthened in his faith that he went with the protection of his Lord. Although he was only twenty-four years old, and despite Cain's allegations, he was a rising figure in the African Methodist Episcopal church. In Georgia he would labor to build the church amid some of the most important events of Reconstruction.

THREE

Georgia: The Making of a Leader

Inspired by the words of the visiting preacher to trust in God for deliverance, Theophilus left Elizabeth in Charleston and went to Macon to help organize the Georgia conference. His limited traveling funds were augmented by assistance from the Reverend Moses B. Salter whom Steward had previously befriended. When he arrived in Augusta, the Reverend Charles L. Bradwell's charity helped him to reach his destination.[1]

Before leaving Augusta, Steward preached in a Baptist church on the subject of the unity of the Christian family. His sermon was not well received by the host pastor, who said, "no union could ever take place until all come to the Baptists." If the African Methodists believed that the freedmen should reject other Methodists for their church, black Baptists believed that they should be the denomination of choice among the African race. Steward, who did not hold orthodox religious views, replied exasperatedly, "take away bigoted preachers and the church would flow together so far as to embrace in its practice an open communion and interchange of pulpits." Do this, he added, "and a sameness of doctrine must inevitably follow." Hardly anyone in the AME church subscribed to this message. This bold inclusiveness was characteristic of Steward; he would in later years write numerous essays and several books outlining in detail his liberal understanding of theology.[2]

Notwithstanding his call for a nonsectarian pulpit, Steward worked hard to establish AME churches in Georgia. He and his fellow missionaries were able to spread the gospel rapidly in the South because the bishops took the radical approach of ordaining the "old leaders" to go out and preach. The fact that so many of these "old leaders" were, like Steward, under the age of thirty, affirmed the church's willingness to entrust the youth with the responsibility to fish for men. Steward and others met in Macon on May 30 to ordain those preachers who were unable to attend the recent South Carolina conference.

The next day, the Georgia conference appointed Steward to Lumpkin, the county seat of Stewart County, a corn and cotton area in the Macon district.[3]

Low in funds but strong in faith, the Stewards departed Charleston on June 27 aboard the steamer *Fannie* for Savannah. The highlight of their brief trip was meeting Robert Smalls, the Civil War hero, who brought a Confederate vessel to the Union's navy. After a brief sojourn in Savannah, the couple arrived in Macon on July 3. Independence Day was boycotted by the white southerners. Throughout Reconstruction the freedmen would jubilantly celebrate July 4 and Emancipation Day as their special holidays.[4]

On July 5 the Stewards took a train from Macon to Cuthbert. Nothing but blind faith compelled them to depart. Theophilus gave the conductor all his cash, including some noncurrent silver. Only the kindness of the conductor allowed them to remain on the train. Cuthbert was the end of the line, but it was still twenty-five miles from Lumpkin. They had no money, no food, and no idea of how they would reach their assignment. Fortunately, they met a friend who lived in Cuthbert, and he arranged passage for them in an open wagon. Lumpkin would be a pleasant place for the young couple. It was in the center of a fine agricultural area. At least they were guaranteed an adequate food supply, not an insignificant concern as food was scarce or very expensive in many parts of the South.[5]

Lumpkin and, later, Macon would test Steward's mettle as a religious and community leader. His involvement in church building, political activism, education, and interracial and intraracial cooperation and conflict would represent in microcosm the plight of the freedmen as the volatile Reconstruction years propelled Georgia on a path that had been unimaginable before the war. The freedmen adamantly wanted their own churches, free from the paternalism of white preachers. At tremendous sacrifice, they built their own churches, took over those abandoned by former masters, worshiped in all types of temporary facilities, or negotiated to acquire legal rights to the churches that they had built before emancipation but were now under the control of white Methodists or Baptists. Two weeks after his arrival, Steward started a school and made arrangements to move a church that had been purchased before his coming. Steward organized the congregation to dismantle and remove the building to its new lot. The Reverend Thomas Crayton, the church's former minister, resented the newcomer's authority and put up a fuss. But Steward efficiently mobilized men, women, and children to raise money for windows, roof, and shingles. On August 25 the congregation worshiped for the first time in its own church.[6]

Steward's ministerial duties required him to bring the Scriptures to the communities of Box Angle and Hard Money. He and his wife operated a day school for a modest tuition of fifty cents a month. Few could consistently make even that small payment, but no one was denied. In an average month, the couple might collect $2 above their actual teaching expenses. Years later he initiated a court case when he learned that Georgia's poor laws would pay the children's tuition. He had kept exact records over the years, detailing the names, attendance records, and accounts of his students. His attorney had no difficulty convincing the court to award payment of these accounts. The financially hard-pressed minister received the money at a time when he was pastoring a small northern church that was unable to provide him with support.[7]

The freedmen made tremendous sacrifices to obtain an education for themselves and their children. Some southern whites were not especially opposed to educating the freedmen, but many were adverse to the introduction of northerners and radicalism. Sarah H. Champney, an AMA teacher who labored in several Georgia cities, noted that before her arrival in Cuthbert whites connived the freedmen into allowing whites to be involved in their educational association. They told them that they had always lived together and that they knew them better than did the northerners. One freedman, who was away, came home and convinced the others to leave the association. "That association *did not* amount to anything," wrote Champney. In Bainbridge, Georgia, local whites sought to lure freedmen to a white school. The freedmen were not interested in having the old planter class or its sympathizers instruct them. Many concurred with the three trustees of a school in Brunswick, Georgia, who praised the AMA teachers who "gained the affection of our people by their great interest in our welfare and understanding our wants and necessities."[8]

Steward had comforts in Lumpkin, but no money; most of his funds had been spent to move the church. Once again, he turned to the AMA. On November 6, 1867, he sought to impress John A. Rockwell in a letter stating that he was "the only colored man in the county with a passable education." He declared that the AME church could not sustain his financial needs but he was unable to leave it because he "was reared at its alters." He asked for a moderate salary until the Lumpkin educational association was able to provide a salary from students' tuition. He reminded Rockwell that aid given to him would uplift "the mental moral and religious improvement of the colored people" for whom he had brought "an understanding heart." Steward sought to meet the AMA's goal of using education to elevate the ex-slaves "to the high plane of Christian civilization."[9]

The AMA was overwhelmed by its inability to pay salaries on time to hundreds of teachers. Steward's request was ignored. Four months later, on March 2, 1868, he contacted Brevet Brigadier General C. C. Sibley, assistant commissioner of the Bureau of Refugees, Freedmen and Abandoned Lands for Georgia, for a salary of $50 a month (he managed to receive $25 a month).[10]

Schools in the Macon area were chaotic. The Reverend Hiram Eddy, an AMA teacher, described teaching in the city as one of confusion caused by "the numbers, the work, the eagerness, the profound ignorance." Yet he, like others, was moved to tears by the freedmen's eagerness to acquire knowledge. Steward faced these same discouragements but he had faith in his brethren that others failed to see. Some white teachers were blinded by the squalor they saw around them and concluded that the environment "must degrade them both morally and physically." Steward did not adopt this paternalistic view. In the fall of 1867 he gave in Lumpkin a concert and exhibition that he claimed was the first ever given by the race in that part of Georgia. He aimed to improve race relations by lecturing on the unity of the races. Later, in Macon during the summer of 1868, he established the Turner Lyceum (named in recognition of the religious and political contribution of Henry M. Turner, AME bishop and Reconstruction politician) with eighteen members. He organized a series of debates aimed at the freedmen's political consciousness. The topics included "Is the Negro inferior to the white man?" "Should the colored people emigrate to Liberia?" "Is money preferable to education?" and "Ought the state provide for the education of the children within its borders?"[11]

These were timely topics that reflected to a large degree concerns or interests of Steward. Like others, he strongly opposed the American Colonization Society's efforts to encourage emigration to Liberia. He suggested that the white supporters of black emigration wanted to maintain white supremacy. "I have no patience," he wrote, "with these white men that are continuing thinking, plotting and doing for the Negro." Later his views would have him at odds with Bishop Turner, who supported a back-to-Africa movement during the 1890s. Other communities developed similar forums. The women of the Charleston Sewing Circle organized six lectures in 1865 that included speeches by E. J. Adams, former missionary to Africa; B. F. Randolph, Civil War chaplain and South Carolina politician; Richard H. Cain; and the Reverend J. C. Gibbs, future secretary of state of Florida.[12]

Steward's leadership qualities and superior education brought him to the attention of blacks and whites. Augusta and Savannah had light-skinned elites dating back to prewar days. Color differences between freedmen did not cause the problems in Lumpkin or Macon that prevailed elsewhere in the South.[13] Differences, of course, existed within the African race, but the differences were attributed to personalities, not class structure. Blacks in Lumpkin and Macon liked Steward because he was smart, articulate, and willing to stand up to whites. Steward was an enigma to many whites: his demeanor and intellectual outlook reminded them of a wealthy planter, businessman, or politician, but blacks were supposed to be inferior.

Violence was common in Georgia. A man shot up the pulpit of a Hawkinsville church. A shot was fired into a crowd of radical freedmen in Camilla; the ensuing riot left nine dead and over thirty wounded. In Americus on January 23, 1869, Steward witnessed two freedmen murdered by a "Democrat nigger," a term reserved for low-down white men.[14]

Fortunately, Steward's encounters with whites were generally civil, if not cordial. While his relationships with his own people were friendly, there were a few exceptional incidents. Steward had an air of self-confidence that some misinterpreted as arrogance. In 1867 a woman in Lumpkin accused Steward of considering yellow women his sisters but not dark ones. Coming from Gouldtown, Steward did not have close association with dark-complexioned people, but there is no evidence that he openly discriminated against them. On another occasion, in Macon, an employee of a local proprietor delivered a carpet to Steward's home. Before entering the gate, he inquired of a woman, "does a Methodist pickpocket live here?" The angry man accused Steward of refusing to bury his stepson. He claimed that the minister said, "get some Democrat white man to [bury him] or else pay me and I [will] do it." Steward countered that he and others attended the funeral. He dismissed the man as "the 'nigger' was a Democrat and doubtless a good one."[15]

He replied uncivilly to the man because he was a perfectionist who did not tolerate sloppiness in speech or behavior. Despite his own humble beginnings, he adopted an unfortunate haughtiness toward the lower class. He visited a teacher in Macon and recorded in his journal that "she has a miserable manner in school. [She] is a poor scholar not knowing whether 'is' is a verb or 'preposition.' [She] is very faulty in pronunciation and awful in articulation."[16] His elitism was shared by some of the AMA teachers, who were unwilling to take into account the enormous limitations the freedmen were encumbered with when they were emancipated. Sarah H. Champney, a teacher in Newton, reported that the community's educational association elected as president an ignorant man who did not even understand how to conduct a business meeting. A more progressive observation came from AMA teacher Mary N. Withington, who noted that despite the brutality of slavery the freedmen had a religious worshiping so emotional that she feared she was faithless in comparison.[17]

AME bishop Henry M. Turner understood clearly that this mockery was unchristian. He declared that the critics "do not consider for a moment the dreadful hardships which these people have endured, and especially those who in any way endeavored to acquire an education."[18]

Despite Steward's self-assurance, he was inexperienced in political matters. He had never voted because New Jersey prohibited blacks from exercising the franchise until the enactment of the Fifteenth Amendment in 1870. Although he would later take an active part in local politics in Georgia, he was in 1867 a political novice. Georgia, unlike South Carolina or Mississippi, never saw the emergence of a viable black political group. They did not have a previously recognized elite that could galvanize the people into political action, nor did they have a group of educated people to provide leadership. Less than 1 percent of the African population was free before 1861.[19]

Steward had no political aspirations when he came to the state. But he was by default made an election registrar by the military in Stewart County because he was one of the few blacks who then could read and write.[20] Reconstruction policies prohibited some whites from voting or holding political office because of prior substantial involvement in the military, judiciary, or legislature of the Confederacy. While they were waiting to have their rights restored, they sought to manipulate politics to their advantage. On August 12, 1867, a Mr. Ottenheimer asked Steward to run as a delegate for the state's constitutional convention. Steward saw through the deception, but "took care not to allow them to see that I suspected sinister designs." He was suspicious because only four whites in the entire county were eligible voters. Steward served as one of the managers of elections in the election for delegates to the state convention to draft the new constitution. This brought him to the attention of the Ku Klux Klan.[21]

Steward's freeborn status and isolation in New Jersey did not condition him to accept whites as superior simply because of their complexion. Steward, to his credit, displayed courage. In 1870 he spoke out forcefully against the practice of limiting jury service to whites, which often left black defendants helpless. He boldly declared, "we want a jury on every case where whites and blacks are litigants composed entirely of [both] men." This statement was notable for its emphasis on "we," which clearly showed that his elitism did not divorce him from the freedmen. He also led a successful protest by Americus freedmen against compulsory labor contracts.[22]

His political activities never brought him harm. The same cannot be said about others. Of the sixty-eight African-American men who were either delegates to the constitutional convention or legislators in Georgia from 1868 to 1872, twenty were intimidated by threats, were shot at, had their houses burned, were arrested, jailed, whipped, or visited by the Klan. One was murdered. Tunis Campbell, AME minister and McIntosh County race leader, built a political machine that controlled the county until 1867, when a counterrevolution removed him from office and restored power to the Democrats. He was falsely indicted, convicted, and jailed for a year at hard labor.[23]

The political situation in Georgia during Steward's stay was highlighted by the Democrat-controlled state legislature, which refused to give seats to twenty-five duly elected African Americans. Bishop Henry M. Turner protested his ouster by exclaiming that he would "neither fawn or cringe . . . nor stoop to beg . . . for my rights." Jefferson Long, a member of Steward's Macon church and a tailor, was also victimized by the legislature's machinations. A correspondent of the New York *Herald* in Macon described Long as a "dangerous rioter." "It is a famous lie," Steward wrote in his journal, "as I heard most of this conversation this [reporter] held with . . . Long. Mr. Long, being only moderately informed and passing more honestly than policy expresses himself indiscreetly but he is no blood stirrer." Long's political action cost him dearly: whites, who were his best customers, boycotted his shop. The excluded legislators eventually received their seats in 1869 after numerous protests were mounted.[24] The spring 1868 state elections foreshadowed the decline of race relations after the election of Grant as president. Sensing victory in the fall gubernatorial election, Democrats harassed agricultural workers. An AMA teacher in Milledgeville reported that many lost their jobs.[25]

Steward was an active campaigner for the Grant-Colfax ticket; as treasurer of the Civil and Political Rights Association, he mailed three thousand copies of the *American Union* as campaign documents. The presidential election passed quietly in Macon, but fraud and violence brought fear elsewhere. A visitor from Americus informed Steward that the polls did not open up until noon and half the people were not given time to vote. In Camilla only one freedman voted, as there was a "great deal of bullying." A mob tried to harm an Englishman who served in the Union Army because he attempted to sell a plantation to benefit the former slaves. Steward observed, "Democrats dissatisfied because Grant is elected and Republican because Georgia went Democratic." Soon after the election the Turner Lyceum debated "will the election of Grant prove beneficial to the colored people."[26]

While Grant would have a warm and close relationship with the nation's black population that would culminate in thousands contributing to the erection of the Grant Memorial in New York City, his election in 1868 did not bode well for the freedmen. Sarah H. Champney, who fled Cuthbert because of Klan activity, reported that Grant's inaugural address was read to an attentive audience of freedmen. Yet whites, she added, boasted that they could treat their former slaves anyway they wanted since the state was now back in their hands. Champney recounted the gruesome story of a woman who was stomped because she refused to plow and testily informed the overseer that she was going to hire herself out to another. "I do hope," Champney pleaded, "Grant will establish military law all over [Georgia]."[27]

Steward was extremely concerned that the Democratic victory in Georgia would lead to race baiting. A few days after the election he sat at his desk to record his thoughts. The editor of a Republican paper read the comments and decided to print them as an unsigned editorial, "Georgia: The Situation." Steward spoke harshly about the state's politics. He complained that those who were defeated on the battlefield were now the victors in the political arena. "Treason," he exclaimed, "instead of being made odious is becoming honorable." "Why," he demanded, "are rebels treated as gallant soldiers and allowed to go scott free?" Not sharing Lincoln's concern for "malice towards none," Steward concluded that traitors should be punished. "If the flag cannot protect its defenders let it be taken down . . . and be buried." Incensed by southern machinations, he cried out, "let us have real peace or open war." He called on Grant to "call out and arm a volunteer force . . . to make Georgia healthy."[28]

His involvement in politics reflected his willingness to help the freedmen cope with all aspects of their new status. His intelligence, race consciousness, and thrift made him an ideal cashier in the Macon branch of the Freedmen's Savings Bank. Established by Congress in April 1865, the bank had about forty branches before it fell victim in 1874 to the economic panic of 1873. Steward, who had lectured the former slaves to save money, attended an enthusiastic meeting in Macon on June 15, 1858, for the purpose of establishing a branch there.[29] Steward practiced the biblical injunction to feed the hungry and clothe the naked. People came to him for loans, which some never repaid. "I accommodated them as I usually do," was his Christian response. The cashier's position was nonsalaried, but cashier Steward opened the bank on November 2 with a deposit of $140. Soon after, he lectured his congregation on the value of banking. The freedmen in Macon heeded his advice and provided the bank with a brisk business.[30]

Steward was chafing in his volunteer position. He wrote on January 20, 1869, to Henry M. Turner, manager of the bank, for a salary. Ten days later, not having heard from Turner, he wrote in his journal his decision to quit. He was under pressure to earn money for his family. "My prospect still appears gloomy with regard to money," he wrote. He continued, however, to lend money to people who, in the example of one man, took a year to repay $5. In mid-March the Freedmen's Savings and Trust Company agreed to pay Steward a salary of $700 a year, nearly double his ministerial salary. He drew his first paycheck from the bank on March 22, which enabled him to give money to Elizabeth as well as to retrieve his watch from the pawn shop. "I can now thank the Lord that I am nearly square with the world," he wrote jubilantly.[31]

Steward diligently balanced his duties to the church, school, and bank, but his main objective was to proselytize for the AME church. In this regard, despite Cain's negative assertions, he was one of the bright lights among the pioneering missionaries. He possessed superb organizational skills, particularly for fund-raising. The Ladies Volunteer Association that he organized in Lumpkin raised in November 1867 $25 for the church, which he described as "very good for this little place." Writing under the pen name "A," Steward informed the *Christian Recorder* that his congregation of fewer than one hundred had raised money through concerts and dinners to help defray some of their expenses. He planned for Christmas a grand exhibition. He requested that the church send at least six more ministers to Stewart County, but that they be men "who have become inured to privations and . . . who are not afraid of hard work."[32]

His tenure in Lumpkin ended in March 1868 when the Georgia conference appointed him to the Macon station as presiding elder overseeing nine other ministers. This added responsibility opened up his ministerial career "at once upon a much broader plan." He was just shy of his twenty-fifth birthday but no longer a naive young man. He had experienced much in his nearly three years laboring for the freedmen. He had survived bouts with self-doubt; he had learned to deal with the greed of others as well as to examine himself in the harsh light of a chaotic region undergoing massive social, political, and economic upheaval.[33]

Prior to taking up his charge at Macon, he visited his family in Gouldtown. En route back to Georgia he stopped in Washington to attend the Thirteenth General Conference of the AME church. The events unfolded at the May meeting affected the church for years. The seating of the southern ministers was one of the major issues confronting the membership. Church law prohibited membership to those without at least eight hundred laymen reported at the previous quadrennial meeting. None of the recently formed conferences of South Carolina, Georgia, Virginia, North Carolina, Florida, Arkansas, Texas, Mississippi, Tennessee, or Kentucky was eligible. Henry M. Turner, the leading southern missionary, presented a motion to admit the southerners as delegates with full voting rights. The motion was defeated but the Reverend William Moore persuaded the delegates to admit them. "It was a radical motion," Steward declared, "but the times demanded it." The enfranchised southerners used their voting strength to elect Turner and, later, Cain bishops. The annulment of an old rule that prohibited ministers from writing and publishing without permission benefitted Steward, who would become a prolific interpreter of theological questions. Despite the historical significance of the 1868 meeting, the minutes were never printed.[34]

After conference, the Stewards traveled to Macon, which would be his longest assignment and the one in which he would hone his leadership skills. Indeed, he worked an unbelievable schedule. His day started at 6:30 A.M. and ended most evenings near midnight. No wonder he exclaimed, "how long I can live at this rate I do not know." Once, he overslept to 7 A.M. Truly alarmed, he wrote, "may God forgive me for this indulgence and enable me to rise earlier hereafter." All of this suggests that he was totally devoted to his duties as minister, counselor, teacher, and community activist. He was so absorbed in his responsibilities that he did not record in his journal Elizabeth's pregnancy until the day before she gave birth. On July 28, 1868, he wrote, "wife still sick." His *second* comment for the following day simply stated, "the baby was . . . born yesterday at 12 m. and is a boy."[35]

His leadership skills were tested almost immediately, when he had to contend with dissenters in his church and legally fight the Methodist Episcopal Church, South over the property issue. Were the churches built by slaves the property of the freedmen and their agent, the AME church, or did they belong to the white Methodists? Shortly after arriving in Macon, Steward visited a Mr. Burke of the Church, South to determine if the African Methodists could obtain title to the church they occupied. This building was originally used by the slave members of the Church, South. Burke replied that church law did not authorize a transfer, but since the African Methodists had possession, no court would remove them. Meanwhile, the Methodist Episcopal Church, North was being shut out in its recruitment efforts. The AME church resented the white Methodists proselytizing among the freedmen but wanted the northerners to supply them with financing. Bishop Jabez Campbell argued that his church had "men without means" and it was the duty of the mother church to provide them with the "means."[36] Instead of cooperating, the Church, North fought the African Methodists to gain converts.

The African Methodists aggressively pursued their property claims. As early as October 1865 the Reverend James Lynch declared that "the colored churches of the Methodist Episcopal Church, South, recently organized under [our] jurisdiction . . . are *de facto* the property of colored people." Whereas the southern Methodists magnanimously supported the exodus of the freedmen from their churches, they failed to display the same Christian charity when it came to valuable property. In 1866 the AME church asked that all church property held in trusteeship for black Methodists by the Methodist Episcopal Church "be permanently and peacefully transferred."[37]

Unwilling to leave proselytizing to the black Methodists, the Church, North sought to recruit worshipers from the AME churches. Steward's journal entry for July 7, 1868, revealed, "learned of a conspiracy on foot to draw members from our church." Richard H. Cain argued that agents of the northern Methodists had offered money to entice desertions. Cain asked, "cannot a colored man be just as good a Christian worshipper under a black bishop as under a white one, who has no interest in his race?" Racial identity was a compelling drawing card for the African Methodists. Steward's journal entry for July 12 reads, "at night I preached on the claims of African Methodism to a large congregation and took in about 20 members." He added, "the work is still in progress and we are still hopeful of victory."[38]

The feud between Methodists was recorded nearly daily in Steward's journal. His entry for July 16 exclaimed, "there seems to be imminent danger of a schism in the body here. In the AME family the conservative and progressive elements are growing daily more antagonistic." William Campbell was the leader of the conservatives. Steward went to the dedication and was appalled that two former slaveholders preached, administered the Lord's Supper, and baptized freedmen. He felt such contempt for his race that he angrily declared,

"I am almost sorry that I am a 'nigger.' " On July 21 he complained that the dissension was the "one general topic among the colored Methodists."[39]

Steward's fight with Campbell came to a head on the night of July 31 at a church meeting. His foe demanded to know if he had done anything "to split the church or had done anything to oppose the AME church." No response came, as Steward had earlier instructed the membership not to engage in a confrontation with Campbell. No one stopped Campbell after he heatedly declared that he was leaving Steward's church. Steward dismissed him as one who preferred to "be a white man's servant than a free man." Campbell vowed to hold onto the present Sunday school. Campbell's move was important; it gave him physical control over the property. One church member lamented to Steward, "Bro. Campbell's plan was very wicked . . . there would be no doubt about our losing the property." On August 2 Steward informed the teachers and students of the Campbell-controlled Sunday school of his intentions to organize a new one. Within two days, Steward had organized twenty teachers. The August 5 meeting was full of good spirit. Steward wrote, "the Campbellites seem to have gone to the caves but doubtless they will come again." The schism attracted the attention of Bishop J. M. Brown, who disapproved of Steward's tactics. Nevertheless, his gamble paid off as the people began to desert Campbell and by the end of August his Sunday school ceased to exist.[40]

Steward, flushed with victory, still had to contend with the larger property question. On August 27 the trustees of the Church, South instructed Steward by letter to turn over the church to Campbell. The court advised Steward not to yield. Two days later the AME trustees declined the Church, South's offer to vacate the church in exchange for a refund of the money they paid for the church's insurance. Two nights later a large crowd voted not to surrender the building. Expecting trouble, a parishioner gave his pastor a gun, which Steward accepted because of a recently attempted burglary at his home.[41]

The approach of fall did little to remove heat from the property issue. On September 3, feeling doubtful about his action, Steward polled the congregation at the church's love feast. He received unanimous support to remain strong against the intrusive Methodists. Although the Sunday school was growing—it now had over fifty students—dissension developed as one teacher declined to be involved in the fuss. The man vowed to serve God, not man. Several Sunday school teachers followed.[42]

Steward inadvertently lightened the situation with humor. On September 20 he preached from Malachi 4:2, which describes how God will destroy evildoers. He read also from Judges 15:4-5, which describes Samson tying torches to the tails of three hundred foxes who ran through the olive orchards and grain of the Philistines, burning them. The words were apropos and the congregation, including his wife, loudly laughed. The stoic minister found the effect not bad, but decided that humor was inappropriate in his sermons.[43]

On October 1 a notice to vacate the property was sent to Steward. Mindful of legally losing the building, Steward four days later visited a potential seller of a lot. At the end of the month he received a summons to answer a bill of eviction brought against him by the Southern Methodists. This blow brought forth his stoic response: "such is the split."[44]

As the calendar moved forward to 1869, the M.E. Church, South tightened the screws. Campbell, Steward's nemesis, was now a presiding elder in their colored division. They voted to hold their next conference in Steward's church. Bishop J. M. Brown was "exercised over it," but Steward thought there was little to fear. Still, the trustees advised him to change the locks. Meanwhile, Congressman Benjamin Butler, a former Union general, introduced a bill to give property rights to black congregations that had built prewar churches. On January 20 Steward wrote to Bishop Brown, asking him to try to persuade the South Carolina conference to endorse the bill. On February 11 Steward influenced the Georgia conference to sign a memorial address to Butler urging passage of the bill.[45]

The dispute came to fruition. On February 17 the sheriff demanded the keys to the church. A trustee was sent to Atlanta to consult with the African Methodists' attorney. Steward faced a dilemma. Should he give up possession of the church, stall, or seek an affordable lot? Southern violence solved his vexing problem: arsonists destroyed the church. Steward rashly blamed the fire on the "Democrat niggers."[46]

A lesser person might have lamented his fate, cursed God, or, at least, ranted about racism. But Steward moved forward with dignity, propelled by his faith. The day after the fire he filed an affidavit before the clerk of the Superior Court, declaring that the church belonged to the African Methodists. He tried to obtain use of city hall for services, but court was in session. He continued to look for a lot the church could afford.[47]

The spirited congregation greeted him on February 21 as he conducted services in a temperance hall. One hundred dollars was collected for the building fund. "Our people," he noted, "have the will and where there is a will there is a way." The people had the will because they had in their minister a leader of the first order. Steward did not harp on the tragedy of the arson nor did he wax for hours about racism. Instead, he took his sermon from Ezekiel 37:12-13, where God promises to raise the dead from the grave. Passionately he told his congregation that like Moses he was not Pharaoh's grandson, but his victim. This humble admission clearly identified him with the freedmen. He was not a carpetbagger, but truly one with the former slaves. For him, to suffer for Christ and the freedmen was greater than the promise of Egypt's or Georgia's wealth.[48]

Steward's faith was justified. On March 5 a lot was purchased for $1,000. Steward quickly applied his superb organizational skills honed in Lumpkin toward erecting a new house of worship in Macon. By the end of March the walls were up, and the cornerstone was laid on April 5. Steward proudly informed the *Christian Recorder*, "we are building a mammoth 'Bethel' in Macon."[49]

Although the church was occupied during the winter of 1870, it remained unfinished for years; it was not dedicated until 1883. So pleased were the people of Macon with their minister that to his embarrassment they named the church Steward AME Church. Years later, Steward argued that it constituted "a great risk . . . to name a church after a living man." He was so concerned that in 1874 he persuaded the Philadelphia conference to adopt a resolution disapproving the naming of churches after living men. Modestly, he wrote that the honor placed "him under the gravest obligations to walk worthy of my own high calling. . . . The Lord help me!"[50]

In the midst of the church's erection, Steward had attacked publicly the Church, North. According to him, the northern whites did not appreciate their "cousins" in the South encouraging their black parishioners to turn their eyes toward the African Methodists. In Steward's estimation the northern Methodists viewed the cooperative effort as "socially, morally and . . . politically wrong." Yet, as he observed, the Church, North believed it "gloriously right" to seek alliances with southern whites. Steward accused them of swallowing "the nigger equality . . . where the success of the church entirely depends upon the adhesion of the blacks only . . . but in every other place . . . they receive colored brethren only as *colored brethren*." He condemned the northerners for perpetuating segregated seating and for having white ministers for black worshipers. "Choose white masters or be free," he emphasized. He urged the editor of the *Christian Recorder* to "keep these facts before the people for the benefit of our race."[51]

Steward's color chauvinism was sharply rebuked by Benjamin T. Tanner, editor of the *Christian Recorder*. Tanner declared that the two branches of

Methodism should become friends over the question of the "maltreated Negro," and that they should emulate Jesus who "came to make peace." He called for African Americans to be the glue that would unite the northern and southern white Methodists. "God is our Father, Christ our Redeemer, Wesley our leader," Tanner declared. "Come," he cried, "let us close ranks and have but one army."[52] In later years, Steward and Tanner would clash over the call for a merger between the British Methodist Episcopal Church and the AME Church.[53]

Steward's disdain for the Church, North was extended to the Colored Methodist Episcopal church, which was formed in 1870 from the black wing of the Church, South. It would become the heir to the numerous slave churches held in trusteeship by the Church, South. This was a blow to the AME church, which had proclaimed itself the rightful heir. On May 1 Bishops W. H. Miles and Richard H. Vanderhorst, a former AME minister, asked their rival to consider the unsettled church property question. Seeking religious peace, they declared, "we believe these little questions in law are injurious to our race." Adding that in the past some AME clergymen were hostile, even to the point of prohibiting them from preaching in "our churches that were occupied by your congregations," they asked that their property be turned over without lawsuits. Since the Georgia Supreme Court had already ruled that the church property belonged to the Church, South, which had relinquished its rights to the CME church, AME Bishops Jabez P. Campbell and T. M. D. Ward wrote on March 26, 1873 to CME officials of their willingness to resolve the conflict amicably.[54]

Despite the property dispute setback, the African Methodists were successful recruiters. They had a crop of zealous missionaries who were, Steward suggested, men of "ability, tact and piety" who "came forward to do or die." Steward possessed ability and piety, but at times he lacked tact. He could be pompous and self-serving, but his virtues were towers of strength. Above all, even though he refused to fawn before either Christian dogma or bishops, he loved the church. His vision was one of his greatest assets. In 1869, amid the church property controversy, Steward called for the clergy to "take up the pen." "Have we no authors?" he inquired. He questioned why the church had not written handbooks of theology, children's biblical stories, or other things worthy of an educated ministry. Tanner, an advocate of a scholarly ministry, replied, "there is hope for a church . . . when their leaders" have vision.[55]

Steward at the end of 1868 developed a Sunday school newspaper, "The Sling and the Stone," described by the *Christian Recorder* as "a perfect little gem." In 1870 or 1871 he wrote a theology handbook, *Hand Book of Theology Designed for Young Ministers of the African Methodist Episcopal Church Who Have Not Had the Benefit of a Theological Training and as a Pocket Manual for All Ministers.*[56] The handbook was simple, for two reasons. First, very few of the ministers in the itineracy had formal theological training, a subject of great concern to Bishop Daniel A. Payne. Second, Steward, a decade away from divinity studies at Philadelphia's Protestant Episcopal Divinity School, was not yet well versed enough in theology to provide more than rudimentary knowledge. His handbook defined terms such as *theology*, offered an explanation of why the Bible had both an Old and New Testament, and how it was "a divine revelation" from God.[57]

Woman suffrage in church matters was another example of Steward's visionary approach to altering dogma. During the summer of 1870 he wrote two essays on the controversial subject. He called for the abolition of regulations that established male supremacy. He believed that women as voters would make the church more progressive because they were less stubborn than men and more apt to take positive action. He boldly suggested that if women voted for trustees there would be female trustees. He called for a vote to end the segregated seating by sex.[58] The question of women's rights was a sensitive issue in the AME church and was the source of heated debates throughout the second half of the nineteenth century. In 1844 and 1852 the General Conferences defeated petitions demanding that women be allowed to preach. Bishop Payne trivialized women who had organized an association patterned after the annual conference. "They held together for a brief time, and *then fell to pieces* like a rope of sand," he wrote contemptuously. Although a number of women preached in AME churches, they were not licensed or ordained. In 1884 the issue was drawn at conference as contradictory resolutions licensing women preachers and prohibiting women preachers passed. In 1885 Bishop Henry M. Turner ordained a female preacher and placed her name on the list of male deacons. The reactionary 1888 General Conference reprimanded Turner for his indiscretion. In the secular area, Frederick Douglass was a staunch supporter of woman suffrage. He was selected in 1866 as one of the three vice presidents of the American Equal Rights Association, which advocated black and woman suffrage.[59]

Steward's vision was hewed from his practical experiences in the South. South Carolina was his baptism; Georgia, with all its dangers and tests, was his crucible. His mettle was tested and he was the victor. His organizational skills, which others observed with marvel, were fully developed in the state.

The 1871 Georgia Conference transferred him to Wilmington, Delaware. (He did not know then that he could choose his assignment.) Years later he recalled that he went where he was sent "without thought other than to do the work." Despite this cavalier attitude, he would later challenge the system that transferred ministers.[60]

On April 23, 1871, Steward gave his farewell address to his sad parishioners. He chose for his text John 16:22, "and ye therefore now have sorrow, but I will see you again, and your heart shall rejoice and your joy shall no man take from you."[61] The genuine affection of his congregation suggests that northerners who labored for the freedmen were not all paragons of puritanical virtues who were cold and distant. He had many deep relationships with the Georgia freedmen and even though his value system was different from theirs, he transcended the cultural differences and warmly embraced his brethren as their brother in Christ and racial solidarity.[62]

Some months after leaving Georgia, Steward delivered a speech in Philadelphia that described his missionary experience. He wrote in a draft, "I found the South with not a rebel visible. I left it full of Ku Klux." He criticized the Reconstruction policies of President Andrew Johnson which, in his estimation, led to Klan influence if not domination in North Carolina, Georgia, Florida, and Mississippi. "The Union," he lamented, "is destroyed. The South is incapable of self-government" as the North was unable to remove the old racist element. Many, including Steward's parishioner Jefferson Long, shared in this sentiment.[63]

Steward left a positive legacy in Georgia. In a large sense, his missionary work was reflective of the progress of the AME church. The Reverend Andrew Brown years later described the missionary work in 1866 as challenging. "When I was presiding Elder of the Marietta Division," he reported, "there was but one colored man that could write his name and read the hymn book. We had to get little white boys and poor white men to act as secretaries of the quarterly conference." Yet within five years the African Methodists were solidly entrenched in Georgia. As Steward noted in 1871, Bishop Richard Vanderhorst of the CME church, who was attempting to recruit ministers from the AME, would have "to offer very liberal inducements to get our ministers and members to leave their work and come to him." Few yielded to the temptation.[64]

Not yet thirty years old, Steward departed Georgia for Delaware, a community socially and politically alien to his southern experience.

FOUR

Delaware and Haiti

Steward came to Delaware with a well-deserved reputation as a builder of churches and congregations. He was also, unfortunately, known for his argumentative personality. His assignment was warmly praised by the Philadelphia Conference. They noted that he "comes to cast in his lot with us." Reflecting on his reputation for controversy, they added, "we feel sure that he will be welcomed."[1]

Steward was profoundly dissatisfied with the physical appearance of Bethel AME Church. Unlike Georgia, "where windows and doors were open and sunlight [was] abundant," Bethel was "wretchedly lighted by day and worse at night by its unsightly and inadequate gas fixtures, the interior was in dark colors, and was dirty withal." Equally depressing to Steward were the spittoons, sawdust on the floor, and the head marks of the sleepers.[2] The sooty factory town lowered his spirits. The Reverend Henry J. Young and W. H. Hunter, a former Civil War chaplain, soon visited and inspired him to get to work in earnest. Singers Sallie Masten and Esther Armstrong did much to encourage him "to get the church out of its material darkness."[3]

The worshipers at Bethel were working-class families. Unlike the freedmen in Georgia, these people were not seeking to alter the social and political order. Nevertheless, in Steward's estimation, they too needed spiritual and secular education.

Steward was a diligent minister who tended to all the needs of his congregation. His duties, however, did not prevent him from engaging in a well-organized schedule of self-study. Sacrificing sleep, he continued his readings in theology, history, and philosophy, and he commenced to learn French. He began tentatively to write about church rituals. A few months after arriving in Wilmington, Steward suggested to the *Christian Recorder* that the church should adopt uniformity in services. He called for "a regular sabbath for the communion service in all our stations," and recommended the first Sunday. He added, "let there be a monthly love feast preceding each communion service . . . on Thursday night, followed by a Friday . . . to observe privately as a day of fasting and prayer." He suggested that the last Sunday of each month be reserved "for receiving into full fellowship those who have served out a probationship, the baptism of such as have not previously been baptized, and the baptism of children."[4] He also wrote about forms in church. For those who considered forms as unmeaning, Steward called for order. He requested that the church service involve more than just the pastor, the choir, or a few select others. The church needed to employ the hearts and tongues of people so that the spiritual environment would increase. In order to bring the church closer, he offered a morning worship order that would lead to the development of "an earnest and holy life in all." He urged that the church adopt his suggested form or a similar one.

Order for Morning Service:

hymn sung by the church
short prayer by minister
Lord's prayer by minister
repeated by congregation
short chant or anthem by choir
reading of scriptures
hymn by congregation
silent prayer and sermon
prayer
choir singing
doxology without announcement
dismissal[5]

Steward's proposal did not generate any response from the readership of the *Christian Recorder*. Nevertheless he sought to improve the service and to make the congregation participate more in the morning service. It was fortunate that he sought to involve the congregation, because his preaching style lacked the emotion or "rousnum" normally associated with Methodism. Levi Jenkins Coppin, a future bishop and a worshiper in Bethel, was influenced by Steward's preaching style. Coppin was in his early twenties when he first heard Steward preach. "I cannot say," he wrote, "that I listened very critically to sermons previously to [the] time that [Steward] became pastor." Although many did not at first take to his Presbyterian style, they were moved more by "what he said than [by] his manner of saying it." Steward disdained worshiping that insulted God with singing that was not in praise of him. "Any worship," he wrote, "that [transforms man] to a singing lumberjack is a disgusting stench in the nostrils of God." Steward believed that man's relationship to God should be as a dog to his master. "We are to crouch before him in humility." He found distasteful those ministers who constantly were blowing their noses, wiping their brows, shouting, and generally "misbehaving" in the pulpit.[6]

Although Steward adjusted to Wilmington, he disagreed with the decision to transfer him from Georgia, where he had been happy. Characteristically, he did not state his grievance in a private letter but boldly placed the issue before the membership of the AME family. In the early winter of 1872 he published several essays on the subject of appointments. "[ask] . . . that all limitations as to the time a minister may remain in one charge or one city be stricken out. Second; that the bishops shall be surrounded with an elected council in which all petitions and propositions coming from churches, shall be considered and consistent with whose advice, all appointments are to be made." It was wrong to send a minister away when he was "in the midst of great enterprise." Steward recommended that each conference form an advisory committee consisting of ministers and laymen "to be elected in part by the annual conferences."[7]

Steward's bold suggestion hit a nerve. He directly attacked the power of the bishops and he was suggesting that ministers be selected by popularity instead of the needs of the churches. Benjamin T. Tanner, editor of the *Christian Recorder*, a supporter of an intellectual ministry, praised his call for reform and asked, "why don't our [other] thinkers do the same?" Tanner's call for others to "set [their] pens to running" was heard by the Reverend Theodore Gould, a cousin of Steward. Blood did not protect Theophilus from his cousin's wrath. "Remove these restrictions," Gould argues, "and our itinerant system would be worth but little more to the church than a man's nose after decapitation." Gould believed that the bishops knew the needs of the people. He added sarcastically that if the bishops waited for the people's whispers, many churches would be without pastors. Others criticized Steward for being naive. One urged him to read Mark 4:15, "go ye into all the world and preach the gospel to every creature."[8]

Steward did not accept the criticism. He lashed out viciously. Typically, when wounded, he questioned the intelligence of his critics. He emphatically stated that his critics actually agreed with him as they did not state anything to negate his viewpoint. To the critic that stated that "our Bishops have a council in each conference," he responded, "I have been all this while asleep. Had I known . . . I need never have written." He added that his critic should have started his sentence with *can*. "Can our Bishops have a council in each conference might read better," he concluded.[9]

One of Steward's strengths was his steadfastness to causes that were good and worthy, although at times this proved to be a fault. Such was the case with the futile argument over appointments. Instead of letting the matter rest, Steward stubbornly pursued the matter at the General Conference in May 1872 in Nashville. His resolution to "affix the appointment of all the traveling preachers" was debated and voted down when amendments were added that would permit a minister to remain in an assignment for as long as six years. His resolution on the subject of transferring itinerants was referred to the committee on revision, which ignored it. One of his resolutions was offered as a snub to Theodore Gould, who had been "foolish" enough to criticize his younger relative. Steward moved that Gould's name be stricken from the New York roll of delegates because "he was practically a member of the Philadelphia Conference." This charge led to an intense debate, and was defeated, but his part in bringing it to the floor did little to endear him to others.[10]

Steward did not shy away from controversies. His good friend Levi J. Coppin admired him for his willingness to advocate "a cause because it was good and worthy, and not on account of what [he] selfishly hoped to get out of it."[11] One cause that Steward devoted his attention to was the sorry state of education in Delaware for blacks. Delaware was a strange state. It was located close to the northern states but it was pro-Confederacy even though it had in 1860 only 1,798 slaves. Slavery was not abolished in the state until the enactment of the Thirteenth Amendment in December 1865. In that year the two feudal counties of Kent and Sussex still sold Africans into servitude for terms up to seven years. Democratic governor Gove Saulsbury used his inaugural address in 1865 to berate Congress for its emancipation plans. Blacks, according to him, were innately unequal. The General Assembly supported this theory and even rejected the Thirteenth, Fourteenth, and Fifteenth amendments.[12]

Steward did not have children old enough to attend school but that did not prevent him from strongly advocating on behalf of the state's twenty thousand African-American citizens. His Gouldtown heritage, with its emphasis on duty and self-reliance, and his six years of labor in the South prepared him for leadership. During the first half of 1873 Steward became the leading voice in Delaware seeking to provide education for his race. His chore was formidable. As late as 1867 there were only seven schools for blacks in the entire state, and three of them were located in Wilmington, a comparatively liberal area.

Two years after the legal eradication of slavery, cooperation among the Freedmen's Bureau, William Hilles, a Quaker merchant, and other whites led to the formation of the Delaware Association for the Moral Improvement and Education of Colored People. Within six months, the association had established fifteen schools with seven hundred students. By 1876 it had organized thirty-two schools, most of which were little better than shanties. Even this modest effort outraged whites, who believed that it was against God's will to educate those who in their estimation were barely above the status of monkeys. Whites in Kent and Sussex counties burned schools or drove teachers away.[13]

White ostracism of blacks from schools, public facilities, the jury box, and churches was due in large part to the latter's political disfranchisement. The ratification of the Fifteenth Amendment in 1870 gave the vote to 4,500 black men but the Democratic tax collectors conveniently reported hundreds of black men as "dead" or "having left the state." Although a legal suit terminated this policy, and the Republicans were able to elect a congressman and win the state for Grant's reelection in 1872, the Democratic-controlled legislature passed a tax law in 1873 that required voters' names to appear on tax rolls. Collectors discouraged the paying of taxes by African Americans or failed to record their names. Thus their ability to participate fully in politics was undermined.[14]

Steward strongly advocated that state funds be utilized for all education. Racial discrimination did not allow this fairness. Tax dollars supported white schools while colored schools were dependent on partial support from the Delaware Association for the Moral Improvement and Education of Colored People and donations. Steward's experience in Georgia taught him that political action was needed. He understood that the vicious cycle of poverty could be broken only by improving the educational opportunities. His decision to fight for equal education for his people thrust him into the political fray. In September 1872 he was elected vice president of the Republican Colored Men's State Convention, and soon after he was placed on the Republican State Central Committee. Recognizing that the state's Republican victory in 1872 was due to the black vote, Steward organized in Dover a convention of colored men in early January 1873. The convention was denounced by the Republicans, who deemed it an opportunity for Steward to puff himself up at their expense.[15]

Steward believed that all people were alike beneath the skin. Delaware must eliminate illiteracy and provide both races with equal school accommodations.

He demanded that the people petition and agitate for equal educational rights. His most significant contribution at the convention was the final report from the committee on address, which he authored. He said that it was a "crying necessity" that funding be equal for white and colored schools. To do otherwise would cause ignorance and breed crime. Educate or incarcerate was his challenge to the white power structure. Convinced that his cause was just, Steward demanded that Delaware provide financial assistance for colored schools or they would ask the federal government "to take charge of [our] education." This approach was widely accepted in the Reconstruction states that faced similar white indifference or hostility.[16]

Steward was an angry man, the leading spokesman for his race in Delaware. It was this prominence that led the Methodist Episcopal Church in Wilmington to invite him to address their preachers' meeting in early 1873. Steward chose for his topic, "Religious and Social Condition of the Colored People of Delaware." Steward reminded them that one-half of the blacks were illiterate and the rest were poorly educated. Speaking frankly, he told the ministers, "I find in every community some wretched [white] leech fattening on the soul life of colored men. If Satan can employ white men with success, why may not God?" He urged the ministers to ponder four suggestions: (1) All Christians demand a public school system "that shall afford the best possible advantages . . . too all the people . . . alike." (2) Convince blacks to abstain from alcohol and to live pure and moral lives. (3) All ministers "set the right example of laboring together for the conversion of God's poor." (4) Give sympathy, "prayers and very potent influence for [our] people."[17]

The poor state of race relations in Delaware was noted by Frederick Douglass, editor of the *New National Era and Citizen*, a Washington newspaper. In its June 12, 1873, editorial, "Lunatics of Delaware," the paper reprinted an article from the *Commercial* of Wilmington that described the dismal school situation in Camden. The schools closed in early May because the commissioners faced a dilemma. They did not want to tax blacks and give them a portion of tax funds for their schools because it would antagonize many whites. But not taxing blacks violated federal law. The commissioners, not being paragons of courage, resigned. The *Commercial* correctly assessed that both the Republican and Democratic parties preferred to close the schools rather than integrate them or have the separate schools equally supported by tax revenue. Perhaps thinking of Steward, the *Commercial* inquired, "is there no preacher in Camden . . . who is fearless enough to denounce the wicked . . . act? Let some brave . . . man stand at the church doors and beg money to send a schoolmaster to Camden . . . and to carry light into a region . . . [where] prejudice . . . keep[s] in the valley of darkness a poor struggling race."[18]

Steward was so demoralized and frustrated by the machinations of both parties that he decided to leave the country for mission work in Haiti. His idea had its genesis in his resolution, presented at the 1872 General Conference, to have the church open a mission in the island then commonly known as San Domingo. As reported in the *Christian Recorder*, "when Bro. Steward introduced his resolution, the heart of the whole body seemed to throb with renewed life."[19] Tanner enthusiastically supported the resolution. In 1867 he had asked, "who is it that is to evangelize the Negroes of the greater and lesser antilles, if it be not" the AME church.[20] Even though the delegates in Nashville supported the resolution, the church lacked the necessary funds to establish, as Steward wanted, a mission in the fall of 1872. "I cannot . . . understand . . . the delay," Steward lamented in July. "If the president of the missionary society would make the proper announcement, the money could be secured." His plea was supported by Thomas S. Malcom's inquiry, "when will the Church raise its banner in Hayti and Domenica?"[21]

Pressure on the bishops and the missionary society finally elicited the desired response, the appointment of a missionary on March 13, 1873. It was no surprise that the pioneer was Theophilus Gould Steward. After all, his 1872 resolution called for the mission to be under the jurisdiction of the Philadelphia Conference, the conference he belonged to. He had studied French and was the architect of the mission idea.[22]

Steward informed the *Christian Recorder* that he planned to sail for Port-au-Prince on or about May 16. Since he had no money and did not expect to obtain a full amount from the missionary society, he pleaded for contributions. The Reverend Washington Hill of Helena, Arkansas, quickly sent $250.[23] The Reverend Thomas S. Malcom, Steward's most consistent supporter (at least in print), asked "have not American Christians strangely neglected the people of Hayti? Let the church speedily send teachers and preachers." Hoping to loose the purse strings of African Methodists, Malcom released the contents of an April 7 letter from a woman in Haiti. She wrote, "the Baptists have no church nor any service at present. Oh my God, sustain me and keep me faithful unto the end of the journey." Malcom called upon every church and Sunday school to send donations for the Haitian missionary work. He noted that Bibles, books, and religious tracts in French were also needed.[24]

As he was preparing for his departure, Steward completed church business at Bethel. He informed the *Christian Recorder* that Bethel had paid off its $800 mortgage, the building was repaired, and the bill paid in full. He had to his delight received his salary for the past two years. Steward was touched that he had received "so many manifestations of kindness and love in the way of surprise donations and valuable presents." In his happiness, he said, "Bethel . . . is [judged by its fruits] the best colored church in the state."[25]

Malcom continued to urge support for the mission. He proposed that all the churches in the conferences take up a special collection to meet Steward's expenses as well as "to bring home [two] promising young men to be educated at Wilberforce . . . Lincoln University, in Pennsylvania, or at Howard University." He urged the AME church to buy land in Liberia so that the profits from cash crops could be applied to the Haitian mission work.[26]

It was not until May 25 that Bishop Payne, senior bishop in the church, publicly expressed his view on Steward's trip to Haiti. Years earlier Payne had stated that African Methodists did not have the financial means to support foreign mission fields. In 1862 he declined a request from James Redpath, chief agent of the Haitian Emigration Bureau, to go to the island as a missionary. Now he suggested that friends of missions be established in Philadelphia or New York and that free-will offerings be solicited on behalf of Steward. Unfortunately, Payne's message was printed in the *Christian Recorder* after Steward had departed.[27]

Steward was not the beneficiary of large funds but he went with the blessings of his congregation. His farewell sermon came from Hebrews 4:14, "seeing then that we have a Great High Priest that is passed into the heavens, Jesus the son of God, let us hold fast our confession." A few hours before departing, on June 5, Steward wrote to Tanner. He indicated his disappointment that his departure had not occurred in the spring of 1872 when he had announced his intention to go to Haiti. He mildly castigated the bishops for waiting until March 1873 before authorizing his selection. "In the meantime," he added, "the first emotions had somewhat subsided." He was upset that he was unable personally to raise sufficient funds. However, he acknowledged that the Philadelphia Conference had provided him with financial support. He asked the church to remember his wife and children, who were staying in Bridgeton with his parents. His final words to Tanner were sober as he pondered what the future would bring. "We *must have success*. Let us hope, labor and pray, and victory will come. A grander and brighter future is dawning upon our church than many would believe. I would not dare utter to say what I feel is in store for African Methodism."[28]

Steward's letter touched Tanner: "there is a rich vein of pathos running all through it, but even a rich one of hope and faith." Tanner described Steward's farewell sermon at Bethel as one whose "solemnity . . . will not soon be forgotten. Enrapt with the thought of the Great High Priest, he forgat the fact that he [was leaving family and friends] and spoke only of Christ." An ardent supporter of foreign missions, Tanner added, "let the whole Church, remember his REQUEST [for money]."[29]

June 13 was a glorious day for Steward as he arrived in Port-au-Prince. There he met James Theodore Holly, the black nationalist Presbyterian minister who had emigrated to Haiti on the eve of the Civil War.[30] During the next few days Steward secured living quarters and met several expatriates who had come to the island in 1824 from Havre de Grace, Maryland. He traveled throughout the city, where he observed that the people were sharp bargainers and were "the only people living that can beat the Jews." Oblivious to his stereotypical thought, he concluded, "they are a nation of traders and sharpers who know how to make money and spend it freely it appears." Throughout his stay in Haiti, he would make similar observations insensitive to cultural differences. He found fault with the market food, which he described as "dirty." The upper-class residents he met were polite, but they were in his perception "very ostentatious, superstitious and overbearing in their manners."[31]

Steward did not understand the culture, and to his dismay, his knowledge of French was insufficient. Holly was important to him. Not only was he a source of information, but he spoke English and shared a similar culture with the overwrought missionary. Steward would remain in Haiti for less than a month and his journal entries clearly reveal a man on the verge of a breakdown. He suffered intermittently from tropical afflictions and was homesick. Full of sentimental thoughts, he recorded, "I live one day at a time. Eighteen days ago I parted from my family since which time I have not heard a word from them but my faith in the Lord will help."[32]

Steward's homesickness, poor health, and inadequate command of French left him unprepared to view fairly Haitians and the French-African culture of the islanders. He rashly judged both the upper-class and lower-class people he met, almost reducing them to caricatures. He thought that the people were invincible in their mountain locales, but that "liquor, licentiousness and superstition" would be their downfall. He made this harsh assessment because he could not understand why a woman would walk around with her breasts exposed. No one else saw any shame in her lack of attire, but Steward was morally outraged. Worse, from his viewpoint, was the number of men and women who openly defecated in the streets. His negative judgment extended to the eagerness of the best Haitian families to marry their daughters to white men. Even though his own ancestry was racially mixed, Steward would on other occasions condemn interracial marriage.[33]

Nothing in his experiences in New Jersey or the American South prepared him for the relationship that existed between Haitian men and women. The wives, he noted, "have not the slightest redress. Socially, the degradation of women is beyond description. She does most of the work and is but little better than a slave. No man," he declared, "ever thinks of appearing on the street with his wife and I have only seen one lady and gentleman walking down the street together." He objected to Haitian men's practice of taking mistresses. The adultery so upset him that he bitterly uttered that outside of Holly there did not appear to be a decent man in Port-au-Prince. "And as for the women," he uncharitably declared, "oh! you could not find one should you pass the whole nation through a sieve."[34]

Many years later a more mature Steward would write positively about Haiti,[35] but in the tropical heat of 1873 his views of Haitian society were uncharitable and would have earned charges of racism if written by a white man.

Some of the drawbacks of Haitian society were not unknown to the freedmen of South Carolina and Georgia, yet Steward never made disparaging remarks about their morals. Even though the freedmen had cultural practices that were alien to Steward, he saw in their liberation the work of God. To him, the freedmen were on the verge of building institutions; they were morally changing American society by participating in politics, building churches, establishing newspapers, and toiling with the demands of a democratic society. In contrast, the Haitians were aliens. Their Africanness defined everything. Steward's immense knowledge hardly touched on African cultures. Like many of his race, he was uninformed about the diversity of African cultures. He saw African customs as primitive and the traditional religious practice as fetishism. Steward saw in Haiti an unstable society, but he failed to take into consideration the social upheaval attributed to the numerous internecine conflicts or wards with neighboring Dominicans.[36]

In early June 1873, when Steward had departed for Haiti, he expected to briefly visit the island, locate surviving African Methodists from the 1824 expedition, and return to the United States to cries of hosanna. It was thought that Steward would gather his family and quickly return to the Caribbean station. Later, when he cited lack of money as his reason for remaining in America, the former missionary heard the old charge of "quitter" hurled at him. The furor over his unwillingness to sacrifice for the good of African Methodism and Steward's cutting responses to his numerous critics would dominate the pages of the *Christian Recorder* for over a year.

Editor Benjamin Tanner wrote in his "Our Swivel" column, "Rev. T. G. Steward has returned from his reconnoiter of Hayti. He brings a glowing report." The following week, Tanner prematurely declared that Steward was planning to return to Haiti in November. Tanner was well aware of Steward's financial needs. He urged the bishops, the ministry, and the people to assure Steward of sufficient funds. "Shall it be done," he declared, or will the church, having to put to "the lips of these famishing souls [in Haiti], the cup of the water of life, will now withdraw it, and leave to . . . die."[37]

Despite Tanner's assertion of Steward's "glowing report," Steward did not present one to the Missionary Society. Losing patience, in August and September Tanner demanded an explanation. Steward had to provide a report if he expected to return to his mission in October or November, argued the editor. Meanwhile, Tanner was concerned about the church's indifference to the fertile Haitian field. "What answer will the church make to the call of our missionary, T. G. Steward? What?" Thomas S. Malcom, still an ardent supporter of a Haitian mission field, called for the church to bring young men from the island to be educated at Wilberforce University. Without any evidence of financial support, Malcom exclaimed, "there is great encouragement to sustain . . . Steward in . . . Hayti."[38]

Steward was frustrated with the dynamics of church politics. He wanted to return to Haiti but he wanted adequate financial support for his wife and three young sons. Early in 1874 the frustrated Steward resigned as missionary to Haiti. But confusion reigned. Bishop J. M. Brown, president of the Missionary Board, declared that the resignation had not been accepted. Benjamin W. Arnett, the board's secretary, was instructed at the February 20 meeting to have Steward explain in writing his absence from the Missionary Board's meetings and, if necessary, to find a replacement if Steward pressed his resignation. Three days earlier, the delegates at the preachers' meeting in Philadelphia discussed the Haitian missionary mess and insisted on "work, not talk."[39]

Talk was what Steward gave everybody. He defended his resignation on the grounds that the church would not give him adequate salary. He indicated his willingness to return to the Caribbean if the church would give him $1,800 for one year's support or $2,800 for two years. He adamantly refused to return without the money in advance, which did not endear him to others. In fairness to Steward, he conceded that he would not object if the church could "find a man with less family who . . . can conduct the work at less expense." He even promised to contribute to another missionary's support if one was sent.[40]

Meanwhile, Theodore Holly inquired, "where is Bro. Steward? His flock here are one and all anxiously inquiring after his coming." Speaking for the supporters of mission work, Tanner asked, "what reply has the Church to make?" An immediate reply came in early March from the Reverend W. B. Derrick, who suggested that one hundred Sunday schools throughout the twenty-five annual conferences raise $30 each to provide Steward with three thousand dollars for a two-year assignment in Haiti. Derrick used as a model his own church, where thirty students used printed cards that requested one cent. They raised $35 for the Haitian field. A dissatisfied New Orleans minister, the Reverend James A. Handy, could not understand how African Methodists with bishops, a publication house, a university, fifteen hundred ministers, and 250,000 members were unable to sustain one missionary.[41]

Steward's refusal to return to Haiti without adequate funding embarrassed the Parent Home and Foreign Missionary Society. Bishop J. M. Brown, president of the society, appealed for money. "*Hayti must be saved*," he stressed. Brown had a missionary besides Steward who would go to Haiti even to face hardships. In a dig at Steward, who was critical of the Missionary Society during his Reconstruction missionary work, Brown concluded that the unnamed missionary "*has no one but a wife*, and she is of a self-denying spirit, and willing to follow her husband."[42]

The Reverend Thomas H. Jackson denounced Steward for having a "nice little pleasure trip at the expense of the Church." He supported Steward's resignation and called for the sending of a man who possessed "the true missionary spirit." Humiliated by the harshness of Jackson's tone, Steward defended himself in the *Christian Recorder*. Reiterating his terms for returning to Haiti, Steward used sarcasm to cover his hurt. He commented that Jackson's viewpoint illustrated Mark Twain's observation that men speak on subjects they know nothing of because there are no facts in the way.[43]

In October 1874 grist was added to the mill. Bishop Brown hoped to have a missionary in Haiti by Christmas. Tanner indicated that Steward should be the missionary because he *"really desires to go."* Steward was close to Tanner and, perhaps, he did want to return to Haiti. He certainly sought ways to raise money for a missionary. He suggested that the recently formed Women's Mite Society devise ways to raise money to support a missionary. He also urged the AME church to stop the "petty jealousies and selfish fears." It was clear from his letters to the *Christian Recorder* that he wanted to see the development of a prosperous Haitian mission field. But it was equally clear that the leadership of the church was divided on the issue of making Steward the basis of their missionary hope.[44]

The mission mess was finally settled on June 19, 1875, nearly two years after Steward's departure from Haiti. Charles W. Mossell was appointed to the island. Yet in September 1875 Mossell was still in the United States. Tanner blamed the situation on the apathy of the Missionary Society and vindicated Steward's refusal to return without proper financial support.[45]

The church, heeding a solicitation from Delaware's Republican leaders, now assigned Steward to Sussex County. He had no doubt that the Republicans wanted him out of Wilmington, where his call for fairness in the distribution of school funds disturbed the party's leadership. Sussex County was dominated by reactionary Democrats who, unlike some Republicans, were not ambivalent about the race question. Although Steward was an active Republican, there was little that he could accomplish politically in conservative Sussex County. He turned his attention to his circuit, which included the seafaring area of Milton, Slaughter Neck, Georgetown, Lewes, and Milford, his home base. The area was a test for him. Unlike South Carolina and Georgia, working with the residents of southern Delaware did not offer the prospect of being on the threshold of a glorious social revolution. The newly freed slaves in the Deep South were ignorant, but they fully expected to wrap themselves in the garment of liberation and improve society. Southern Delaware was "feudal" and "primitive." There, the "ox was still harnessed to wagon and plow. Illiteracy prevailed to an astounding extent among both white and colored people," wrote Steward. He was dismayed that "there was not a map nor a blackboard in a rural school in the whole county." Religiously, he was bemused by the camp meetings, which were "occasions for weird singing with the accompaniment of hand clapping." Steward, a gifted orator, considered the singing of greater importance to the people than the preaching. A contributor to the *Christian Recorder* described the region as an area where the colored people preferred the Methodist Episcopal church to their AME rivals. Despite Steward's doubts about the significance of camp meetings, the correspondent observed that "the Wood's meeting of Rev. T. G. Steward seemed to make a ripple though in the monotony of Milford and I hope left some effect."[46]

Steward was disillusioned with his assignment. The white population was uncompromising on racial issues. Blacks seemed indifferent to the social and political changes occurring among former slaves elsewhere in the nation. They were unorganized and unable or unwilling to challenge an educational system that virtually excluded them. Not able to arouse the people in Sussex, Steward devoted his spare time to writing. Tanner was a staunch supporter of Steward's literary efforts. On February 15, 1874, Steward was a guest preacher at Bethel and Allen chapels in Philadelphia, preaching to enthusiastic congregations. Tanner was delighted with the sermons: "we hope it will not be long till he gives the Church in book form a series of sermons." Few would disagree with the editor's conclusion that "we know of none more capable."[47]

Encouraged by Tanner's interest and having some free time in Sussex County, Steward provided for the *Christian Recorder* sermons titled "Death and Life" and "Covenanting With God," which implored people to practice temperance and to speak the truth or else remain silent, a message that clearly was intended for his critics. He attacked white Christians for their prejudice and questioned whether they had "consented unto the law of God or have long since gone backslide. Either the Bible is a myth, salvation a dream, Heaven a passing fancy and Hell a scarecrow or all oppression . . . a sin."[48]

From March 1874 to March 1876, Steward would write for the *Christian Recorder* a series of sketches of Bible characters. Jacob was examined as "a character of energy, perseverance and success that does not seem to betray a single weakness nor to know a failure." Some of the sketches were about biblical women, who clearly matched his criteria for true womanhood. Rebecca was the "pure and chaste virgin" who assisted her son, Jacob, fraudulently to obtain from his blind father, Isaac, Esau's birthright. Ironically, although he wrote this essay to warn parents to treat their children equally, he absolved Jacob of blame, but was not as charitable toward Rebecca's action.[49]

His description of Rebecca is revealing of his estimation of women. In his support of females voting in church matters, Steward was an advocate of women's rights. Yet some of his views were chauvinistic. In his *Christian Recorder* description of Deborah, Steward wrote, "it is thought by many that female character is very monotonous and uniform and in the main negative; made of innocence, affection and other domestic virtues occasionally accompanied with puerile wickedness." Admitting to the correctness of that view, he noted in women's defense that "there is variety in character and circumstances belonging to them." Interestingly, he likened the condition of Deborah to that of the formerly enslaved American population. Praising Deborah for creating song, he noted that "poetry of this style to live must be associated with events in which were displayed great virtues." Implying that the African American was lacking in virtue, Steward believed that this accounted "for the absence of song among our poetic race [as] the only song that owe their origin to the African race that live among them are mostly religious songs." Steward believed that complete freedom and participation in the life of the nation would lead to the unlocking of "a great . . . unopened treasure of song. Till that day come," he insisted, we "will be like captive Israel unable to sing in a strange land."[50]

Steward was in Sussex County because Bishop James A. Shorter had heeded the Republicans' demands to remove him from Wilmington. But in 1874, when Shorter was a guest in Steward's Milford home, he admitted that sending him down there was "all foolishness." A remorseful Shorter, recognizing that Steward was wasting his time, arranged for Steward to take charge of Brooklyn's Bridge Street Church.

The assignment to Bridge Street was a prize. It was the city's oldest AME church, having developed from Sands Street M. E. Church in 1818 under the leadership of Bishop Richard Allen, African Methodism's first bishop.[51] It was here that Steward would meet Mrs. Susan McKinney, the state's first African-American female physician, who, in 1896, would become the second Mrs. Theophilus Steward.[52]

FIVE

Brooklyn, 1874-1879

Steward arrived in Brooklyn to a cordial reception on December 6, 1874. He replaced the Reverend William H. W. Winder as pastor of the historic African Wesleyan Methodist Episcopal Church, commonly known as Bridge Street Church for its location at 309 Bridge Street. Several years before Steward's arrival, Bridge Street faced severe financial difficulties. In 1872 six members paid the church's debt to prevent foreclosure. Later, a grateful church repurchased itself for the sum of $7,975 from Robert Jackson, Willis and Ellen Jones, Robert Cousin, Stephen Overton, and Alvin Spenser. Bridge Street was a church that actively supported its pastors.[1]

Steward's priority was to find lodging for his family. Bridge Street, like nearly every other black church in New York City, did not have a parsonage. Renting a home in the mid-1870s was a challenge for a family with four small children. Steward's race made this task formidable. Some landlords gave him "polite" excuses; others curtly refused him space. One landlady so angered Steward that he told her bluntly that he hoped that "she would never hear herself addressed as mother."[2] To wish for barrenness in a woman was the ultimate insult that he could conjure.

Despite the difficulty in securing adequate lodging for his family, Steward did not attempt to pass for a Cuban. Cubans were popular at this time, because of their revolutionary efforts against Spain. Steward and his family lived at various addresses during their stay in Brooklyn, and always within the black community.

Brooklyn was far different in many respects from his previous assignments. For the first time since his brief stay in South Camden a decade earlier, Steward was preaching to people who did not share a common slavery experience. Brooklyn had only 6,178 African Americans in 1875, yet it had nine black churches or missions. (Manhattan, by comparison, had nine churches for its 20,000 blacks.)[3]

Many of these churches were activist, with ministers and congregations committed to civil and human rights issues. Both Bridge Street and Siloam

Presbyterian were active in helping slaves escape via the Underground Railroad. The Reverend A. N. Freeman, pastor of Siloam, labored to repeal the obnoxious 1850 Fugitive Slave Law. He was a strong supporter of the Fourteenth and Fifteenth amendments. In 1872 Freeman formed the Siloam Benevolent Society, patterned after antebellum societies.[4] Other important churches were Manhattan's Abyssinian Baptist, organized in 1809; and Shiloh Presbyterian, founded in 1822 by the Reverend Samuel E. Cornish, who, along with John Russwurm, founded in 1827 *Freedom's Journal*, the nation's first African-American newspaper. Later, Shiloh would have two distinguished ministers, the Reverend Theodore Wright, the first black to graduate from Princeton Theological Seminary, and the famed abolitionist civil rights advocate, diplomat, and Pan-Africanist, Henry Highland Garnet.[5] Henry Ward Beecher, pastor of Plymouth Church, was representative of the progressive white clergy in the metropolitan area.

Churchgoers in Brooklyn, particularly those who belonged to the old colored families, chose their churches, in part, by the oratorical powers of the minister. Steward was a powerful orator, and he had other attractive qualities. Although many of these "aristocrats of color" lacked huge incomes, they emphasized "education, pride in family heritage and tradition, and adherence to a rigid moral code and Victorian decorum." Steward shared these values. Steward's major task during his stay at Bridge Street was to maintain a harmonious, or at least cordial, relationship between the church's two elements. Unlike Bethel Church in Delaware or his previous southern assignments, he faced a congregation that had the potential for class division. There was an element of old worshipers who were part African, European, and Shinnecock or Montauk Indian from Suffolk County. They were a conservative lot, "resolute in manner and method." Susan McKinney belonged to this class. This group married into select families from the New York or Philadelphia areas. Many of them knew several foreign languages. They kept well-furnished homes and entertained lavishly. To have this type of person in your church did much to increase the prestige of the pastor. Steward was elated when Susan McKinney, the church's organist, "came forward and united with the church" on May 6, 1877.[6]

Brooklyn's colored elite included Samuel Scottron, an inventor famed for his adjustable mirror for barbers and hairdressers, and his imitation marble; Civil War surgeon and druggist, Peter W. Ray; Lewis H. Latimer, electrical engineer; educators Charles H. Dorsey and Charles L. Reason. Other elites were undertakers, dentists, letter carriers, or skilled craftsmen or vestrymen.

Not all of them, of course, worshiped at Bridge Street. But enough did to concern Steward about the potential for disagreement with the second element, the working class.[7] These men and women were the day laborers, porters, whitewashers, cartmen, street sweepers, and domestic servants. Most were underpaid, as there was discrimination in apprenticeships and labor unions. All of this combined "to develop a triangular conflict with cupidity, caste and callousness."[8] Approximately one-half of the city's black population was not native born. Many were migrants from the South, particularly North Carolina, and they were, according to Steward, "aggressive and progressive, but quite easily influenced toward the right [way]." His southern experience with the freedmen and his own aristocratic bearing helped him to understand the group mentality of both elements. Despite the potential for class conflict, Steward, by his own admission, maintained a harmonious relationship between the two elements.[9]

Like all ministers, Steward made frequent visits to the homes of his parishioners, consoling the bereaved, visiting the sick, or just getting better acquainted with members of the congregation.[10] Steward was an astute observer of human behavior. His pastoral visits to the homes of the elite and the working class inspired him to write a series of essays on "Colored Society" for the *Christian Recorder* in 1876 and 1877. His studies were not scientific, but he believed that they were probably "the first broad sociological papers written with respect to the colored people of this country. They were quoted to some extent," he proudly added.[11] Steward wrote eight essays, which to some degree antedated E. Franklin Frazier's scathing *The Black Bourgeoisie*. He observed that outside forces molded colored society and did not represent "the tastes and powers of the colored people themselves." Steward was proud of his African blood, but he noted that many others rejected the appellation "African" or "Negro" and exclaimed that "I am an American citizen." He understood that many of his race were voluntary blacks who could pass into white society. The problem of the race was its inability to claim a common experience. Slavery, he argued, was not the glue that would bind because "slave history is no history. The colored people have made no history which has the least tendency to unite, outside of the religious." Unlike Jews, blacks would not admit to a slave past because they felt ashamed of their degradation. Although Steward belonged to the AME church, it was not a separatist organization. Whites chose not to join, but under no circumstances were they prohibited from worshiping. Steward, who on later occasions preached in white churches and who was a member of many black organizations, condemned his people for having separate organizations instead of challenging white supremacy and exclusiveness. He thought that the race imitated white society too much, but noted that while blacks honored white men such as John Brown, Charles Sumner, or Abraham Lincoln, they didn't honor white preachers. Preachers "express the feelings of the people and win their *love*." In contrast, "the public men claim their ears and win their applause." Not all of his observations were critical. Steward believed that blacks were more compassionate than whites and less willing to condemn a man because of his occupation. Because discrimination made it difficult for blacks to obtain good jobs, they understood that people could engage in menial labor but not be servile.[12]

To some degree Steward's comments reflected his own ambivalence. His education had focused on European and American philosophers, historians, theologians, and scientists. Yet he would later advocate a study of blacks' contributions to American and world history, and on several occasions he would defend blacks as being superior to whites in physical conditioning and equal to them in intellectual attainments. Throughout his life he would struggle with conflicts over color and race, and like his friend W. E. B. Du Bois, he felt the "twoness of the American Negro" who felt torn between allegiance to his African and his European blood.[13]

Steward's critical observations were, of course, not original. Others accused the elite of aping the white middle and upper classes and dismissed them as "lamp black whites."[14] Despite his frankness and provocative comments, Steward garnered the attention of Benjamin Tanner, who, despite his own elite status, shared Steward's racial pride. Tanner wrote that his friend had "no right to tantalize his readers with much *tastes*. Having created the appetite he should be generous enough to satisfy it."[15] Steward's essays were a fair assessment of the behavior and attitudes of black residents of Brooklyn. They contrasted with the general white newspaper coverage that depicted Africans as "darkies" who lived "in ricketty old houses, who walls, floors and staircases are begrimed with dirt."[16] While this description was apt for many of the city's poor, it could as easily have been applied to whites as well as blacks.

Steward used his tenure at Bridge Street Church to write frequently. During the next two decades he would be a constant contributor to the *Christian Recorder*. While not all of his pieces would "tantalize," all were informative and some were even controversial. In the spring of 1875, a few months after his arrival, he wrote a two-part essay on marriage. Steward was a voracious reader with eclectic tastes. Undoubtedly he read about free love or proposals to eliminate marriage and felt the need to defend the institution. He urged readers to view marriage as a lifelong pact. Free love advocates were no better than lustful brutes who violated women. A marriage that accepted free love was, in his estimation, "bestial." Steward believed that women should have the same opportunities as men, but he had no sympathy for those "woman's righters who complain of woman's hardships under the Gospel." No, a Christian marriage "is the profoundest sympathy with the actual condition of woman." The key to his argument was "Christian"; he believed that a home without Christian practices or a home where only one partner was a Christian inevitably led to friction. He called upon young women to "love God! Love Jesus! Be not deceived with your own heart, nor the pretensions or appearance of an ungodly suitor." He warned them to "trust reason, experience, God; but distrust your own heart."[17]

"Marriage" and other activities on behalf of his congregation brought him attention, but it was the publication of *My First Four Years in the Itineracy of the African Methodist Episcopal Church* that embarked him on a literary effort that would place him among the leadership of the African Methodist's theological interpreters. He acknowledged in his introduction that this slim book was "an experiment, and if successful, a beginning, for the author proposes to follow it with publications of a more important and comprehensive character." Benjamin Tanner, a consistent supporter of an intellectual clergy, praised the book. "The only wonder," he commented, "is that he could have restrained himself from giving more fully the store of facts which he has on hand. He tantalizes us . . . but, says, not now. The Church certainly has the right to expect that they are kept safely, for when the time comes to write up African Methodism in the South, they will be more precious than gold."[18]

Steward shared Tanner's love of intellectual stimulation. He was a prolific reader, and he studied French, Greek, and Hebrew. Moreover, he encouraged others to pursue such interests. Just as he had established a lyceum and debating society among the freedmen, Steward believed in developing the intellectual capacity of the residents of Brooklyn. He organized a series of lectures, the Richard Allen Course, that were presented on Wednesday evenings in November and December 1875. The first lecture was delivered by James Theodore Holly, now a bishop in the Protestant Episcopal church, who spoke about "Hayti: Its Past, Present, and Future in Its Relation to Negro Destiny." Holly was a dedicated black nationalist who believed that Haiti should represent to the African world what England meant to the European world—the centerpiece of civilization.[19] Other prominent speakers, representing some of the finest minds in Metropolitan New York, included William Johnson, Henry Highland Garnet, Benjamin Tanner, and Susan McKinney. Steward closed the series with "The Proper Attitude of the Colored People in the Next National Election." Tanner viewed the Allen Course as "one of the most hopeful signs of the times in our churches." He asked, "why should not the AME Church lead off in this general enlightenment of the people?"[20] Tanner recognized that the AME church, through the instrumentality of its clergy, had a responsibility to do more for the nonreligious needs of the people. Steward agreed, and he arranged to have some of his sermons, which emphasized both religious and secular viewpoints, published in the *National Monitor*.

Steward continued throughout 1876 to contribute to Brooklyn's and Bridge Street Church's intellectual development. On May 9 he lectured before the Young Men's Literary Association on literature, learning, and education that were related to the AME ministry. The attentive audience heard him say that blacks were miseducated "or worse, badly educated." He stressed that the role of the church was to inculcate "the doctrine of self-reliant Christian manhood. Its object is to take the stoop from the Negro's shoulders, the cringe from his knee and enable him to stand erect." The AME church was fulfilling the mandate for self-reliance, he noted, by publishing a weekly newspaper, maintaining a university, and preparing to erect a monument to Richard Allen, African Methodism's founder. All of this reflected Steward's pride in the AME church and in the capabilities of African people. Yet his ambivalence about racial distinctions caused him to add that the elimination of prejudice and caste distinction and the establishment and maintenance of "a Church which shall have no white ministers or no black members" were goals that the church should seek. Steward believed in the brotherhood of man, but he defended the AME use of the appellation "African" as a name that "came to us by necessity." In separating from the Methodist Episcopal church because of its colorphobia, Steward emphasized that the African Methodists "did not know enough to call themselves the Reformed M. E. Church." Despite its name, Steward boasted that his church was the only religious body in the country that was "teaching a Christianity in opposition to caste." He concluded his lecture by urging the audience "to cast down at a single stroke the whole temple of lies respecting our race and to believe ourselves men in spite of the world." Some months later, he attacked white Protestants, especially Methodist Episcopalians, for their failure to abolish caste. Even though he had a religious bias against the Catholic church, he credited them with withholding the last sacraments to slaveholders. "Today," he declared, "in Catholic countries, the Negro see more of the Church in Christ than he can in Protestant America."[21]

Steward's view that African Americans were badly educated was a subject that others agreed with. Brooklyn, like other northern communities, practiced both de jure and de facto racial segregation in the school system. Despite the state's passage of a civil rights bill in 1873 that prohibited racial discrimination in public facilities and in the assigning of children to schools, the Brooklyn Board of Education refused during the mid-1870s to integrate approximately five hundred black students into a system that enrolled 43,000 white pupils. Rufus Perry, publisher of the *National Monitor*, called the city's black schools "an outrage on taxpayers and Republicanism. . . . Abuse us no longer, your hands are all stained with blood. In the name of God we beseech you to *wash* them." Although 173 petitioners called on the board to abolish the black schools, which were "seriously detrimental . . . to the educational interests of their children, regardless of either the color or the qualifications of the teacher," the board voted 33-2 to maintain the status quo.[22] Two years later a Brooklyn Supreme Court ruled that no violation of the 1873 law had occurred. It was no more wrong to separate the races than it was to prohibit coeducational schools.[23] Steward, who raised objections to separate schools in Delaware, and who later would criticize separate schools in Baltimore, was surprisingly quiet about the Brooklyn school situation. If Steward agreed with the protesters, he did not mention his sympathy in his autobiography and there is no evidence that he submitted essays to any of the local newspapers. Despite the numerous outcries against the separate schools, Brooklyn had many fine African-American teachers. Notable among them were Maritcha R. Lyons, who spent forty-eight years in the system; Charles L. Reason; Charles H. Dorsey; and Sarah Garnet, wife of Henry Highland Garnet, who taught in both Brooklyn and Manhattan. It is probable that Steward's school age children were privately tutored, and he did not thrust himself into the fight. The struggle to integrate schools in New York State, although the goal of many, was not supported by those who feared that integration would cost the blacks employment and control over educational matters. This internal battle within the African-American community was repeated in Manhattan, Buffalo, and elsewhere.[24]

The beginning of 1876 was marred by tragedy. On February 26, Stephen, Steward's fifteen-month-old son, died of tuberculosis.[25] The Stewards, while mourning their son, never lost faith or questioned God for their loss. Instead, they gave their attention to Bridge Street. On March 13, 1876 they joined one hundred others in a love feast. Elizabeth Steward was filled with the Holy Ghost "while we were singing a chorus, 'help me my Lord when I'm in trouble.' " Steward brought in a dozen or more members to the church at this time. On another occasion, five came forward for prayers, and one became a convert. By the end of March Steward had brought around fifty into membership. According to Tanner, the members of Bridge Street "think him one of the most gifted and pious" ministers in the itineracy.[26]

Steward differed, at times, with some of the traditions of his parishioners. In 1877 he publicly expressed his dissatisfaction with the Grand Concerts, which he described as grand only in "the circular, and cake walks where nothing is grand but the humbuggery that gathers around them." He found this type of behavior boorish. Although he had previously yielded to the custom, and Bridge Street was sponsoring a concert on May 23, he vowed never to yield again. He considered it ludicrous to sit in a hot church "till 2 a.m. eating and drinking." Steward's own class-consciousness was coming through. Like others of Brooklyn's "best society," Steward disapproved of ostentation. He asked Tanner to write a column on the subject, as he feared that "the evil fostered . . . outweigh[ed] the good accomplished."[27]

Steward was quick to obtain assistance from Tanner when he needed it, but he was no fawning admirer of the editor. He described Tanner as "a small man with canine features and brusque manners. Learned, but lacking in dignity, and faulty in pronunciation."[28] He accused Tanner and Henry M. Turner, the business manager of the *Christian Recorder*, of lacking "creative genius" when Turner complained in the summer of 1876 that about one-half of the paper's five thousand subscribers were in arrears and that ministers did not aggressively sell the paper to their congregations. Steward believed that he was smarter than both men and boldly called on the AME Book Concern to issue stock and reduce expenditures. Concerned that Turner would reduce the pages from eight to four, Steward urged him to "cease heralding your own death! Stop preaching your own funeral [for] creditors hug up close around a dying debtor saying 'nothing you bought, nothing you shall carry.' " Despite Steward's criticisms, he sold the paper.[29] The paper's debt was not erased until 1879, when Fanny Jackson Coppin organized a week's display of items made by blacks to show the creative talent of African Americans. This "World's Fair" was a successful fund-raiser.[30]

Steward's busy schedule, at times, left him haggard. He was able to take a three-week vacation in August 1876, a time when many of the church elite took to the mountains or shore. On August 16, the day before his vacation started, Steward attended a camp meeting in Chester Heights, near Philadelphia. He delivered a powerful, emotion-provoking sermon on the punishment of sinners. After this event, he went to Gouldtown, where he "was not Rev. Mr. Steward, Mr. Steward or even Brother Steward, but simply 'Theop' "[31] He used his leisure time to enjoy himself with his parents, brothers, sisters, and numerous relatives. He was at home and left there well rested.

Steward labored mightily in Brooklyn until the call of the itineracy beckoned him to Zion mission in South Philadelphia. He was departing from one of the best-supported churches in African Methodism to pastor a small mission. Steward accepted the move without any public protest. At least he had the consolation of being assigned close to the ancestral home in Gouldtown. He would in later years remember with fondness his stay in Brooklyn.

SIX

Pennsylvania and Delaware: Time of Personal Crisis, 1877-1883

A few months before Steward left Brooklyn, Rutherford B. Hayes, Republican, was inaugurated president after a political compromise settled the disputed election. The Democratic candidate, Samuel Tilden, had 184 electoral votes, one short of the minimum. A committee of fifteen, composed of five each from the Senate, House, and Supreme Court, determined that Hayes won the disputed states of South Carolina, Florida, Louisiana, and Oregon, thus giving him 185 electoral votes. Southern representatives in Congress agreed to the committee's choice in exchange for a cabinet position and, more important, the removal of federal troops. This "betrayal of the Negro" left African Americans at the mercy of southern Bourbon machinations. The exodus of forty thousand blacks for Kansas two years later clearly underlined the growing dissatisfaction of African Americans with the Republicans, a dissatisfaction that would eventually result in them deserting the Republican ship for the social welfare principles of Franklin D. Roosevelt's Democratic Party.[1] This distancing of the African Americans from their former Republican supporters would occupy some of Steward's time in Pennsylvania and Delaware during the next decade. Meanwhile, his immediate attention was devoted to family and personal crises.

Zion's congregation was from the lower class. There were about ninety members to greet their new pastor and his growing family of five sons. Although it was called a mission, Zion was responsible for Steward's support. Barely half of the church members were able to make a financial contribution to their pastor's support. Once again, Steward faced financial uncertainty. The poor worshipers came from southern Delaware, a region that was feudal in his estimation. These people lacked money, but they were blessed with many children, which provided Steward with good opportunities for Sunday school work. He formally took charge of Zion on June 3, 1877.[2]

Philadelphia was a city where like-minded individuals of cultural and intellectual taste resided. Benjamin Tanner introduced Steward to the city's elite families and he rekindled his friendship with those he knew from previous visits to the city. Steward was pastor to a humble congregation, but otherwise had little personal contact with the lower class. He socialized with those like him who had a love of literature, politics, and philosophy. There were three distinctive groups of elites representing Philadelphia's best colored families. There were the old native families who had lived in the city for decades. There was a French-speaking group that had emigrated from Haiti during the late eighteenth and early nineteenth centuries. The third element were Southern mulattoes, quadroons, and octoroons, who had migrated from South Carolina, Virginia, and Maryland.[3]

Steward's social status in the community and his reputation as an intellectual in African Methodism made him an attractive guest. But parties and receptions, while diversions, commanded only a small portion of his time. Zion's humble status in the itineracy demanded considerable energy from its pastor. Everywhere Steward worked, he struggled to make the church and the congregation better than when he found them. On June 24, 1877, three weeks after delivering his first sermon at Zion, he began "a series of discourses on the prophecies respecting Jesus Christ." Several months later he organized a Sunday School Missionary Society with an initial membership of eighty-seven. He also renovated Zion's mission, which precipitated a minor conflict between the minister and his congregation. Steward was opposed to the presence of a pulpit because he wanted to make the service less ostentatious.[4]

Steward's involvement in upgrading his churches reflected his strong sense of loyalty to the itineracy and his interest in improving the whole person of the parishioners. In this context, he was similar to other elite Philadelphians who sought to expose the masses to reform, be it educational, moral, or political. As suggested by a recent study of nineteenth-century African-American elites, "the upper tens" had little social contact with the lower class but they believed that it was their responsibility to labor for the betterment of this group. The Quaker city's African-American elite, motivated by a sense of noblesse oblige, had a long history of activism in assisting fugitive slaves, establishing self-reliance institutions, or tending to the needs of the elderly or poor. Representative of this group was Fanny Jackson Coppin, wife of AME

Bishop Levi J. Coppin, who was born a slave in 1837 but freed in her youth. She was a graduate of Oberlin College, and served for thirty-seven years as principal of the Institute for Colored Youth—the only high school in Philadelphia for African Americans. Coppin endeavored to provide students with a classical training and an industrial education to prepare them for opportunities in the skilled trades as increased European immigration and racial discrimination lowered the number of black craftsmen and entrepreneurs. After several years of struggle, Coppin and her supporters persuaded the Quaker managers of the ICY in 1885 to add an industrial component to the school's curriculum. Although Philadelphia had more African Americans in businesses such as coal merchants, real estate, and the skilled crafts than did other cities, these were limited to areas far removed from the viable business center of Market and Chestnut streets.[5]

A sense of social responsibility was a legacy Steward had received from his mother. Years after her death, Rebecca Steward was described by the Women's Parent Mite Missionary Society as one "whose influences for good and for service were instilled in the members of her family and permeated their lives for usefulness among the lowly." Rebecca, more than anyone in his immediate family, encouraged Theophilus. Her motto, "aim at the sun! If you do not bring it down, you will shoot higher than if you had aimed at the earth," sustained him throughout low moments in his life.[6]

His dependence on his mother's wisdom and his extraordinarily close relationship with her came to a tragic end on June 8, 1877 when Rebecca died at the age of fifty-seven, three weeks after the deaths of her mother and her older sister. The passing of Rebecca brought extreme gloom to Steward's life. Nearly forty years after her death, he wrote, "I have never been able to speak of my mother in public, on account of emotions which arise . . . but of her I can write: she was among the most intelligent and most holy of women." Rebecca's interpretation of the Lord's Prayer included this summation: "we are not taught to address God . . . as our master, president, lord or king, but as our Father. What name so dear as Father? What home so bright as Heaven?"[7]

Steward's love for his mother was expressed in 1877 in *The Memoirs of Mrs. Rebecca Steward*. Steward dedicated the book to Bishop Daniel A. Payne, "as a testimonial to his high appreciation of female excellence." The devoted son published the book as "an act of obedience to the feelings of [his] own heart . . . to discharge this duty in obedience to the wish of many relatives . . . [and because] the interests of Christianity seem to demand this." Citing spiritual guidance, he added, "a voice from above which I regard as that of the Master urges me to lay before the Christian world this life, as a help and solace to the many struggling ones." The Philadelphia *Sunday Press* commented that "every married man should present [it] to his wife." Rev. S. B. Jones, presiding elder of the Marietta District in Georgia, noted that if people knew the value of Steward's tribute, "a hundred thousand [copies] would not supply the demand." "Her writings," he added, "will give her a rank in the future that scarcely one minister of the gospel in a thousand will get." He was so moved by his reading of the memoirs that he promised to see "that every preacher in [his] district reads it."[8]

In 1878 Steward entered Philadelphia's Protestant Episcopal Church Divinity School. Based on his previous education, much of it self-learned, Steward was assigned to the junior class. He enrolled in a Hebrew language class without revealing to his fellow students or the faculty that he had previously studied the language in Brooklyn. Like others of his race, Steward viewed himself as a symbol of blacks' potential. He was competing with white graduates of the nation's best schools, and he was unwilling to do poorly. After completing Hebrew and Greek (another course that he had previously studied), he rose to the top of his class. The class in theology was his first effort at a formal examination of the subject. He quickly began to discard some of his "erroneous notions." An ecumenicalist, he "found genuine religion among the Episcopalians." Benjamin Tanner, his intellectual mentor, approved of his admission into the school and wrote, "if our ministers generally were actuated by a similar spirit a more general enlightenment would prevail."[9]

Steward's theological education flourished in Philadelphia, where he met the Reverend John Inskip and his wife, both of whom were professors and preachers of the doctrine of Christian perfection. To Steward, "they were earnest and real, free from all sham and pretense; no self seeking or greed of 'filthy lucre' marred their heart searching efforts. By them," he humbly exclaimed, "I was gloriously helped."[10]

His enrollment at divinity school taxed his already busy schedule, but Steward was able to budget his time among church duties, reading, writing, and studying. He was a man of inestimable energy. Wanting to improve his already formidable speaking skills, he took an evening course at the National School of Elocution and Oratory. He wrote several essays for the *Christian Recorder* on the subject of sanctification. He even promised Tanner a romantic book in installments, but here his commitments overwhelmed him. He did not evade his responsibility to Zion, however. The *Christian Recorder* praised him for bringing in twenty-two new members in early 1878. Tanner was pleased that among this group was "a set of wild young men, who will be as bright and shining lights in the service [of God] as they were wild and daring in the . . . wilderness." In March Tanner praised Steward for raising money for the foreign mission field. On May 12 Steward spoke at the Central Presbyterian Church in Philadelphia, taking his text from Isaiah 50:6, "I gave my back to the smiters, and my cheeks to them that plucked off the hair. I hid my face from shame and spitting."[11]

Steward was still concerned about political and social issues. He was a member of the Philadelphia Annual Conference's African Emigration and Education committees. (His participation in the former committee was an anomaly; Steward thought emigration to Africa an impractical solution to America's race problem.)[12] Steward wrote the Education Committee's report. Unanimously adopted, it condemned segregated schools as unchristian because they were supported by tax dollars. He wrote angrily, "the whole power of the states is invoked to force the colored people to send their children into schoolhouses, badgered with a disgrace as incurable as the ancient leprosy." At this time he indicated that he favored black churches and schools because they were supported by private funds. His concerns were that his people paid taxes that supported white schools, but tax funds were not distributed for the support of black schools.[13] Steward had a very personal interest in the Philadelphia school situation. His son James would graduate from the Institute for Colored Youth in 1886; at this time, 1878, none of his children were old enough to enroll in that prestigious institution. Although Philadelphia offered a variety of private schools as alternatives to the inferior segregated black schools, the majority of African Americans could not afford the tuition. The black schools had a majority of white teachers, a practice that was soundly criticized by many. Few blacks disagreed with the Reverend Francis J. Grimké's call for "colored men as professors in colored institutions." It was not until 1881 that a state law prohibited segregated schools, but it would be years before schools were effectively integrated.[14]

Steward again attacked the bishops' appointing powers. Although he was intelligent enough to make his attacks appear that he was devil's advocate for all ministers, Steward's real concern was personal. The dissenting minister argued that the bishops were only representatives of the church and that their power was to take the names of eligible ministers provided by the various annual conferences and distribute "them among the list of appointments established by the conference." He further argued that the bishops had no choice but to put church and pastor together. He harshly concluded that "the present period in our church is somewhat marked by episcopal lawlessness, and the tendency is increasing." Benjamin Tanner, who generally supported Steward's opinions, vehemently disagreed: "the hands of our bishops must not be tied." Two years later, the mercurial and temperamental Steward came to the conclusion that "the harsh personal rule of [the] Bishops . . . was a necessity." He offered no explanation for this change of heart.[15]

Steward's combative nature was on display at the AME church's sixteenth quadrennial conference that met in St. Louis from May 3 to May 24, 1880. The conference was disorderly, as delegates fought over numerous issues. Despite his assertion that "my part in the General Conference . . . was not very conspicuous, for I was at that time finishing my course in the seminary," he was at the center of some of the disorder as he attacked fellow delegates and, later, alienated the bishops in his critique of the meeting.[16]

After completing his divinity studies, Steward, not satisfied with his intemperate remarks about fellow delegates, launched a major attack against the 1880 General Conference, which brought upon him the condemnation of many in the church.[17] From mid-August to late October 1880 he outraged readers of the *Christian Recorder* with his divisive comments. He blamed much of the conference's disorders on the young delegates who were only fifteen years removed from slavery. Expressing class snobbery, he observed that many had intelligence, but they lacked training. Few, if any, were graduates of colleges or seminaries. It was incomprehensible why he, who up to 1877 had no formal divinity training, would criticize others. He blamed the delegates for not dealing adequately with "the relations of the Episcopacy to the conference and laity" and for their failure to sort out the church's financial problems. He deplored the selection of Richard Harvey Cain to the bishopric. Additionally, he insinuated that unnamed bishops were receiving more traveling money than they deserved. He expressed, also, concern about the pressure placed on ministers to produce dollar money (each member contributed one dollar a week) or face severe reprimands including removal from the itineracy. He offered additional criticisms about the conference's inability to dispose of no more than five of the 125 bills presented for revision in the Book of Discipline. Again expressing snobbery, he attacked the quality of the conference's leadership by accusing delegates of murdering the English language in their presentations. Although he excluded himself, he blamed others for declining "to assume . . . leadership," which led to a struggle between the unknown leaders and obstructionists. In an effort to blunt his raw criticism, Steward added a sweetener. He believed that history would note that the delegates did well in electing to the bishopric Henry M. Turner, Richard H. Cain, and W. F. Dickerson. "No brother," said Steward, "who was a member of this body need ever blush at this epoch in his history, even though he was like the writer uncompromisingly opposed to it."[18]

Both clergy and bishops aimed their thunderbolts at the meddling Steward. The Reverend P. W. Jefferson of Marion, South Carolina, defended his fellow southerners who had labored under the overseer's lash. "I say," commented Jefferson, "his name is hardly known among the people . . . whether as a minister or a teacher, from a well bred family or from a college [because] when troubles beset him he fled and left the [freedmen] still in darkness." Reviving Cain's charge of Steward as a quitter, Jefferson concluded, "he had his day in the South and . . . failed; he had his day in Hayti and failed worse still."[19]

Bishops Richard H. Cain, J. M. Brown, and Daniel A. Payne attacked Steward's logic and personality. Taking personally Steward's generalization that bishops had more money than they deserved, Payne responded, "I challenge [anyone] . . . to put his finger upon an instance wherein I received more than my lawful right." Outraged, Payne added, "where and when will he stop this kind of writing? If he belongs to the Clerical Association for the Promotion of Virtue he had better stop now and forever."[20]

While Steward's criticisms of the General Conference were harsh and, in the estimation of many, intemperate, they were also valid in certain respects. The delegates, despite their vow to eschew discord in order to "soften [race] prejudice," made fools of themselves in front of the invited white press as they argued incessantly over minor points.[21] Steward's concerns were genuine, but his method of protesting was outrageous. He was more a creator of ideas than a leader of men. Many of his ideas were practical and useful in guiding the AME church during its troubled times. Despite his undiplomatic questioning of dollar money, his raising of the issue forced the bishops to send out a pastoral letter explaining that the dollar money paid for the salaries of bishops, *Christian Recorder*'s editor, business manager, and two secretaries, as well as the expenses of the AME Book Concern, the publishing house of the church.[22]

Steward's outburst about the General Conference may have been attributable in part to his reassignment from Zion to Frankfort, Pennsylvania. Although the support at Zion was, in his words, "barely sufficient to keep the wolf from the door," he considered his three years there among the happiest in the itineracy.[23]

Once again, Steward found himself in a community where the school situation was intolerable. "I found a poor little 'colored school' to which I was expected to send my children," he exclaimed. The minister had three school age boys but "as [he] did not expect to remain there [he] did not care to precipitate a fight." Later, after leaving Frankfort, the local paper accused him of advocating mixed schools, a charge he denied. He was also accused of trying to get his children into a white school, the Henry Herbert School. Although he denied this charge too, it was probably true; he was adamant about providing his sons with the best available education. If his race could provide it, fine. If not, he would educate them in a mixed setting.[24]

There were happier moments for him during 1880. An important event for him and his family was his graduation from the divinity school of the Protestant Episcopal church. Steward had developed a close relationship with his professors, all of whom wrote glowing endorsements. When it was rumored that he would be named to a theological professorship at Wilberforce University, four white professors, including the dean of theology, Daniel R. Goodwin, issued a proclamation praising their prize student "for character, scholarship, fidelity and ability." They believed that he had the potential to become "a teacher of high distinction." Goodwin wrote, at Steward's request, an evaluation of his gifted student: "His essays are of the very highest order . . . for philosophical and theological accuracy. . . . I have had few men under my instruction . . . who have so thoroughly mastered the subjects and the system of Christian theology."[25]

Steward's intellect and giftedness were expressed in his prolific writings and his vision for the church. He suggested in July 1880 that a Richard Allen professorship be established at Wilberforce, calling for "an endowed professorship of Biblical Learning." It is probable, in light of his request for recommendations and his suggestion of a professorship, that Steward was angling for a position for himself.[26]

Bishop Payne supported him in this issue. Payne called upon people to forsake their cigars and other pleasures and help to raise $500,000 to make Wilberforce a first-rate institution. He asked the nearly 88,000 African Methodists to give up for five years their picnics, camp meetings, excursions, and other unnecessary pleasures. He asked that up to 1,000 of the most prominent AME members petition the Reverend Joshua P. B. Eddy "to endow one or two professorships . . . each of which shall bear his name." This grandiose plan came to nothing, as Eddy died in 1882 and his will allocated no money to either Wilberforce University or to the AME church. The

Bishops Council, meeting in Newport, Rhode Island, in August, endorsed Steward's proposal. The following April, Wilberforce University notified Steward by letter that a special meeting of the executive committee had elected him "to solicit for our university." The letter was a formality, for Steward had for several months been attempting to raise $25,000 for an endowment.[27]

A happier occasion was his deliverance on June 13 of the annual sermon at Wilberforce's commencement. His subject, "the incarnation of the Son of God" was taken from John 1:14, "and the word was made flesh and dwelt among us." The sermon was published in 1881 as *The Incarnation of the Son of God*.[28] It gave him the confidence to try for a prize offered by Bishop J. P. Campbell. Money prizes were offered for the three best essays on "the scriptural means of producing an immediate revival of pure Christianity in the ministry and laity of our church." Steward's essay won the second prize, of $15.[29] This increased his popularity among African Methodists as a rising scriptural interpreter.

Once again, in 1881, the itinerant preacher moved. Frankfort's congregation found their pastor too controversial for their taste. The church's trustees "semiofficially notified [him] that they would learn with pleasure of his acceptance of a call in some other locality."[30] He was thirty-eight years old and had the responsibility of a wife, seven children (only three of them of school age), and a new baby. He was returning to Wilmington, Delaware, a locale that he had left nearly seven years earlier in an unhappy mood. But "he [was] in high favor with the Wilmingtonians" of Bethel Church.[31]

Bishop A. W. Wayman heard Steward preach in February 1882 and agreed with Steward's supporters that he was "uncommonly gifted in possessing the power of eloquence." Wayman described the Bethel congregation as earnestly waiting for their pastor to speak. "I was struck at once by the deep and searching tone of the quiet prayer. It was as if we each one prayed for ourselves, so truly did he touch upon our individual needs. Such prayers indeed must cleanse from sin." Wayman described the sermon as one that brought forth a joyous demonstration, yet "in one short, low spoken sentence, he had quiet fully restored." Wayman, an accomplished speaker himself, left Bethel in tears, so moved was he by Steward.[32]

Steward's views on prayers were clear. In "The Doctrine of Prayer," Steward cited Joseph Le Conte's *Religion and Science*. Le Conte, a professor of geology and natural history at the University of California, argued that people can pray for themselves but that prayers cannot influence external nature. Steward believed that God had the power to "modify the application of

77

[natural] laws . . . [but people] ought not to expect it." Rather, they should "ask for wisdom and strength to obey . . . the government of God . . . and only in extreme cases cry to God for a deliverance that would ever seem to involve a departure from the usual cause of law."[33]

Not all of Steward's peers shared Bishop Wayman's adulation of the Bethel minister. Steward's aggressive personality and sharp tongue caused some to dislike him intensely. From May 3 to 9, 1882, Steward attended the Philadelphia Annual Conference in West Chester. For unknown reasons, the Reverends James H. Payton and A. A. Robinson raised their hands against Steward's "moral, religious and official character." Enraged, Steward demanded that the charges be put into writing and that he be given time to prepare a defense. He complained that "a motion to this effect was made but not put; but [rather] certain very dangerous remarks were made publicly affecting my moral and religious standing, after which, on motion the conference proceeded to pass my character without deciding as to my guilt or innocence and leaving these key grave charges uninvestigated." Steward insisted on a speedy trial and vowed not "to end the matter with a mere demand."[34] It is not known how this matter was resolved. Perhaps it was out of spite that Steward wrote an extremely critical analysis of the conference's published minutes, which he criticized as the worst in the conference's sixty-seven years. "I am ashamed of the book and pronounce it utterly indefensible or inexcusable," Steward wrote.[35] While his frankness angered some, it did not affect his reappointment to Bethel nor did it prevent Wilberforce University from bestowing on him an honorary doctor of divinity degree at their June commencement.

That summer Steward returned to Macon, Georgia, for the dedication of the church he built years earlier. Since his departure in the early 1870s, the material condition of the people in Macon had improved. He was pleased that the dedicatory services brought in $400 despite the lack of vigor and organization. Steward returned to Wilmington in a lighter mood.[36]

Normally a serious writer of theology, in the fall he wrote a satirical essay, "Other People's Children." He made fun of those who think that their children are perfect whereas other people's children are rude. He observed that others think of our children as spoiled. "Gracious!" he exclaimed, "suppose this is true. How blind they must be not to see the virtues of all of our children." The solution would be to have the parents of "our children" and the parents of "other people's children" meet at a convention. The results would be to have the children happily playing together while the parents forgot that there are "other people's children." In a more serious vein, he suggested that ministers set examples of hospitality or be barred from holding a position "longer than is absolutely necessary." Maybe he had some personal unpleasant experience in mind when he added that if ministers refused lodging or food to other ministers, the people might follow suit and conferences that depended on laymen putting up ministers would not be able to function.[37]

More serious for Steward was the Wilmington school situation. In 1875 the Delaware legislature had passed a law that authorized taxation of blacks for the support of black schools. The near poverty of this group accounted for only one-third of the funds needed for running these separate schools. In 1881 the legislature appropriated $2,400 annually for distribution among the black schools on a per capita basis. Steward, an advocate of using tax dollars for educating all children, criticized both political parties for not advocating 100 percent state support for education of black children. In 1882, an election year, the Democrats accused the Republicans of advocating mixed schools, a subject intensely disliked in Delaware and elsewhere. The Republicans quickly denounced the unpopular concept. Steward was a member of the Delaware State Central Committee, but he was so upset with the Republicans' unwillingness to support the concept of equal education that he withdrew from the fall campaign in protest. His belief caused him problems at Bethel Church, many of whose parishioners were loyal Republicans. Steward spoke in his church on November 23 on the subject of mixed schools. He emphasized that schools were considered mixed only when the children were not white; that the presence of Germans, Irish, or Jews did not make schools mixed. He urged people not to vote for candidates who supported discrimination. Angry at Republicans who sought to drive a wedge between the congregation and their controversial minister, Steward accused politicians of selling him "for old rags if thereby they could increase the value of their political charms." Steward informed T. Thomas Fortune, editor of the New York *Globe* and a major advocate of independence in politics, "henceforth, I, too, am an independent in politics, and am prepared for . . . barks and bites of false friends or open foes."[38]

The school situation was of great interest to Bethel's congregation. They wanted a good education for their children but they were undecided on tactics. This sentiment was shared by others in Wilmington, who met on February 9, 1883 at Zion AME Church "to consider what action the colored people ought to take with regard to their school relations." Steward attended this meeting and remarked that while the people were "quite earnest," they remained "remarkably undecided as to what is best to do." The people were confused because outside of Wilmington, blacks had no part in a free school system. Later, these schools came under the jurisdiction of the state's superintendent of schools. Steward was so serious that he called for an interracial national convention to address the problem of racism. (A convention met in Louisville on September 24, 1883.)[39] In April he asked if whites would ever change their racial attitudes and use the uniqueness of America's geographical isolation to develop a society that was a blend of the best elements of the European, African, and Asian races. Optimistic, he suggested that this would be the America of the future. A mass meeting was held on May 16 in Philadelphia to discuss issues raised by Steward's concern, which had the support of the Philadelphia Annual Conference.[40]

Steward's controversial views caused a rift between him and his congregation. Republican politicians had convinced people that Steward was seeking to develop a power base at their expense. Many in his congregation did not want integrated schools because they feared that blacks would lose what little authority they had in the separate schools. Despite Steward's claim that he did not advocate integrated schools, he clearly did in a letter to the Wilmington *Morning News*. "I believe," he wrote, "that in this country there ought to be one set of public schools in which all the children can be educated. These have been my views publicly for the last ten years." Fortunately, the itineracy system that he criticized saved him from the embarrassment of remaining in a church that did not want him. Despite his less than happy departure, he was proud of his record at Bethel. He had received over one hundred into the church, and he had raised $8,200 in two years. "No two years in the history of the church can show a similar record, and no church of colored people in [Delaware] ever did the like," he boasted. Expressing no bitterness over his departure, he added that he had many friends in Wilmington and that he left with "no change in my own feelings toward the enterprising colored people of that city."[41]

In May 1883 Steward took charge of Philadelphia's Union AME Church, a congregation that openly bemoaned the arrival of "Mr. Controversy."

Return to Pennsylvania, 1883-1886

Steward returned to Philadelphia in extremely low spirits. Prior to receiving his official assignment to Union, he preached a guest sermon in the dilapidated building and undiplomatically expressed the desire "that after the people were entirely cleared from the church the [unsightly] building might fall down and thus go out of existence." The unamused congregation unsuccessfully petitioned the Philadelphia Annual Conference to allow them to retain the services of their outgoing minister, the Reverend J. W. Beckett. Steward was discredited. He did not want to go to Union, which would be hostile to him. He gave some serious thought to requesting another assignment, but his controversial reputation made him undesirable to other churches. It was only the advice of the Reverend W. H. Davis that convinced Steward to go to Union and gain the confidence of the people. He wrote in his autobiography that the assignment to Union was "the supreme test of my life."[1]

His first few weeks at Union were troubling ones, as Steward sought to win over recalcitrant members. After Steward was presented to the congregation, the chief of stewards requested that the members come forward and meet their new pastor. A woman sitting next to Elizabeth Steward, not knowing her identity, said, "why, I understand he does not allow his family to associate with the people."[2] This was true. Steward, like other elites, labored for the betterment of the masses and faithfully carried out his pastoral duties on their behalf, but he did not socialize with the lower classes.

Steward's authority at Union was challenged by Beckett when he was invited back to conduct a wedding in the church. Steward was upset that the couple did not ask him to perform the ceremony, and he retaliated by locking his study to prevent Beckett from using it. When some in the church questioned this action, he replied, "a man is sometimes obliged to leave his hat in his seat . . . in order to retain his seat." He had forcefully established his authority, and no other ministers conducted weddings or funerals in his church without his invitation.[3]

As usual, Steward moved quickly to improve Union. On the plus side, Union had "a fine Sunday School, a well organized church, an overflowing night congregation, but a very small Sunday morning congregation." Previously, no more than two dozen came to the morning service, but Steward soon increased attendance to over seventy. Still, Union Church was housed in an inadequate building. It needed a larger house to worship in "or worse things will befall them," observed the *Christian Recorder*.[4]

Steward used his skills that had led to the purchase of churches in Georgia. He arranged to buy the former Trinity Methodist Episcopal Church, furniture, and parsonage for approximately $25,000. The new Union Church was opened to the public on December 13, 1883, with dedicatory services a month later. Nearly $3,000 was raised at this service, which he believed was the largest amount collected in one day's offering in the AME church. Steward adopted a military style collection system, organizing Union into five departments: right wing, left wing, center column, advance guard, and rear guard. He perfected the scheme by organizing "three divisions under three generals assisted by twenty-seven captains." This system, effectively combined with grand rallies and the sale of some church property, enabled Steward to eliminate a debt of $22,000 within sixteen months of his arrival. Pleased with his fund-raising efforts, Steward announced that other churches should adopt this method and stop attempting to erase deficits "by promiscuous begging."[5]

Steward was a minister who sought to elevate people's spirits, educate their minds, and help them save their souls. He was at the center of activities that occupied the attention of Union's congregation and by extension the larger African-American community in Philadelphia. On February 10, 1884, he ended the period of dedicatory services with a local preachers' day at Union. In an ecumenical gesture, Steward invited all local preachers from the branches of Methodism and other denominations.[6]

A devout supporter of temperance, Steward used the old Union building for temperance meetings, and in September 1884 it was used by Steward and presiding elder, C. C. Felts, for a novel camp meeting that brought in twenty members. It was ironic that he sponsored a camp meeting; he agreed with the *State Journal's* assertion that camp meetings attracted a low element that corrupted the morals of others. Steward had no choice. He wanted to increase

Union's membership, and Philadelphia's elite had other options for church attendance.[7]

Steward's activism proved to be a tonic that lifted his spirits. In contrast to his feelings a year earlier, he was in a happy mood when the Philadelphia Annual Conference met in April 1884. "Seeing myself dangerously near the pit as conference adjourned in 1883, I had thrown myself wholly upon God for guidance and strength and He brought me to the conference of 1884 with a 'new song in my mouth,' and I felt 'my goings' were established. Praise the Lord!" He was active in the 1884 conference that met in Chambersburg, Pennsylvania, where he introduced a resolution on divorce and a report on education.[8]

Events in 1884 projected him once again into the spotlight of controversy. Delegates to the 1883 Philadelphia Annual Conference, like their counterparts from New York, for the first time elected candidates to attend the church's General Conference in 1884. Many of the older church leaders such as Theodore Gould, C. C. Felts, and Theophilus Steward were not elected. Steward was not amused at being excluded from the church's quadrennial meeting. His essay "Ripeness in the Gospel Ministry" argued that mature men (he was forty-one) should be the church's leaders. This was his point when he had criticized the southern delegates four years earlier. He stated forcefully that it was time "to look this boyism in the face, and to set up a rule of seniority in the ministerial ranks." Although he was not a delegate to the conference, he sought to influence some of its deliberations. In September 1883 he had notified the *Christian Recorder* that the Philadelphia Annual Conference adopted a resolution calling on the General Conference to appoint a commission "to consider the property of establishing a method of administration in the Lord's Supper, that shall secure order and decency, and promote the solemnity and spiritual value of the sacrament." Steward supported uniformity because its adoption "would give us more of law and less of men; and this is an essential point in moulding character." A few days before the May General Conference, the *Christian Recorder* printed Steward's essay "Confirmation," in which he asked that those who favored restoring "the beautiful and scriptural rite of confirmation in our church, as the proper complement of infant baptism," send him a postcard of support that he would forward to the Baltimore meeting.[9]

His exclusion from the conference was a minor controversy compared to his involvement by proxy in Wilberforce University's presidential search fiasco. The comedy of errors began on June 17 when the teachers' committee presented two reports to the trustees to replace President Benjamin F. Lee, who had resigned to take over the editorship of the *Christian Recorder*. The majority report endorsed Steward for president, whereas the minority report recommended John G. Mitchell. "Ignoring the reports, the [trustees] . . . placed in nomination from the floor . . . the names of John G. Mitchell, T. G. Steward, and J. T. Jenifer." Mitchell received seventeen votes, one more than the minimum. Steward and Jenifer trailed with twelve and two votes respectively. Unhappy with the vote, Steward's supporters, who believed that their man had been "cheated," submitted a motion the next morning to rescind the previous decision. Before the motion was voted on, the trustees adjourned to observe the commencement exercises. An individual or individuals lobbied on behalf of Mitchell, but ironically it was for Samuel Mitchell, John's brother and a faculty member. To everyone's shock, Samuel Mitchell was selected for the presidency. Hoping to save face, the trustees offered Steward a teaching position but he turned down the position. It would not be until 1907 that Steward would join the faculty of Wilberforce.[10]

Steward's combative nature led him to engage in yet another fight over church policy. While he supported grand rallies and tolerated camp meetings, he did not support, in the fall of 1884, the right of Sunday schools to hold regular sessions without interruptions. Using the provocative phrase "Sunday School heresies," Steward criticized the Reverend C. S. Smith, corresponding secretary of the Sunday School Union, for writing that Sunday school sessions should not be interrupted or dismissed to benefit other services. This benign statement became grist for Steward's mill and he responded with characteristic overkill. Smith and his defenders reminded Steward that Jesus said "suffer little children to come unto me," adding that Jesus told Peter, "feed my lambs." Smith offered to resign if anyone could prove that he had, in Steward's words, committed "heresy." Displaying a customary arrogance, Steward "graciously" indicated that he did not want Smith to resign over such a small "mishap." Steward had the last word, which was his practice in these "debates." "I oppose this nonsense of children's rights because I want some children in the church!" Perhaps realizing his vituperation was costing him support, Steward belatedly sought to extricate himself by concluding that children needed to be taught principles and duties "and Brother Smith is doing a good work in quickening thought with regard to them."[11]

This incident reveals a lot about Steward's character. He had a tremendous need to be correct. He would debate a point way beyond its original horizons in order to "win." This latest controversy also revealed that Steward was a rigid figure who did not afford children any rights in the home or in the church. Sunday school sessions lasted only one hour and it would be easy to schedule them without interruptions, but his nature did not permit this flexibility.

People were willing to follow Steward's leadership when he articulated issues that were compatible with the community's betterment. One important issue that confronted the black Philadelphians in the mid-1880s was their relationship to the Republican Party. In 1884, seven years after the notorious compromise that ended Reconstruction, the nation's African-American population had at best a tenuous relationship with their former savior, the Republican Party. Philadelphia's black politicians and civic leaders wanted more benefits from the relationship. African Americans in the nation were recipients of several prestigious appointments, such as recorder of the deeds in Washington, D.C., custom collectors in major cities, auditor of the navy's books, treasurer of the United States, and postmasters general of small southern communities whenever Republicans occupied the White House. But this meant little to the masses or elites beyond the level of racial pride. Philadelphia's colored elite wanted more opportunities for economic advancement, and, like white reformers, they wanted an end to municipal corruption. Although Philadelphia offered more opportunities for blacks than did other northern cities, racism and discrimination were alive and well in The City of Brotherly Love. During the early 1880s some gains were achieved. Thomas T. Henry was admitted to the bar; *The Press*, a daily newspaper, hired a black reporter, a graduate of Howard University, causing a stir among his white coworkers; and Miles Tucker, a man described as "black as coal" by *The New York Times*, was appointed a United States customhouse weigher. By 1885 the *New York Freeman* reported that Philadelphia had more colored men in business than other cities. While this was true, Philadelphia could not boast of a visible African American in either banking or brokerage houses and there was none among the city's wholesale jobbers.[12]

Municipal corruption affected political allegiance. Staunch supporters of the Republican Party, by 1874 the elite were disillusioned. Robert Purvis and William Still of Underground Railroad fame supported for mayor an independent who ran with Democratic Party support against Republican corruption. Many, who saw Democrats, regardless of their ideology, as allies of the Ku Klux Klan, were outraged by Purvis and Still's defection. Others, in 1881, supported Samuel G. King for mayor. This coalition of Democrats, nonmachine Republicans, and independents was victorious. The city's black politicians sided with Democrat King, hoping now to achieve what the Republicans had denied them. Reform-minded King made a concerted effort to help them and the city's African-American population. He appointed four blacks to the police department, a first in the North. By 1884, thirty-five of the city's 1,400 police officers were black. In his reelection bid, King had the support of 200 of Philadelphia's leading African Americans, but Republican William Smith won. He fired Lewis Carroll, one of King's four original appointees to the police force, and had nearly all the others removed from duty. Philadelphia's black politicians, who were initially flushed with the power of independence, quickly came back to the Republican fold, leaving insurgency for another generation.[13]

Nationally, African Americans were torn between maintaining an allegiance to the Republican Party, supporting the Democrats who were viewed as being affiliated with mob rule and the former slavocracy, or joining or forming an independent party. A few prominent race leaders such as George T. Downing, a Rhode Island caterer and restaurateur, T. McCants Stewart, a Brooklyn attorney and AME minister, Monroe Trotter, a former member of the Fifty-fourth Massachusetts Colored Infantry, and Peter Clark, a Cincinnati principal, all defected. Clark became a well-known advocate of socialism.

The eve of the 1884 presidential election found African Americans lukewarm in their support for partisan politics. The Republican-dominated Supreme Court had declared in 1883 that the 1875 Civil Rights Act was unconstitutional as only states had the rights to prohibit discrimination involving public accommodation. Demoralized, many agreed with militant New York *Globe* editor Timothy Thomas Fortune that the race felt like it was "baptized in ice water." "We do not ask the corrupt Republican party for its sympathy," he wrote. "We spurn it with loathing contempt." While most would not embrace this extremism, many lauded the 1883 National Convention of Colored People meeting's decision not to endorse Chester A. Arthur's bid for president. Few shed tears when James G. Blaine wrestled the party's nomination away from Arthur. New York attorney John F. Quarles assessed in the spring of 1883 that "there is a great dissatisfaction among the colored people about their position in the Republican party. The colored vote is drifting from it." George T. Downing told the *New York Evening Post* that the race should divide its vote in order to gain respect. Many heard the message but saw the Democratic Party as antithetical to their political beliefs. A former Virginia slave voted for the Democrats in a local election. He died soon after and "the Negroes refused to attend the funeral, and the service was conducted by . . . a white minister, and he was buried by white men."[14]

Steward, mindful of the hysteria that would accompany a Democratic victory, did not believe the rumor that Cleveland's victory would lead to reenslavement. He did not campaign for the Blaine/Logan ticket, citing as justification his busy schedule (it was more likely that he was still miffed at the party's refusal to support him in the Wilmington school fight). Yet he was not unconcerned about the election result. On November 9, prior to the final tally, he spoke in Union Church to a large crowd composed of blacks and whites. They came, according to *The Press*, because of his reputation "as an organized thinker and speaker." His text came from Psalms 47:7, "for God is the king of all the earth." He cautioned the people to be calm and to avoid a riot. *The Press* described him as both "earnest and eloquent; showing that he keenly felt the truth of his statements, the foundations of his fears and the importance of his warnings and advise."[15]

As the election outcome remained in doubt, Steward stated that a Republican defeat would be "providential retribution for their indifference and pusillanimity in dealing with the Negro vote." Meanwhile, as the votes were slowly coming in, some Democrats went on a rampage in Baltimore and held a "victory" parade while the police did little to quell the wild disturbance.[16]

Once Cleveland was declared the victor, Steward attacked the incoming administration in a sermon. The Democratic Party, and by inference Cleveland, represented to Steward "a party of assassination . . . that . . . has murdered . . . ten thousand . . . for their political opinions." Others did not share his outrage. Frederick Douglass, who was known as "Mr. Republican," "was prepared to give Cleveland a fair trial [because] . . . he had done some good things in . . . New York as governor, and he may do some good things for the colored people when he shall be president." Neither former South Carolina Congressman Joseph H. Rainey nor William Still believed that Cleveland would revive slavery. Timothy Thomas Fortune, as editor of the New York *Freeman*, initially did not expect much from a Democrat president, but later he offered praise for Cleveland's first administration. Concern about Cleveland's victory and its political implication led *The AME Church Review* to devote over thirty pages to the return of the Democrats to national power.[17] Despite Steward's flirtation with political independence, he, like the majority of African Americans, would continue, albeit reluctantly, to support the Republican Party for the next half century.

Meanwhile, the controversial minister continued to delight his supporters and alienate his detractors when he wrote between 1883 and 1885 several theological pieces that vaulted him into the forefront of African Methodist writers. Both *Divine Attributes* and *Death, Hades and Resurrection* were acclaimed by prominent ministerial colleagues and laymen. Steward's two theological publications were the first in a series of textbooks on theology known as the Tawawa Series. He organized the Tawawa Theological, Scientific, and Literary Association in late 1883. Steward was the dean of Theology, Bishop J. P. Campbell was president, Bishop Daniel A. Payne was vice president, Dr. Benjamin W. Arnett was general manager, and Dr. T. H. Jackson was secretary. Students took correspondence courses or purchased textbooks for home study. Henry M. Turner considered the Tawawa Series the work of Steward's life and urged all ministers to read it or "miss a rare theological treat and a vast store of valuable information."[18]

Steward was not an orthodox theological thinker. Tanner and others accepted the Bible literally. Steward's mother's insistence on searching for the truth, his own questioning nature, and his prolific reading led him to believe that the Bible offered broad truths, but there was latitude for interpretation. To those who believed that certain truths were infallible, Steward's interpretations bordered on heresy. In late 1884 the Florida Annual Conference passed a resolution condemning both of Steward's books. He defended himself by citing the numerous endorsements he had received. He urged the Florida clergymen "to read and weigh them, and if they are worthless, appropriate them for kindling." Steward raised serious questions about man's relationship with God and he shocked unenlightened thinkers with his inquiries into resurrection. Are bodies reunited with souls? Do loved ones meet again in heaven? Can humans really communicate with the dead? These and other questions Steward debated with himself and then raised in devout groups, forcing people to reexamine their beliefs.[19]

The controversial nature of his books, particularly *Death, Hades and Resurrection*, brought him praise from enlightened circles. Financially, he expressed doubts about the AME Book Concern's accounting. He wrote in his scrapbook that the Methodist Episcopalian bookstore in Philadelphia strictly accounted for his books, whereas the AME Book Concern was sloppy in its bookkeeping. For the meticulous writer, this was unacceptable.[20]

Steward created more controversy with his interpretation of evolution. The publication in 1859 of Charles Darwin's *On the Origin of Species* caused an uproar among fundamentalists. Religious leaders questioned if scientists had empirical evidence to refute the Genesis account of creation. *The Catholic World* was one of the religious journals that devoted issue after issue to the evolution debate. Many agreed with the Reverend George M. Searle's argument that "you may be scientific or religious but surely not both, unless you have altogether lost your mental balance and proprieties." Steward disagreed. In 1881 he wrote two essays. In "The Modern Controversy: Science and Religion," he wrote that it was a mistake to assume that scientists were infidels. He believed that the controversy would make theology more human and science more Christian. He argued that scientists could question the literal interpretation of Genesis while still believing that the mystery of the universe was the creation of God. His second essay, "The Inspiration of the Scriptures," led to criticism from orthodox religionists who were outraged over his contention that the Bible "may have been inspired."[21] Yet these reactions were minor compared to the reception fundamentalists heaped upon Steward's 1885 publication of *Genesis Re-read*.

Steward was too well read in science and theology to accept simple dogma. He knew that the Bible was written by men who lived at a different time and that it reflected the cultural and political times of its writers. *Genesis Re-read* offered a view that one historian described as placing "the evolutionary process within the context of divine plan." David Wills noted that "though he affirmed the Mosaic authorship of the pentateuch, Steward dealt with Moses . . . as 'an historian reviewing events as the knowledge of them had reached' him. This emphasis on Moses' sources was . . . crucial . . . for it allowed Steward to make a sharp distinction between Moses' description of events . . . which he could have known by oral tradition, written records, and public engravings, and the events of creation itself, which clearly lay beyond the reach of those sources." Daniel Payne considered Steward to be "frank, bold and fearless," but he cautioned that African Methodists had reason "to watch the Christian apologist . . . but so long as we know him to be fighting our battles, we should . . . consider the arduousness of the task of him who contends with advanced science, and [have] the patience to wait long enough to understand him before passing upon his work."[22]

Genesis Re-read's controversial reception did not prevent its inclusion in 1888 in the Doctrine and Discipline of the AME Church "as a secondary source for the fourth year of ministerial study." This backhanded compliment indicated that the church recognized its literary quality but was unwilling to make it primary reading. Its inclusion into the curriculum did not guarantee its popularity among laymen and preachers. Steward complained that the AME

Book Concern did not reprint the book after one thousand copies were sold. Although he ascribed this to a "lack of enterprise," the church had a legitimate reason for not reprinting *Genesis Re-read*. The book was difficult to sell. J. C. Embry advertised two hundred copies in the July 1, 1886 issue at $1.50, with 50¢ going to agents who sold copies. Although it was a natural fund-raiser for churches, a year later Embry was forced by slow sales to offer two hundred copies at 75¢ each.[23]

In 1888 Steward wrote his most provocative examination of theology, *The End of the World; or, Clearing the Way for the Fullness of Gentiles*. His thesis challenged Anglo-Saxon superiority by stating that the world would not end in the biblical sense of a fiery destruction but in the destruction of Anglo-Saxon supremacy. It would be at this time that "Ethiopia will stretch out her hands unto God."[24]

His book contended that the Anglo-Saxon was the retiring man and that out of Africa and Asia would come the world's new leaders. These leaders would be spiritual and walk in God's footsteps. Unlike the Anglo-Saxon, they would not destroy the culture of others or try to control the world. He was influenced by Josiah Strong's *Our Country* (1885). Strong argued that Anglo-Saxons were destined to "dispossess many weaker races, assimilate others and mould the remainder." Unlike Strong, Steward did not view Anglo-Saxons as the savior of civilization. He argued that anarchy would rise as capitalism was challenged. The destruction of law and order in Europe would result in a tide of immigrants coming to America and in his estimation, America "will soon become the seething cauldron into which these elements will fall." He believed that God would someday punish Anglo-Saxons and other whites for misusing Christianity to enslave Africans, and exterminate Indians. He declared that the destruction of Anglo-Saxons would lead to the world embracing Christianity as the African, the new prophet of a bigotry-free Christianity, would represent a society free of corruption and evil.[25]

Steward's thesis excited some and appalled others. J. C. Embry, business manager of AME Book Publications, predicted a large sale because its contents were "foretold by Daniel and confirmed by the prophecy and teaching of Jesus and his apostles." He requested that ministers send in their orders, as ten thousand, he believed, would want to read *The End of the World*. Sarah C. Bierce Scarborough, a Wilberforce faculty member, wrote Steward that "we have just finish reading your latest work with much pleasure and admiration for the scholarly trend of its author's mind. . . . We deeply regret that we cannot have your literary companionship in our isolated life here."[26]

The AME publications responded predictably. Benjamin F. Lee, editor of the *Christian Recorder*, reviewed *End of the World* not to "show that the popular idea of millennium is about to be realized," but to show that Anglo-Saxonism has "no place in Christian development." Benjamin Tanner, who constantly urged ministers to write, viewed Steward's prophecies as cloudy and even heretical. He questioned Steward's declaration that the end of the world meant "simply a change of hands in the work of disseminating the grace of the Kingdom of God." Tanner argued that the world's end meant resurrection, not a transfer of power, spiritual or otherwise.[27]

Steward was outraged by Tanner's charge of heresy. Privately, he wrote, "I bow to his authority in some other things [but] I cannot say so much for his judgment of what is logical as for his ability to follow a line of argumentation." Incensed, he accused his mentor of acting "impetuously."[28]

Overlooked in the criticism of Steward's book was the place of African-American Christianity in the realm of Christianity as practiced in America. Steward—unlike his critics, who accepted literally the biblical interpretation of the end of the world—went farther and questioned the true role of Christian behavior. It made perfect sense to him that the world's end would come when God's subjects were spiritually returned to his grace. He raised this thought in 1889 in "A New Reading of an Old Phase; The End of the World." He asked if Judgment Day was the same as the end of the world, and wondered if it was possible that not everything would be destroyed simultaneously. He believed that the end would come when Israel was returned to God. Steward predicted that the "sinister of race will melt away . . . and a new fraternal world will emerge." Once again he repeated his theme of *The End of the World*: "Africa and Asia will come to the ensign lifted up, and an era of brotherhood . . . will dawn upon the world." Nearly a year later he wrote that he recently heard a lecture by Bishop W. R. Nicholson of the Reformed Church, who confirmed his interpretations of the prophecies.[29]

Steward's theological interpretation, while dissimilar to Bishop Henry M. Turner's bold religious nationalism that declared "God is a Negro," did, as suggested by David Wills, connect theology to blackness. With few exceptions, Steward's contemporaries were unable to see their religiosity divorced from white American Christianity. Steward, suggests Wills, showed that African-American Christian culture "would not emerge as a subculture within Christian America nor as the gradual result of the colonization and Christianization of Africa."[30] His writings made him one of the leading thinkers in African Methodism. Indeed, he was by 1890 one of the most prominent African

Americans of his generation. Yet a major publication in 1887 that provided biographical sketches of 170 black men such as Booker T. Washington, Timothy Thomas Fortune, Frederick Douglass, Alexander Crummell, Henry Highland Garnet, and Daniel A. Payne excluded Theophilus Steward. Although it was the author's contention that he had to draw the line in making selections and that many worthy men were left out, the only plausible explanation for his exclusion is that Steward was too controversial.[31]

Steward was an active minister who lent his name and talents to many civic causes. He was a popular preacher who frequently delivered guest sermons. On April 6, 1884, he returned to Brooklyn to preach the Sunday evening service at Bridge Street AME Church. He spoke from John 14, where Jesus said to his disciples that he was in God and they were in Him and He was in them. The New York *Globe* described Steward's presentation as "a masterly production of deep thought. A very large number greeted him with a hearty welcome after seven years' absence from the pastorate."[32]

By tradition, upbringing, and Christian faith, Steward was a community-minded person. He spoke out against injustice, be it racial or judicial. On November 16, 1885, Steward, William Still, and a delegation visited the governor of Pennsylvania to ask him to mitigate the sentence of Annie Cutler, a convicted murderer. Her lover had beaten and robbed her, and then betrayed her affections by marrying someone else. Under the influence of alcohol, Annie Cutler killed him. Steward was among the six hundred individuals who signed a petition seeking clemency. Their pleas were not ignored and the pardon board commuted her sentence to eight years.[33] Such actions helped him attract more worshipers to Union Church. Unfortunately, by the time the congregation was reconciled with their minister and he was happy in his assignment, the itineracy system moved him on to Washington's Metropolitan Church. His worth as a minister was recognized by the Philadelphia Annual Conference, which unanimously adopted a resolution signed by Benjamin T. Tanner and Levi J. Coppin that read, "we beg to bear witness to his strict integrity of character, his broad intellectual acquirements and his fearless devotion to the right as it presents itself to him."[34]

EIGHT

Washington, Baltimore, and the End of Itineracy, 1886-1891

On the surface, Metropolitan African Methodist Episcopal Church represented a plum assignment for Theophilus Steward. It was organized in 1836 as Union Bethel but in 1872 the delegates to the general conference in Nashville voted to erect a new building to reflect the glory of African Methodism. The succeeding conferences of 1876, 1880, and 1884 arranged for the church to be the largest in the connectional. Metropolitan was to be built as "a monument to the love of the race, for the church of God, and for the good of man."[1]

Metropolitan represented Steward's most formidable challenge. As the nation's capital, Washington was a magnet for the country's colored aristocrats, who came from Charleston, Baltimore, Memphis, Philadelphia, New Orleans, New York, and other cities to seek their fame and fortune in the federal bureaucracy. Many of these elites worshiped at Fifteenth Street Presbyterian Church. Steward described his congregation as ranging from "persons of character and literary taste" to "common laborers, washer women, servants . . . and a few mechanics." The congregation had a "warm, loving spirit," and Metropolitan was for him a place "simply glorious to preach," but the church was poor.[2]

The church wanted Metropolitan to be a showcase for African Methodists but it was unwilling to offer sufficient financial support. That task was handed to Steward, who, despite his excellent fund-raising skills, faced a difficult if not impossible task. This problem was temporarily put aside as special trains brought worshipers from Baltimore, Annapolis, and other cities for the May 30, 1886, dedication. Frederick Douglass and Robert Smalls, the Civil War hero, were among the luminaries who spoke during the dedicatory week. The excitement of dedication had barely subsided when Steward had to devise ways to erase the deficit of $51,000. Creditors were impatient and the congregation was not "of the extraordinary self-sacrificing class." Steward's two years at Metropolitan were troubled ones, as "creditors harassed [him] in person and by letter."[3]

Steward was task oriented. He officially took charge of Metropolitan on June 13 and the next day he provided the church's board with a plan to liquidate the debt. The plan was unanimously adopted by the board, which also voted 4-3 to pay him $600 a year for his board, bringing his board and salary to $1,000.[4]

Steward was a proud man. He sought during the hot and humid summer of 1886 to extricate Metropolitan from its financial situation. In August he reported to the *Christian Recorder* that his predecessor had mismanaged affairs. Citing race pride, he pleaded with African Methodists to support Metropolitan, as it represented "the glory of the American Negro." Clearly he understood that critics of the race would cite Metropolitan's financial situation as proof that blacks were incapable of leadership. "Oh!" Steward exclaimed, "that I might touch just one sympathetic heart by these utterances." His cry was echoed by editor Benjamin F. Lee, who demanded that the laity "get hold of the handle fairly and relieve the connection of this small responsibility."[5]

Financial support was slow in coming. The September 2 issue of the *Christian Recorder* printed Steward's new plea to save Metropolitan or have critics ridicule its erection as "the most prominent, striking, expressive and expansive moment of folly." He had collected $700 at a recent service, but most of it went to normal maintenance expenses. The Washington correspondent of the New York *Freeman* heralded his efforts and praised him as one of the "ablest preachers in this city." This was an important observation; Washington's churches were extremely competitive. Steward had to compete with twenty-eight AME churches there, not to mention the Catholic, Presbyterian, or Congregational churches that also attracted colored aristocrats.[6]

The burden of raising funds left Steward in low spirits. In early November 1886, less than six months after taking over Metropolitan, *The People's Advocate* reported that Steward had resigned. John W. Cromwell, editor of the *Advocate*, was a friend of Steward. Steward may have mentioned to Cromwell his dissatisfaction and even an intention to resign. Regardless, it was with relief that the *Christian Recorder* reported in late November that "we are glad that [Steward] still remains at . . . Metropolitan."[7]

Near the end of 1886, Steward reported that he had raised $500 at an October fair. His bold, even reckless, prose called on the AME church to lend Metropolitan $4,000 with low interest. "As a church," he explained, "we have never had a grander opportunity to display our business ability." The emotional, accusatory letter immediately caused editor Lee to view its contents as controversial and possibly injurious to Metropolitan, and he decided not to publish it. However, while he was away from the office, someone set the essay in type. Soon after, Steward asked that the letter not be published. But it was too late. While his frankness disturbed many, Theodore Gould, after visiting Metropolitan in January 1887, declared emphatically that Steward was the right man for Metropolitan. Gould urged pastors to raise $2,000 annually to erase the debt, which Steward had lowered to $47,000.[8]

Steward was not above embarrassing others. He informed the *Christian Recorder* that his loving congregation gave his family for Thanksgiving 1886 three turkeys and $10. Several weeks later they gave the Stewards a Christmas present of food worth $50. He provided this information so that readers would understand that "a grand and noble souled people" worshiped at Metropolitan. He was hoping, too, to embarrass the leadership of the AME church to support his debt-ridden church. A March 26, 1887, fund-raiser netted $600. An excursion to Harper's Ferry in September added $200. Other affairs brought in more funds, but he was unable to lower appreciably the church's debt because neither his immediate congregation nor the AME church viewed the debt as the most pressing problem. Steward's pulpit mastery increased average attendance from three hundred when he arrived to nearly a thousand throughout 1887. Yet only about half were members. The AME church had to consider the debt of other churches, not to mention financial support for Wilberforce University and its poorly supported foreign mission program.[9]

Not overlooked in the church's unending battle to reduce its debt was the question of Steward's salary. Metropolitan's board minutes indicate that Steward's salary was always in arrears. With monthly expenses of $500, the board could hardly maintain Steward's salary and make debt payments. Often the board offered him portions of his regular salary.[10]

His chronic money problems prevented Elizabeth Steward and other family members from attending the funeral of Martha Gadsden, Elizabeth's mother, who died in Charleston, South Carolina.[11] His spirits were not lifted by circumstances that led to the funeral service of his nemesis, Richard Harvey Cain, being held in Metropolitan in 1887.[12]

Not all was gloom for Steward in Washington. Steward was pleased with the educational system of the district. Although schools were segregated until 1901, the black schools had excellent reputations and outstanding teachers. M Street High School, under the direction of Francis L. Cardoza, was the nation's premier preparatory school for black youth. The majority of its graduates, including Steward's sons Frank and Charles, went to Harvard College.[13]

Frederick Douglass, who spoke in Union Church when Steward preached in Philadelphia, was a frequent visitor to Metropolitan. The abolitionist, journalist, and human rights advocate had a reputation as a humanist who thought little of religion. Puzzled by Douglass's presence in his church, Steward on July 26, 1886, wrote to him that he "had heard that he was not a believer in Christianity, and . . . that he had little respect for ministers or religion." Douglass, an admirer of the younger man, replied the next day in a five-page handwritten letter. Annoyed by the message, but not by the messenger, Douglass wrote, "ignorant men, inside and outside the pulpit . . . [have] called me infidel, atheist and a disorganizer." These critics, complained Douglass, have never quoted from his speeches or writings. This was not entirely true; Douglass had on several occasions disturbed people with his lack of "reverence" for God. In 1870 he praised the ratification of the Fifteenth Amendment with thanks to the efforts of Wendell Phillips, Charles Sumner, Thaddeus Stevens, Benjamin F. Butler, Ulysses S. Grant, John Brown, Abraham Lincoln, and other abolitionists. African-American clergymen were upset that Douglass did not list God as a major force in their victory for equal male suffrage. He further alienated himself from the clergy when he addressed the final meeting of the American Anti-Slavery Society on April 26, 1870 with these words: "I dwell here in no hackneyed cant about thanking God for this deliverance." He was bitter because too many had said that God would destroy slavery when He felt the need to do so. Thus, he believed it important to thank those who labored with their God-given intelligence to eradicate slavery. Douglass continued in his letter to Steward to state that he regularly read the *Christian Recorder* and the *AME Church Review* as well as contributed to Metropolitan's treasury. He made it clear that his "line of action in this matter is not determined by any approval of the theological dogma often promulgated from the pulpit." Steward did not preach dogma, a practice that he shunned. Douglass reminded Steward that his sermon on July 25 "called upon us to give for the glory of God and the good of man." This message was the motivating factor in Douglass's life. He believed that it was more Christian to feed the poor, clothe the naked, tend to the afflicted, and help one's neighbor than to wear the trappings of organized religion while ignoring the plight of others. Douglass believed in God but he added that one can glorify him by living a life harmonious "with the laws of man's creation. God is good! God is light! God is truth! God is love!" Douglass gave money to Metropolitan and other churches because they promoted "character and conduct." A scholar recently suggested that Douglass was a humanist who believed that "the final hope for social liberation was located within the human command rather than . . . Jesus." This view has merit because he believed that too many depended on God for their deliverance without lifting a hand or using their intellect to solve their problems. Douglass questioned the acceptance of the Bible as God's truth. "[I] have no time or inclination for correspondence on the subject of its plenary or other inspiration," he wrote. Douglass considered more important the Bible's views on peace or war, love or hate, and "whether it welcomes men of all races and colors to the same communion, or whether it excludes a part and compels it to go off in a church by itself, as in the case of your church." While Douglass objected to color caste, he was also proud that blacks could establish and operate a religious order that had its own printing house and university. (Steward did not reply to Douglass's letter, but he was so convinced that his friend was a Christian that he reprinted his letter in his autobiography.) While it was true that Douglass "not only lacked a tie to the black church but repudiated its mystical, evangelical rhetoric," he found in Steward's Metropolitan Church a place where sermons appealed to his intellect and not to his emotion. Steward represented to Douglass a minister who saw his role as addressing the whole person, not his soul only.[14]

Douglass's marriage to Helen Pitts, a white woman, in 1884, deeply disturbed many African Americans who thought he had betrayed his black sisters.[15] During the 1880s many openly questioned Douglass's leadership as age and allegiance to the Republican Party placed him on the wrong side of racial issues. But despite his declining popularity, his name was still magical for many. During the fall of 1886 and throughout the first half of 1887, the Douglasses traveled throughout England, France, Italy, and Egypt. Paying homage to Douglass and using his name to raise funds for Metropolitan, Steward invited Douglass to a banquet. Douglass happily accepted. Two thousand of Washington's elite attended the September 22 reception.[16]

Two years later, on July 26, 1889, Steward wrote to Douglass after President Benjamin Harrison appointed him to a diplomatic post in Haiti. Concerned about his friend's physical and political health, Steward wrote, "I am exceedingly anxious that you may be spared to finish your ministry to the full satisfaction of your own country and not against the good will of the Haytians themselves." Steward's words were prophetic, as Douglass was expected to persuade the Haitians to cede to the United States the Môle St. Nicholas to be used as a naval base and coaling station. This base would open up American military and economic expansion in the Caribbean. To the dismay of American businessmen, Douglass proved to be neither a willing nor an unwitting accomplice in this unsavory act of diplomacy. Haiti refused to sign a lease.[17]

The traits that attracted Frederick Douglass to Steward were the same ones that others admired. Steward was a forceful speaker with a wide command of eclectic information. He was the principal speaker at the opening of the sixth season of Washington's Bethel Literary and Historical Association. This forum attracted well-known speakers such as Douglass, Booker T. Washington, and Mary Church Terrell. This association, like its counterparts in Brooklyn, Philadelphia, Baltimore, and elsewhere, represented an august gathering place for aristocrats to discuss literature, history, and African-American themes. Steward spoke at some of their meetings during the 1887-1888 season.[18] In the fall of 1887, Steward presented one of the thirty-six lectures at the centennial celebration of the AME church held at Bethel Church in Philadelphia. His lecture, "The AME Church and Its Relationship to the Elevation of the Race," drew a large and attentive audience. On November 14, he participated in a convention of District of Columbia Protestant black ministers at Metropolitan, where "questions of vital importance [were] considered."[19]

In the spring of 1887 the delegates to the Baltimore Annual Conference, mindful of Steward's controversial nature but appreciative of his leadership qualities, had elected him as a delegate to the quadrennial meeting in Indianapolis the following year. Shortly after returning from Baltimore, he lived up to his reputation by raising questions for the forthcoming general conference. In an essay, "Questions for 1888," Steward questioned the selection of bishops. As many names, including his, were rumored for the bishopric, he opined that men should not be made bishops as a reward for great work or service. If that were true, he argued that women "would occupy all the bishoprics for many years to come." Men, he insisted, should be considered for the bishopric only if they were "noted for their piety. Do they believe in . . . repentance, regeneration and sanctification?" There were too many bishops, in his estimation, and if more were needed, they should be appointed to have "more efficient control of the missionary, educational, Sunday School and church extension work." He added forcefully, "down with ambition and divisions and up with harmony and unity."[20]

Steward had his supporters and dissenters on the bishop question. Southerners, who wanted more control in administering the affairs of the AME church, welcomed calls for more bishops whether they were needed for "efficient control" or not. A major critic of Steward's nonsupport for more bishops was the Reverend J. H. A. Johnson of Baltimore. Johnson, whom some considered "the brainiest man" in the AME connection, wrote twenty essays on the bishop question that matched Steward's for their tenacity. In one essay Johnson called for eight new bishops.[21] Steward responded, "It is not bishops and ministers we need now as much as it is members and churches. What we want now is members! Members! Members!" Enraged, he added, "the millions are perishing while we are disputing as to who shall be chief among the disciples."[22]

In the spring of 1888, shortly before departing for a conference in Indianapolis, Steward was transferred to Baltimore's Bethel AME Church, which was started in the early 1800s by Daniel Coker, who later went to Africa as a missionary. Steward, who had associated with elites from New York to Charleston, found that color was not as important in Baltimore as in other cities. He noticed that among his fellow African Americans, the color line was most rigid in Washington's social and religious circles. Steward surmised that this was due to the absence of business and political affiliations "to compel the people to associate." John Cromwell, editor of the *People's Advocate*, believed that Washington's colored elite were too occupied with selfish pleasures and needed "to elevate the moral and intellectual tone of the *whole* community." Others were less diplomatic. The Reverend J. M. Townsend denounced "the Negro aristocracy in this country and especially in [Washington] as a farce and a disgrace." Calvin Chase, editor of the *Bee*, accused the aristocrats of practicing color discrimination and limiting membership to those whose blue veins were visible. Chase, who came from a prestigious Virginia family, saw his family excluded from the city's top stratum of colored society.[23]

Steward was one of the elites who devoted his time and talents to those social, political, and religious issues that would elevate the community. He was active in the growing temperance movement in the District of Columbia. His departure from Metropolitan was marked by sadness by the church. Benjamin Arnett noted in 1888 that Steward brought Metropolitan to an important status in the community. "People no longer shake their heads at . . . Metropolitan," he declared. "It is now the center of culture, refinement and Christian zeal." Praise came from the Ministers Union in Washington, Bishop J. P. Campbell, and the Reverend Charles H. Shorter, who predicted that Steward would be "the standard other Metropolitan ministers will be judged by." After his departure, the trustees of Metropolitan passed a resolution commending their former pastor for his "urbane manner, exemplary piety, Christian bearing, and pulpit oratory."[24]

Although he was unable to reduce greatly Metropolitan's debt, the failure was not Steward's but rather an indictment of African Methodism. He boarded the train in Washington for the trip to the Indianapolis conference feeling at peace with himself.

Steward was at the center of much of the discussion, as his name was bantered about for the bishopric. Steward stated in his autobiography that the thought of responsibility always destroyed any fleeting thoughts about the bishopric. Modesty was not a characteristic of his personality. In light of his defeat for the presidency of Wilberforce, Steward perhaps did not want to risk the humiliation of defeat. Years later he wrote, "as Napoleon missed his destiny at Acre, so I missed mine at Indianapolis; but I missed mine with eyes wide open and willingly not willfully." Even though a supporter believed that "the ecclesiastical mantle could [not] fall upon worthier shoulders than his," Steward discouraged support. He was also approached by several ministers to seek the editorship of the *Christian Recorder*. He declined, most likely because it would have meant competing with his cousin. Benjamin F. Lee easily won reelection on the first ballot.[25]

The meeting was raucous. Bishop Daniel A. Payne viewed the delegates as "determined to be put into office themselves or to put their favorites in by hook or crook." He accused them of lacking "moral character." Regardless, the delegates, many of whom were rebelling against the old leadership, had their way and elected four bishops.[26]

The convention was divided over several issues, notably the question of merger with the British Methodist Episcopal Church and the liturgy question. A report on the merger between the two branches of Methodism, ordered at the 1884 gathering, was not available. Steward supported the merger and his motion to recognize the merger action taken four years earlier caused heated discussion, with Bishop Payne leading the opposition.[27] The liturgical question became the source of much discussion and, later, Steward led the postconvention opposition with vigor if not logic. The question was originally raised in 1880, when Henry M. Turner called for the adoption of "ritualism and the use of clerical vestments in order to create an atmosphere of formality and dignity in [the] worship services." On May 21 the debate was so intense that a motion to adopt ritualism was tabled. As reported by the *Christian Recorder*, "rash expressions were made, and some uncomplimentary personalities were indulged." Steward vigorously opposed a ritualistic service with a reading of the commandments, Apostles' Creed, etc., because he considered it an incongruity. Yet sixteen years earlier he had called on African Methodists to employ order in their morning worship. Now in 1888 he stood before his peers and said, "every morning we stand up here and go through a rigmarole which we call a ritual and then plunge into the most riotous disorder." Bishop Payne, who at times was enraged by Steward, replied in contemptuous tones.[28]

The "rash expressions" and the dominance of the "uncomplimentary personalities" so annoyed Reverend A. J. Kershaw of Tallahassee, Florida, that he several months later publicly rated Steward and six other leading clergymen. He prefaced his remarks by explaining that his estimation of their speaking power was not a reflection on their brain power, as he preferred to "leave that part of the work for the brethren who understand the true meaning of the terms, 'common sense,' 'common gumption,' 'wisdom,' and 'refined learning.' " Steward was "not an orator . . . but he is a forceful talker, from the fact that he buries himself beneath the subject that he attempts to discuss, and hence, he is a formidable antagonist upon the field of discussion." In contrast, his assessment of Steward's cousin, B. F. Lee, helps in part to explain why Lee was elected president of Wilberforce, editor of the *Christian Recorder*, and, later, bishop of the AME church. "Dr. B. F. Lee seems to have learned that a pound of sense is worth a thousand pounds of nonsense, and hence he always gets a hearing from his audience because he has something to say worth saying."[29]

The liturgy question, not settled in Indianapolis, became a focus of discussion for nearly a year. It was a topic in which Steward would "bury" himself in a forceful manner. He had formidable opposition from a young, unknown minister, J. M. Henderson. The debate started in August 1888, when the Reverend I. H. Welch suggested that a "limited use of the liturgy or ritual would elevate and unify our mode of worship." Steward responded that the liturgy would only develop "the uniformity of a retroacting revolution."[30]

For months Steward and Henderson would excite and then eventually bore readers with their overkill. Both used debating tricks and character assassination. Essentially Henderson argued that John Wesley had established a ritual for marriage, baptism, and funerals but many of the early American Methodists did not follow them. They were unaware of his ideas since his letter to the American pioneers was withheld from them, and the prayer books sent by him were destroyed. Henderson spent over $50 for books and documents on the liturgy question.[31]

Steward dismissed Wesley's contribution to African Methodism and argued that it was better to follow Richard Allen, who preached "the simple gospel" so both the learned and untutored could understand.[32] The debate finally ended when, coincidentally, both men submitted their last essays to the *Christian Recorder* one day apart. Editor Lee asked, "have these two brethren indeed found the end of an endless chain?"[33] Henderson's was contrite. Acknowledging that he had been "warned that no matter how right I might be . . . I would be made to suffer that it was foolish . . . to challenge a Goliath," and that Steward was more obsessed with winning an argument than he was in obtaining the truth, the little "David" put away his stones. Showing an annoying arrogance, Steward admitted that he wanted to prove that he was more logical than Henderson. He admitted that he "may have 'hit' someone whom it were better to 'leave alone in his glory.' " Uncharitably, but in character, he concluded with an " 'adieu,' with kindest sympathies for that little dog that gets bit for the big dog's sins." The debate was costly to Steward in one respect. As intimated by Henderson, Steward ended the debate because he had "received some heavy blows from headquarters." Venting his spleen on Henderson was a reflection of a character flaw when it came to relationships.[34] The only apparent victor in the lengthy debate was J. C. Embry, business manager of AME Book Publications, who was able to sell extra copies of a book by Steward. "The more he talks the more we sell," he noted. "Now if someone will be kind enough to do us like service for 'Genesis Re-read' and 'End of the World,' . . . we shall be exceedingly thankful."[35]

It was amazing that Steward was able to engage in a lengthy debate with Henderson; his involvement with Bethel demanded a considerable amount of time. An indefatigable worker, Steward joined other aristocrats in an effort to improve the lives of black Baltimoreans. Unlike Delaware, Steward could not enter the community as the self-proclaimed savior of the masses. He had to adjust to the existing leadership of Isaac Myers, a union leader, who ran Bethel's Sunday school. Along with the Reverend J. H. A. Johnson, William

H. Bishop, Dr. H. J. Brown, and others, Myers sought to improve black schools. Maryland statutes did not prohibit instruction for freedmen or slaves. Yet most whites were indifferent to educating members of these groups. Like other cities, education for blacks was provided by charitable organizations or the religious efforts of progressive Quakers, Methodists, Presbyterians, and Catholics. In 1859 there were fifteen self-sustaining schools for blacks that did not receive state or local government funds. In 1867 the Baltimore Association for the Moral and Educational Improvement of the Colored People pressured successfully the mayor and the city council to take control of these schools. The city refurbished some and relocated others. Thirteen primary schools were established for blacks. In late 1868 all thirteen schools employed only white teachers. The Board of Commissioners of public schools decided against establishing a grammar and high school for blacks because it was thought "neither advisable nor practicable to provide such grades or schools for this class of people as are in use by the children of white parents." All the black teachers who taught in the pre-1867 schools were dismissed. It was not until September 1, 1868, that community pressure led to the establishment of a grammar school for black children.[36] Throughout the 1870s and after Steward's arrival, Baltimore's black leadership, including many who worshipped at Bethel, raised the issue of black teachers. The community argued in mass meetings for control over their own schools as white teachers would not mingle with the children's parents nor did they make an effort to understand the culture of their pupils. It was not until 1888 that the community received a high school. Two years later, it finally received black teachers. By 1907 the race had complete control of the schools that served them.[37]

This was the situation that faced Steward as he considered schools for three of his sons. A proud and erudite man, Steward wanted the best education for his children. He evaluated the Baltimore public schools as the poorest he had seen anywhere. "The teachers were uniformly white and perhaps uniformly unfit for the positions they held." Unlike the other aristocrats, the Stewards lacked the funds to enroll their boys in a private school. In a visit to his children's school, he was shocked to see the principal and two assistants throw candy to the "dirty brick pavement for the children (including his) to pick up." He complained to the mayor "and my story appeared to take proper effect."[38] Steward's concern for a decent education for his sons and the city's other youth, consistent with his civic concerns in all his assignments, brought him into direct conflict with Baltimore's black leadership. In 1888 the city decided to construct a black high school and to hire black teachers as an experiment.

Steward supported this endeavor. The proposal was, in his view, "just as necessary as it was to try whether the gas supplied by our city would burn." Yet once the school was built, it was impossible to find a dozen qualified teachers. Steward incensed many when he declared flippantly that he could obtain enough black teachers in twenty-four hours from Washington or Philadelphia, but that there were none in Baltimore. Steward's assessment was correct, but saying so was boorish.[39]

Despite his rash comment, Steward had a fairly good relationship with his Bethel congregation. His parishioners took to him and assisted him in improving Bethel. Steward enjoyed his stay at Bethel. "It was a beautiful and spacious building of the established churchly type, made to worship in, rather than for holding mass meetings." Although many of Bethel's worshipers were involved in community betterment societies, they were conservatives in church matters. Slowly he moved the church forward. Isaac Myers, who in 1869 developed the Colored National Labor Union, was the key to Steward's success in the church. Steward acknowledged years after leaving Baltimore that "Bethel Church in the eighties was very much what Isaac Myers determined it to be." Steward was astute enough to maintain cordial relations with Myers. In August 1888 William H. Barnes, a presiding elder in the Baltimore area, credited Steward with renovating Bethel, "which will make it the equal, if not the superior, of any colored church in the city." Barnes added that Steward was regarded by the people "as a preacher of great ability." He was beloved by the congregation for his church leadership.[40]

Steward's contributions to Baltimore's civic endeavors showed his concern for racial progress. He supported the efforts of Isaac Myers, Jacob A. Seaton, Thomas I. Hall, Malachi Gibson, Joseph Warren, and Samuel E. Young to organize in October 1888 an Industrial Exhibition, testament to the progress of the freedmen in Maryland since emancipation.[41] Patterned after Fanny Jackson Coppin's successful World's Fair of 1879, the exhibition was a catalyst that encouraged blacks to display their technical skills to a grateful city, state, and nation. The fair attracted twenty thousand visitors. Inspired by its success, Steward "secured promise of space at the [forthcoming 1889] Paris Exhibition for the colored people of this country." Steward's ambitious design to display diverse examples of blacks' scientific and technical skills was scaled back considerably by space limitations, which limited the display to "the progress of the colored people in school work and . . . mechanical arts." Steward's efforts showed his pride in the achievement of African people.[42]

Steward willingly lent a hand to fellow ministers, particularly when they sought funds. Near the end of 1888, as president of the AME Preacher's Meeting, he worked to help St. James AME mission escape debt. Envelopes were placed in nine churches, which raised $600.[43]

Steward lent his name to other worthy causes. On April 8, 1888, Isaac Myers requested that the Baltimore Annual Conference build a home for aged and infirm ministers and their wives or widows. Nearly a year later Steward joined forces with delegates from Philadelphia, Baltimore, New York, New Jersey, and New England to organize the Aged Minister Association. It was officially dedicated in August 1889, with Isaac Myers as president. In July 1889 Steward organized the National Christian Home Guard, with the objective "to develop, cultivate and strengthen moral character." The organization sought primarily to aid blacks, but it vowed not to close their doors to anyone. Later in the year, he planned to host a national conference of black ministers to "consider the special, moral and religious difficulties and dangers which beset the colored people." This ideology of self-reliance, which had its origins in slavery days, was emulated by eight physicians who in 1894 organized a faculty of medicine and opened a hospital and free dispensary known as Providence Hospital. Providence was the first hospital "in the South controlled and attended by Negro physicians."[44]

Not one to stay out of controversy, Steward in May 1889 engaged in a verbal fistfight with Bishop Henry M. Turner. Turner, a vocal advocate of bishops' rights, maligned the General Conference of 1888 when he protested that "by law all general officers are members of the General Conference and cannot be deprived of that right except by general convention of the entire church." Steward, ready to pounce on an illogical thought, publicized his dissatisfaction with Turner. Under church discipline, argued Steward, "no one is licensed to malign the General Conference at a whole or speak evil of any of its members and bishops above all others should avoid giving countenance to a course at once so disorderly and injurious." Steward's opposition was that general officers should not also be ex-officio members of the General Conference. Surprisingly, considering how long Steward had hung onto the liturgy issue, he accused Turner of writing about a subject that had "been gone over *ad nauseam*. If ridicule were in order I would . . . think of the classic animal who finds plenty of substance upon the meal when all is gone, except thistles, tin cans, and defunct paper."[45]

By attacking Turner, Steward indirectly took on other bishops. They, too, were afflicted with the sins of men. During the summer and fall of 1889, the

AME bishops engaged in a major fight over the advisability of retaining the services of the secretary of the AME missions. Ten bishops supported the secretary, but Bishop Payne strongly opposed him, as there were questions about missing funds. The ugly quarrel upset many in the AME family. Steward was shocked at the behavior of the bishops. "Reared from my infancy to venerate your persons and respect your office . . . I . . . invite you to look with me upon the sad spectacle now standing before the church and world." He was saddened that the majority of the bishops supported the secretary, while Payne viewed him as a criminal. Ashamed of their behavior and concerned about how the rift would affect African Methodism, Steward wrote, "on my knees, on the graves of my ancestors who lived and died in the church, I beg of you, remove this sad and serious bone of unholy strife." Wanting to alleviate the tension caused by the affair, and to raise money, Steward near the end of 1889 suggested that money could be raised if the bishops contributed 5 percent of their income to the support of foreign missions. He thought this example would inspire laymen to do likewise. "Many of us are holding back the Lord's money," he commented. His suggestion, which the *Christian Recorder* noted was "a little presumptuous," received that paper's endorsement because "a movement of that kind would start a mighty missionary revolution."[46]

Steward had a deep and abiding love for the church and the people who supported African Methodism. In mid-June 1889 he wrote about the South. A trip to Virginia, Georgia, and the Carolinas convinced him that the material condition of the people had declined. "The South as it appears to me, is poor, poor, poor, and apparently growing poorer." He praised the AME preachers for performing miraculously despite the overt race hostility. "One wrong step," he warned, "may plunge a whole community into strife and bloodshed." Reverend I. S. Grant of Clarendon County, South Carolina, reported that southern preachers received only eight or nine dollars monthly "and a part of that is in corn, meat, coffee and molasses." Grant added, "we trust the doctor [Steward] will give us some more of his sympathizing talk . . . though he speaks up north, we hear the sound down here."[47]

Steward's concern about the plight of southern ministers reflected his interest in the material and spiritual needs of African Methodism. For the spiritual growth of his congregation and fellow ministers, Steward set a very fine table. In the fall of 1889 he organized a theological class for young ministers in the Baltimore area. B. F. Lee, who heard his cousin preach, wrote that Bethel Church was "a model of strength, beauty and comfort in worship.

Dr. Steward is advancing the cause of Christ . . . in his usual dignified but decided manner." In December Steward gave a series of Bible readings in Philadelphia's Central Presbyterian Church. In January 1891, at a ministerial meeting, Steward suggested that a theological college be established in the Baltimore Conference. A few days later he proposed that the church needed to buy a larger building to house the AME Publishing Concerns. Steward contributed $100 toward the purchase price.[48]

Steward enjoyed his work at Bethel Church. Unfortunately, the itineracy claimed him once more. In late April 1890 he was transferred to Mt. Pisgah Church in Washington, D.C. Mt. Pisgah was a very poor church. As usual, he devoted his energies to hauling "in the silver and the gold." The *Christian Recorder* expressed regret that his assignment there was not "one commensurate with the character of the man." Editor Lee urged the public to assist Steward in paying off the church's $7,000 debt. To help Mt. Pisgah with its financial embarrassment, several church choirs gave a benefit concert on December 4, 1890.[49]

Despite poor health, Steward sometime in 1889 or 1890 presented a major paper, "The Causes Which Retard the Moral, Material and Educational Progress of the Colored People of the United States." At a later date he would debate with himself the use of racial nomenclatures, but here he purposefully used the term "colored." He did not generally use "Afro-American," then in vogue among some intellectuals, as he saw his destiny to reside in America, not Africa. At this time Senator Matthew Butler introduced a bill to help ex-slaves settle outside the South. Although Africa was not mentioned, it was clear that he intended that continent for the area of resettlement. The bill never came to a vote; it received a tremendous negative response from the nation's black press. Steward criticized Edward Blyden (who was visiting from Liberia to drum up support for African emigration) for "thrusting a practical distinction between the persons of mixed blood and those suppose to be purity of Negro blood." He believed that all blacks shared a common African ancestry. His speech echoed many of the points made popular by Booker T. Washington regarding the vices of the race. Like many others, Steward in 1890, while not a gung-ho supporter of Washington, shared his views on racial pride, self-reliance, and economic development.[50]

It was ironic that Steward, the epitome of a well-educated clergy, would become embroiled in a controversy over the educational deficiencies of southern preachers. The issue of an educated and pious ministry was one that had confronted the AME church for years. Yet it was Booker T. Washington's criticism in 1890 that led to a major debate. A few years earlier, W. Calvin Chase, editor of the Washington *Bee*, had accused fellow journalist John W. Cromwell, editor of the *People's Advocate*, of classifying Washington's black preachers as unscrupulous, cardplayers, alcoholics, and seducers of women. There was no outcry in print against Cromwell.[51]

The reaction was different for Booker T. Washington's frank declaration in August 1890 that the majority of the black Baptist and Methodist clergy were "unfit, either mentally or morally, or both, to preach the Gospel." Washington based his blunt assessment on his own observations and reports from other ministers.[52] The response was swift but mixed. Daniel A. Payne, senior bishop in the AME church, whose earlier call for an educated clergy had promoted some to call him an "infidel" and a "devil," wrote to Washington to support him. Citing his own southern experience, Payne confirmed Washington's observation that many left the cotton and corn fields for the ministry, which they considered easier work. Payne specified that "not more than one-third of all the ministers, Baptists and Methodists, in the South are morally and intellectually gifted." Payne acknowledged that he would be criticized for his remarks, and he was.[53] Washington also received major support from other ministers.[54] A major supporter of both Payne and Washington was the puritanical intellectual Francis J. Grimké, who wrote Washington on December 12, "every word that you say is true. The condition of the colored ministry . . . is unquestionably a deplorable one."[55] Perhaps due to chronic illness, Steward did not join the debate until January 1891. Commenting on a recent ministers' meeting that he attended, Steward wrote, "as soon as I saw it I knew it could be productive of only evil." He introduced a resolution to condemn Washington but the ministers, perhaps fearful of Payne or Washington or both, tabled the resolution. Steward, who had public quarrels with Payne before, considered the senior bishop's opinion as not adding "a feather's weight to the case." Praising the southern brethren for their sacrifices, he added, "the man who would arise either to oppress or slander that class of men, sinks himself below Christian respect." Surprising considering his intellectual attainments, Steward proudly exclaimed that he too belonged to the two-thirds condemned by Booker T. Washington. His formative preaching years in Georgia and South Carolina had provided Steward with an opportunity to develop intimate relationships with many ministers who lacked both material comfort and academic attainment. The genesis of his defense can be traced also to his address at the quarter-century conference of the AME church held in Charleston in 1889. Steward was ill and did not make the trip;

his paper was read. He praised southern preachers for bringing converts to African Methodism and was pleased that the region was represented by the election of bishops in 1888 because it helped "to silence calumny on one hand, and furnish inspiration on the other." In 1889 he published six sermons that he had preached in South Carolina and Georgia between 1866 and 1871. It was dedicated "to the memory of those who labored to plant our Church in the South."[56]

Payne and Steward had clashed over the years, which explains his willingness to attack his bishop's support of Washington. Less explainable is Steward's agreement with Grimké's 1892 speech before the Ministers' Union in Washington, D.C. Grimké declared that there were too many ignorant preachers. Worse was the large number of morally unfit preachers. His accusation that the leading characteristics of pulpit ministrations were emotionalism, frivolity, and greed was in accord with Steward's own views. After receiving a copy of Grimké's speech, Steward informed him, "I . . . wish 20,000 copies of it might be . . . circulated free. My name goes with the Ministers' Union in [its] endorsement."[57]

Once again, the itineracy called and Steward was assigned in 1891 to Waters Chapel in Baltimore. He would remain in his new assignment for only a few months—his appointment to a military chaplaincy would end his twenty-seven years as an itinerant preacher.[58]

Theophilus Steward did not come easily to his decision to leave the itineracy. In part, the church and Steward fought one battle too many. His controversial opinions cost him election in 1891 as a delegate to the 1892 General Conference. He noted privately that his 1888 fight against the rights and privileges of the general officers had created a hostile climate against him. "I have been informed," he confessed, "that I am to be punished the remainder of my days for the part I took in this movement." Steward noted that "the church is not altogether a man made institution, and . . . with God's grace I can wait, watch and pray, and strive to keep a warm heart and a helpful hand."[59]

His years in the itineracy were bittersweet ones. He was a brilliant pulpit orator who possessed outstanding organizational skills. Despite his tremendous success in organizing, renovating, and improving AME churches from Georgia to Brooklyn, his achievements were flawed by his failure in Haiti, and his argumentative personality cost him the presidency of Wilberforce University and election to the bishopric. But Steward was resourceful. He would take his prodigious skills to start anew on the frontier, miles away from bishops and church politics, where he would labor to save souls.

NINE

Fort Missoula, 1891-1898

In February 1891 the chaplaincy of the Twenty-fifth U.S. Colored Infantry became available. John R. Lynch, former Reconstruction congressman from Mississippi, urged Francis J. Grimké to apply for the position.[1]

Grimké declined and suggested that Steward might be interested in the position. Steward informed Lynch that "I do not dare to refuse it for it may be the Lord's way to provide for me, but I must consult my wife before I can give you an answer." He could not ignore Elizabeth's wishes. Not only would they have to uproot their family and take their younger sons to Montana, but the couple would be far removed from family and comforts. Elizabeth prayed and concluded that it was God's will for her husband to accept the chaplaincy.[2]

Former U.S. senator Blanche Kelso Bruce supported Steward's candidacy: "I want to see you fixed for life where you will not have to care for the wherewithal to live." Advised by Bruce and Lynch to keep the probable appointment quiet until Benjamin Harrison made a public statement, Steward confided only in Postmaster General John Wanamaker. Steward depended on white benefactors. Unlike black aristocrats who acquired their status after 1900 and who depended on their own race for employment or recognition, men like Steward needed assistance from wealthy or politically connected whites.[3]

Once Steward's name was publicly mentioned as the leading candidate, support for him was widespread. Between March and June 1891, numerous endorsements, including ones from Frederick Douglass, John Wanamaker, John R. Lynch, Blanche K. Bruce, the faculty of the West Philadelphia Divinity School of the Protestant Episcopal Church, and AME ministers in the Baltimore area were forwarded to Redford Proctor, secretary of war.

On July 25, 1891, Steward became the third African American appointed to the chaplaincy since the end of the Civil War. He was ordered to depart for

Fort Missoula by August 21. Throughout his ministerial career, he had been hard-pressed financially. His annual chaplain's salary was $1,500, plus a 10 percent increase for every five years of service. Other benefits included free government housing, one servant, and the use of a horse.[4]

While Steward had his critics in the African Methodist connection, he had many supporters who knew that the church had lost a faithful worker. The *Christian Recorder* expressed regret in losing him from the itineracy. Isaiah C. Wears asked, "how will the church do without him?"[5]

Steward was joining a regiment that had been formed in 1869 when Congress consolidated the Thirty-ninth and Fortieth infantries to make the Twenty-fifth U.S. Colored Infantry. By 1880, after serving in Texas for ten years, the regiment was assigned to the Dakotas and Minnesota. Eight years later it was assigned to Montana, with headquarters at Fort Missoula. The Twenty-fifth had two distinctions not shared by white regiments. White troops rotated between western and eastern assignments, thus minimizing their hardship on the frontier to only a few years. But belief in the stereotypical brute negro who lusted after white women or who was a criminal kept black men at isolated frontier posts. Second, the Act of 1866 that organized the colored regiments specified that a chaplain be assigned to teach the illiterate recruits as well as to provide for their spiritual guidance. This law did not provide chaplains for every white regiment, as most were near cities that had established churches.[6]

Steward bid his wife and children a temporary farewell and traveled to Philadelphia, where on August 3 his former parishioners at Union AME Church gave him a farewell reception. Soon after, he boarded the train to Montana. He passed through the grain fields and the "barren hills" of the Dakotas. He was particularly moved by Little Bighorn, which reminded him that the potential for Indian uprising was only an incident away. He anticipated what the future would bring. He knew his way around the politics of the itineracy, but the military, with its rigid division of command, still remained an unknown. He arrived at Fort Missoula on August 24 and quickly began his official duties of administering to the soldiers' religious and educational needs. He also operated the garrison's library as well as beginning a Sunday school and elementary school for the children at the fort. He and his family were warmly received by the fort commander and his wife, much to Steward's pleasure.[7]

Contrary to the fears of his fellow ministers, Chaplain Steward did not have it physically hard on the frontier. "I became possessed of the army spirit and identified myself with its discipline and training as well as its outdoor life," he wrote soon after his arrival. He purposely exposed a macho personality to the young recruits, some of whom initially stereotyped him as an effete easterner. He actively participated in driving mules, hunting, riding horses, and hiking to endear himself to the men. Even his well-tended garden helped him to reach the soldiers. "Work, work, work, is the special gift by which the chaplain succeeds," he wrote. His work, although far removed from the AME itineracy, did much to represent the church that he had faithfully served. Chaplain Allen Allensworth, Twenty-fourth U.S. Colored Infantry, informed the *Christian Recorder*, "your church needed just such a man to represent it in the army [for] . . . you have but little idea how much good for the race and cause of Christ, he can and is doing where he is, as chaplain."[8]

Steward readily took to his new duties. He was full of energy and willing to accommodate the spiritual and educational needs of the soldiers and their families. There were 321 people at Fort Missoula, 45 of them under the age of fifteen. They provided him with a good nucleus for his Sunday school. The adult church membership was small; only thirty-one professed membership in a Christian church. His temperance work was developing. Twenty-four men witnessed on November 11 for the installation of officers in the Blanche Kelso Bruce Temperance Society.[9]

Colonel Andrews was pleased with Steward. He wrote that Steward was "well educated, gentlemanly, refined and respected by all. He has assumed his duties with zeal and prosecuted them with intelligence and the results "will be satisfactory." Steward's duties varied. In addition to chapel services and Sunday school, he was the treasurer of the fort's bakery and he conducted baptisms, funerals, and wedding ceremonies.[10]

Theophilus Steward was more than a mere functionary. Above all, he was cognizant of the economy of the region, the political factions that existed, and the state of race relations. Within six months of his appointment, he commented on the paucity of Afro-Americans in the army's officer corps. Having spent most of his adult years in urban areas, Steward viewed cities as negative environments for human development. While blacks could go far in the ministry, opportunities for advancement in other professions were usually nonexistent, or at best limited. Steward believed that the military offered opportunities. He urged the young black men to "earnestly seek . . . commissions in the army." The military's educational program greatly impressed Steward: "any soldier has a better opportunity to secure education than . . . thousands of young men in New York, much better than I enjoyed

Theophilus Gould Steward, Chaplain, 25th U.S. Infantry, ca. 1891. Photograph courtesy of the Schomburg Center for Research in Black Culture, NYPL.

From Walzl's Imperial Portrait Studios.
N. E. Cor. Eutaw & Franklin Sts., } BALTIMORE.
21 E. Balto. Near Charles St.

Elizabeth Gadsden Steward, ca. 1890. Photograph courtesy of the Schomburg Center for Research in Black Culture, NYPL.

115

in my youth."[11]

Whether the Army would be the vehicle for race advancement was an issue of hot debate. Some years earlier, a letter from Chirrachan, Arizona, to the editor of the New York *Freeman* presented the army as a better alternative to "waiting on tables in hotels . . . or driving carriages." A dissenting view was provided by G. H. Burton, a former soldier of ten years' experience. He complained that musicians had to perform "menial services in the houses of their . . . officers . . . in addition to their regular duties." He added, "I pity the intelligent colored men who have fine feelings and are . . . in the United States army." Another soldier, who described himself as "an educated colored man," informed *The Army and Navy Journal*, "we are always receiving nice notices about colored men making such good soldiers, but never a good station. Many officers do their best to transfer because of what they have to take and stand because they are in a colored regiment."[12]

Other negative views condemned the military for racism in the officer corps. It was their belief that "these commissioned snobs and colorphobists . . . will always stand between the Afro-American private and the first step to a general's epaulets." Steward's view of the army as a place for opportunity was blinded by his own personal acceptance. The evidence did not support his position. As late as 1904 there were only four African-American commissioned officers, and Steward himself was denied promotion. As one soldier remarked in 1896, "never sing 'my country, tis of thee' until our country recognizes the black man as a citizen from every cardinal point of this country."[13]

Steward was fortunate that his commanding officer at Fort Missoula accepted him as an equal. Colonel Andrews' retirement from the service on April 22, 1892, was sadly noted by Steward, who described his commanding officer as "a typical American gentleman and soldier, a useful object lesson for the youth of the nation." Andrews's departure from Fort Missoula was described by the chaplain as "a beautiful sight . . . men . . . hardened by years of . . . discipline . . . manifesting a friendship as tender and rich as can be found anywhere in America."[14]

Colonel Andrews's presence at chapel services had emphatically informed the garrison that he approved of a professed moral observation. Many other officers also regularly attended chapel services. While their presence proved helpful for Steward's conversion efforts, he was dismayed that the military provided soldiers with wine and beer in the garrison's canteen. Steward was an eyewitness to the ravaging effect of liquor on the minds and bodies of young men. He believed in abstinence in practice and prohibition in principle.

Writing in *Harper's Weekly* in 1892, Steward expressed the wish that changing the name of the canteen to post exchange might eventually lead to the elimination of liquor in the garrison. His view was a minority one. The army believed that if men drank in a base facility where food and recreation existed, they would be less inclined to act in a rowdy manner. Later, when the canteen was abolished, supporters blamed its closing for an increase in alcoholism. Now sellers of cheap whiskey supplied the soldiers' off-base supply.[15]

Although drinking eroded attendance at Fort Missoula's Sunday evening services, not all avoided chapel services because of the influence of liquor. The April 24, 1892, service was affected by "baseball fever"; only forty-one came to hear Steward preach. Three weeks earlier, ninety-seven had attended service. The summer weather hurt attendance, as target practice, heat, and mosquitoes affected the turnout. Steward rationalized, "I shall look for improvement as the evenings lengthened." Indeed, sixty-four came to a service in August. Steward formerly preached to hundreds, but he admirably adjusted to a congregation of fifty or sixty. "I never preached with more interest and satisfaction than I do here, and I cannot feel that in any sense it is labor thrown away."[16]

Steward struggled to get the attention of the enlisted men. He reported in January 1893 that over one hundred dollars worth of religious books were purchased by the soldiers. The "relish for such books . . . developed" after they heard Walter, Steward's seven-year-old son, read from *The Story of the Gospel*. Attendance at services improved, too. Defending the soldiers, he wrote that "the *worst men* of the country are not *always* found in the army." There were "*many* who . . . feel the restraints of religious principles. Many of them I should class from a moral stand point as 'good men.' "[17]

Besides saving souls, Steward had in early 1893 pressing professional and personal issues to contend with. In January the *AME Church Review* printed his views on incarnation. He wrote that Scriptures showed that God was embodied in the physical form of Jesus Christ. Steward asked, "can the infinite (God) join itself to the finite (man)? Here stands the great central fact of all religion, morals, history and science. *God is revealed through a human life.*"[18]

Steward was a race-conscious man who wanted to see blacks progress. The Chicago World Fair of 1893 received his attention as early as 1891 when he informed the New York *Tribune* that his race "could present a respectable exhibit in educational and literary work and some creditable scientific and artistic work." On January 25, 1893, he requested from the adjutant general's office in Washington, D.C., that he be ordered to the fair for approximately six weeks. He wanted to "attend the educational exhibits, in order to better qualify [himself] to direct the educational work of the regiment." He also wanted to participate in a "world's parliament of religion . . . of which body I am a member . . . with a view to . . . increasing my efficiency as chaplain." Steward was a member of the Ecumenical Methodist Conference and his appointment to the army had prevented him in 1891 from delivering his paper "The Lord's Day" at the Washington gathering. He was determined not to miss the 1893 meeting. His superiors approved his request for leave, but the adjutant general ruled that only officers who had duty assignment to Chicago would be permitted to leave. Steward would meet the same fate two years later when the Cotton States and International Exposition Company requested that the War Department send a military exhibit to Atlanta. The War Department agreed to send two companies from Fort McPherson, Georgia. Seeking fair play, J. Garland Penn, chief of the Negro Department for the Cotton States and International Exposition Company requested that the army send some colored troops and Chaplain Steward as recognition of his literary work. Penn's request was denied and fate provided Booker T. Washington with the forum for his famous speech on racial accommodation.[19]

His disappointment at not going to Chicago was overshadowed by gloomy news he received from Washington. James, Steward's firstborn, was severely ill. Steward left Montana in early March to be at James's bedside. On June 5 James died. "Oh, how my heart aches when I think of his sufferings; but I can praise God for the assurance that he rests in Heaven," Steward lamented.[20] Relying on his personal motto, "save the pieces, never despair," he returned to Montana to tend to the men's spiritual needs. But his efforts were again interrupted by an illness of Elizabeth, which lasted for six weeks until her death on November 2. Although he heroically divided his attention between his army duties and caring for his wife, Steward had little enthusiasm for church services. Elizabeth's death cast a pall over the entire base. Elizabeth always had a kind word for the soldiers. The men recognized the loss of a "zealous promoter of [their] interests, [who was] . . . devoted to [their] welfare and prosperity." With Elizabeth's death, Steward lost the second most important woman in his life. His mother had inspired him to attain heights. Elizabeth had supported him during all the low points of his life. Never once did she question his actions or judgment. In later years he wrote, "the year 1893 must stand in my history as the year of deep and harrowing grief."[21]

Striving to put the tragedies behind him, Steward devoted himself to the care of his surviving six sons and busied himself in his religious work. His December report stated that "there has been some progress made in stimulating a love of good reading. The school teachers and a few others are striving to cultivate themselves in manners, morale and intelligence." He was pleased that there was no drunkenness displayed by the soldiers during the Christmas holidays. "I venture that few communities . . . passed through the Christmas season more orderly and quietly than did this garrison."[22]

Sunday, December 31, found him "barely able to get out for a short time to the Sunday School, and to the evening service." His illness continued into 1894. During the first two weeks of the new year he could do no more "than merely keep up the Sabbath service and visit the hospital." He was forced to cancel two Sunday school services. Despite his illness, he sought to improve attendance at chapel services. Following a timely suggestion, Steward and Sergeant Chambers of Company H visited three saloonkeepers and requested that they close their establishments during the Sunday evening worship hours. They agreed, and attendance on January 23 shot up to ninety, who displayed "a genuine interest in the service."[23]

Although Steward believed that his work was "necessary and proper," he found it disappointing that the enlisted men made excuses. "I can't lead a Christian life in the army," and "it's no use playing the hypocrite" were common rationales for not attending services. He was frustrated because he believed that they were "men of *conscience* and of fair moral habits." Steward's frustration went beyond that of a minister who was unable to persuade men to live moral lives. Like other race-conscious aristocrats, he had an intense interest in uplifting the race. To some degree, he was upset with the men's behavior because their drunkenness, their liaisons with prostitutes, and their gambling reflected poorly on African Americans. His zealous efforts to improve their moral behavior was motivated by both religious and racial concerns.[24]

Steward's diligence paid off in 1895. A Major McKibbin reported at the end of June that Steward possessed special skills in preaching and teaching. Throughout the year the garrison was "orderly" and the guardhouse was "empty," according to Steward's monthly reports. He proudly wrote that both the "officers and men seem to take pride in maintaining the good name and high standing of the garrison." He added, "while I would not claim too much for religion, I do believe that the preaching of the gospel here has something to do with the general good conduct prevailing." In February of 1896, Steward received a letter from a former soldier who wrote: "your illustrated sermons . . . I still cherish and . . . speak to *any* and all who care to listen. Among other things fresh in my memory is your visit to me in the hospital."[25]

Nevertheless, there was a continuing problem. Men were apt to show their appreciation for their chaplain after leaving the army but peer pressure made many ambivalent about practicing their religious or moral beliefs on base. Steward was upset by the presence of nearby "disreputable houses." "How to deal with them I do not know," he wrote painfully. "I cannot but *feel* that there has been a decided but I trust temporary outbreak *towards* gross and reckless immorality." Not understanding the mens' desires, Steward questioned why they patronized the disreputable places even though the garrison was "amply supplied with means of amusement and recreation." Fed up with the soldiers' impulses that drove them to the prostitutes, he boldly took action. His circular announced in large print, SOLDIERS! DOES IT PAY TO SIN?

> Two young men cut off already this year. Both were in good health; but had fair prospect for forty years more of life; but both have met bloody dishonorable deaths. They died for no cause; their deaths stand for nothing. No slab can be raised to their honor; nothing can ever be said about them by tongue or pen, they were simply killed. Their best friends cannot pay a tribute to their memories. In silence they must rest, with God alone as their judge. To His all merciful hands their souls are commended. DOES IT PAY TO SIN? Let us meet and talk about it tonight at church call.
>
> Sincerely your friend
> Chaplain T. G. Steward

His sincerity and personal intervention resulted in sixty-two soldiers attending the service. They had no pressure to attend except for their own feelings of guilt and fear about their own mortality. By the beginning of November 1896, Fort Missoula was a quiet place, where "the feeling of contentment [was] well nigh universal."[26]

He was contented with the men's behavior, but he was lonely. In late October he took a six-week leave of absence to travel to Brooklyn to marry Dr. Susan McKinney, the widow of the Reverend William McKinney. Susan, who came from an old elite Long Island family, was the first African-American female physician in the state of New York and the third in the nation. She was a successful and wealthy physician who was active in temperance, women's rights, and church mission societies. She was an ideal mate for Steward.[27]

Susan's arrival at Fort Missoula provided his remaining sons with a devoted stepmother and her musical talents and medical skills were welcome additions to the frontier. With the assistance of Susan, Steward worked hard to convert the enlisted men to a higher morality. Religious services were held in the drab

Susan Smith Steward, the first black female physician in the State of New York, ca. 1870. Photograph courtesy of the Schomburg Center for Research in Black Culture, NYPL.

121

post hall "in the midst of . . . everyday scenes, so that there [was] no novelty of place or persons as may be found in the ordinary place of worship." Steward believed that the absence of a real chapel with the "look" of a church, with a traditional altar, stained glass, and other ornamentation contributed to his difficulty in attracting recruits. Steward understood that God's presence was everywhere and that Christians did not need physical trappings or ornamentation to feel close to God. He certainly knew from his work among the freedmen that true worshipers needed only to be in God's presence to feel spiritual. So he should have been above excuses. But he was frustrated.[28]

Steward's preaching skills, recognized by his superior officers, also gained the attention of the white residents in the Missoula area. On July 18, 1895, he and his family went to the Bitterroot Valley, eighteen miles away, to preach to the residents of Carleton. The citizens, some of whom were among the approximately three hundred ex-Confederate soldiers in the state, extended to him Christian brotherhood. In July 1897 he preached at a Baptist church in Missoula for two Sundays. In January 1898, at the unanimous request of a Missoula Presbyterian church, he preached on four consecutive Sundays when the congregation was between pastors. A local journalist wrote of his desire that the regiment remain in the state for a long time so that they would have Chaplain Steward's services.[29]

His acceptance was all the more remarkable when it is considered that Montana had very few African Americans. Their numbers increased from 183 in 1870 to only 1,490 in 1890. Yet racism was virtually absent. The state's schools, integrated since 1883, provided an education for all children.[30]

The popular chaplain presented numerous lectures to the officers of the garrison and, occasionally, to the women at Fort Missoula. He presented three lectures on Queen Elizabeth and one on Catherine II of Prussia, as well as Marie Antoinette, Empress Josephine, Toussaint L'Overture, Antonio Maceo, and the role of Haitians in the 1779 Siege of Savannah.[31]

Steward used the solitude of Montana to write numerous essays for newspapers and journals, particularly in 1894 and 1895. Several of his essays were inspired by his observation of army life, for example "The Colored American as a Soldier," a frank declaration of racial equality. As race relations declined during the 1890s, bigots sought to prove the superiority of whites. Steward countered this trend with his assessment that whites had a higher death rate in the military than colored soldiers. He cited the 1892 surgeon general's report to prove his point. To those who believed that blacks were better suited to hot climates, Steward argued that they could withstand temperatures of twenty to thirty degrees below zero. Steward was proud of his African ancestry, but he longed for a color-blind society. He proudly quoted Brigadier General Wesley Merritt's observation that "the day will come when there will be no more colored soldiers in the army . . . but the special defenders of the flag shall be simply Americans-all."[32]

Unlike some of his contemporaries, Steward did not believe that the military was a hired gun available to suppress social unrest. This was the view of a United States senator who, in 1895, condemned the army for acting as strike breakers. Steward defended the soldier's action when he had to bring "the bayonet against . . . his own countrymen." He was in these circumstances "a patriot; true to his oath and loyal to his flag." Interestingly, he viewed the problem of "starving laborers" as a socioeconomic problem that did not call for the army to act as enforcers. Instead of charity, he called for jobs for the nation's four million unemployed, many of whom were foreigners. He suggested that the government provide jobs "at such rates as would not draw unnecessarily from other channels. Let work be given at wages not high enough to interfere seriously with those employed, and men would come and go accordingly as the time rose and fell around them." Predating by forty years the action of the New Deal's recovery acts, Steward suggested that jobs be developed to provide irrigation and road building "within the new states, and the consequent drawing of the unemployed to the less crowded portions of the country."[33] Although he left it unstated, Steward was probably thinking of unemployment benefits for African Americans who, like immigrants, suffered economic deprivations.

Steward was never one to shy away from controversy. Whenever he sensed that African Americans were under attack simply because of their race, he was quick to come to their defense. In 1895, when white physicians attributed black deaths in southern cities to poor food, inadequate housing, and immoral living, Steward challenged their thesis. He countered that the population of Port-au-Prince, a poor Caribbean city, doubled in twenty years. He frankly asked why people were dying of consumption in cities under white political control but not in the Haitian city where the doctors and politicians were of African descent. He cited the excellent health of the colored soldiers and added, "the American Negro will not die out. He will soon be fixed so that he can look after his own health." In this matter, Steward had allies who believed that many of the consumption deaths were due to environmental reasons, not congenital ones.[34]

In 1893, and then again in 1897, he observed the Flathead Indians on a reservation, where he observed that they were "badly mixed with white blood." Despite his family's own mixed ancestry, he declared, "no people are too filthy for the white men to mingle with." Contrary to popular belief, Steward did not think that mixed bloods were genetically weaker. The "white" Indians were, in his estimation, bigger, stronger, and more alert than other Flatheads. This observation applied also to an African-looking Indian whom Steward spotted while he was boarding a train. He noted that she "was quicker in motion and brighter in expression than any of her sisters."[35]

Steward stated his mind. He was intelligent, articulate, and believed that he was the equal (if not the superior) of any man. On July 25, 1894, he went to Missoula's Florence Hotel to meet Chaplain J. Newton Ritner, a white minister from Fort Keogh. Ritner, a guest at the hotel, invited Steward to dine with him. The manager refused to serve Steward. Instead of embarrassing his colleague, Ritner declined to eat alone. Incensed by the insult, Steward wrote letters to the local newspapers criticizing the manager. He informed the newspapers, "I can feel my individuality and my responsibility, but my consciousness fails to give any response to" the word "colored." Expressing an assimilationist view, he added, "the African element . . . is thoroughly American . . . and enthusiastically loyal." Despite this assertion, Steward had ambivalent views about race and color. While it would be nice to be simply an American, he was classified by his color and race. This ambivalence resulted in him and others asserting at times their cultural superiority. Steward added that cultivated black men were superior to their white counterparts in "conversational ability and refinement." Steward had the backing of his superior officer. The manager of the Florence Hotel, fearing a military boycott, apologized in writing to the offended chaplain.[36]

The military supported Steward on this issue, but later his commanding officer, Colonel A. S. Burt, openly showed himself to be a bigot. On March 9, 1896, Steward applied to fill a vacancy at West Point. Naively, Steward believed, as he explained in a letter to his son Frank, that his scholarship, training, experience, and manners qualified him for the position. He added, "owing to my color, I believe my presence . . . would tend to promote a breadth of character, and develop a truly American spirit." Steward wanted to return to the East because Frank, age twenty-four, and his son Charles, twenty-six, were graduating from Harvard in 1896. "I wish," he wrote in his application, "to be where I can assist them in getting a start in life." He also wanted to return to make university arrangements for Benjamin, Theophilus

Bolden, and Gustavus, who ranged in age from fifteen to nineteen. Steward believed that as an American he was entitled to all the benefits of citizenship. The West Point Military Academy was, in the words of New York *Age*'s Timothy Thomas Fortune, "the rankest charity cesspool of snobbery and colorphobia, outside the University of Virginia." The cadets annually hosted a "Color Line" satire in which they used "nigger jokes" and, on one occasion, three cadets sang about "three curly headed coons." Colonel A. S. Burt made Steward's application moot when he declined to endorse it, even though he considered him "a scholar of high attainments, a true Christian, and a refined gentleman." Steward was furious. In his letter to Frank, he suggested that Burt felt the two were in competition.[37]

Steward's difficulty with Colonel Burt represented a classic dilemma for him and other black aristocrats. These elites had over the years, before and after emancipation, cultivated a close relationship with the upper-class whites, who provided them with appointments or other privileges. Unfortunately, they were rarely able to attain all the rights or privileges they believed they deserved. Steward, however, because he was aggressive, often obtained his wants. By 1898 his sons Frank and Charles were in professional schools (Frank was at Harvard Law and Charles was attending Tufts dental school). Steward's dependence on whites met a setback in 1898, when he sought a cadetship for one of his sons aboard a steamer. In response to his inquiry, John T. Dallas, superintendent of a steamship line, wrote frankly that there was a long waiting list and "I am afraid your race would be against him, the boys room together . . . and you can readily understand that a colored boy would make trouble. We carry winch boys who are colored but there are no chances for promotion." In a paternal tone, he added, "pick out some other vocation for your son as I am convinced he would have no other show under white officers."[38]

This was typical of the state of race relations in the last decade of the nineteenth century. Southern states were sanctioning lynching, disfranchisement, convict-lease systems, Jim Crow schools, and public facilities to hammer home the ideology of white supremacy. As noted by Alexander Crummell, the American creed in 1898 told African Americans, "thus far and no farther."[39] Steward was concerned about the future of blacks in America. He wanted his children to achieve success in the land of their birth, hindered by neither color nor race. After his run-in with Colonel Burt, Steward sought to determine the exact feelings the races had about social equality. He asked a prominent but unidentified woman to survey the issue for him. Not believing herself competent, she referred his request to another woman, who was "almost white." The reply forwarded to Steward from an eastern city emphasized that the better classes of both races associated "freely in religious, charitable and educational movements" but "that such connection is limited, temporary, and bounded by confines." The informant believed that true social intercourse would come only after the social patterns generated by slavery "will be but a vague and musty tradition."[40]

Throughout his life Steward sought to erase the barriers that divided the races. In his later years he was affiliated with organizations that sought to make American society color-blind.[41] But in 1897 Steward accepted what he hoped would be a temporary racial segregation in the church, the military, and elsewhere because he believed that if whites understood that both shared many ideals and aspirations, whites would accept them as equal. This philosophy would be declared irrelevant in later years, but in the 1890s it had the support of many, like Alexander Crummell, Booker T. Washington, and W. E. B. DuBois. Meanwhile, in 1897 Steward accepted an invitation to join the newly organized American Negro Academy as one of the founding members. The ANA sought to have the black intellectual elite disseminate knowledge about the achievements of African Americans.[42]

Serving in the military was an example of patriotism. Steward was proud of his service and pleased that the garrison was orderly during the early part of 1898. The calmness at Fort Missoula was shattered, however, by the sinking of the battleship *Maine* in Havana harbor. The nation was soon at war with Spain. On March 29 the War Department ordered the Twenty-fifth U.S. Colored Infantry to transfer to the Dry Tortugas, Florida, to await orders. The prevailing viewpoint was that "the Negro is better able to withstand the Cuban climate than the white man." This was an ironic assumption since the regiment had spent nearly twenty years enduring Montana's frigid winters. It was assumed that race alone would make them immune to the feverish tropical climate, a mistaken belief that sent many young men to their graves, victims of Cuban mosquitoes.[43]

The people of Montana were sad to see the regiment depart. *The Daily Missoulian* praised the troops: "the fortunes of the [men] will be followed with intense interest by the people of Missoula who are satisfied that though it is a dark regiment not a white feather [of surrender] will be shown." The ministers of Missoula's churches signed an open letter commending the soldiers for their good behavior, a compliment to Steward's work.[44]

Steward packed his bags. Would he and the regiment see combat in Cuba? Would death be his fate? These and other questions raced through his mind as he bade farewell to Susan and Gustavus and Walter, his two remaining sons at Fort Missoula. His heart was sad at the prospect of leaving his family, but he was proud to be serving his country. Steward and the men basked in the goodwill of Missoulians who cheered them as they left the fort. They were off to war, but before reaching their destination they would fight bigotry and prejudice.

TEN

Spanish-American War and Philippine Pacification

The origin of the Spanish-American War was clouded with accusations of sabotage fueled by the yellow journalism of William Randolph Hearst.[1] Motivated by patriotism, an opportunity for adventure, and a mission for overseas expansion, Americans eagerly supported "the splendid little war." As a group, African Americans were ambivalent. Some believed that it was their duty as American citizens, albeit second-class ones, to support the nation's war effort. Others, distrustful of a government that could not protect them from domestic injustice, were unwilling to participate in a war that would lead to an expansion of a Jim Crow system to the Caribbean and Asia. Lewis Douglass, a Civil War veteran, thought it hypocritical for black men to fight for a government that did not protect their basic human rights. There were some who agreed with Benjamin T. Tanner that President William McKinley would not recognize a liberated Cuba because of that island's large African population.[2]

The men of the Ninth and Tenth cavalries and the Twenty-fourth and Twenty-fifth infantries, collectively known as "The Colored Regulars," would view the developing crisis with ambivalence. Trained to fight, they welcomed the opportunity. Nevertheless, an opportunity to behave heroically on the battlefield was overshadowed by their concerns that they were aiding American imperialism. Later this ambivalence would extend to the American occupation and pacification of the Philippines.[3]

African Americans attempted to enlist in the volunteer army, but governors, North and South, refused to include black men in the volunteer forces. Few African Americans belonged to the militia and volunteers came primarily from militiamen. Later, after McKinley called for additional volunteers, the governors of Illinois, Kansas, Virginia, Indiana, and North Carolina accepted African Americans in response to pressure from politicians or because of a need to fill quotas when sufficient whites failed to volunteer. Only one volunteer black unit, Company L, Sixth Massachusetts Regiment, saw action in the Caribbean.[4]

Meanwhile, the men of the Twenty-fifth Infantry left Montana on April 10, Easter Sunday. All was well until they reached the South. Then the soldiers "crossed the line that divide[d] the world." Instead of cheers, the men received hostilities. Steward was denied eating privileges in the railroad dining room in Nashville. "These men," he wrote "whose brawny arms are expected to uphold the flag . . . had a 'realizing sense' of the weakness of their flag as they saw the government blue spit upon." He predicted profoundly that "a glorious dilemma that will be for the Cuban Negro to usher him in to the condition of the American Negro." The men of the Colored Regulars, unused to blatant racism, continued on their journey to Tampa with mixed feelings. The absurdity of the color question was noted by Steward in Chattanooga. A dark-complexioned woman boarded the "wrong" train car and was rudely told by the conductor to move to the "colored" car. "I'm not colored," she retorted hotly, "I'm a Mexican woman, born in Monterey, old Mexico." The perplexed conductor allowed her to remain in the white section. He did not even question Steward, who was also in the "wrong" section. Evidently he was afraid of repeating his earlier "mistake." The regiment was not as fortunate; they were ordered to the "nigger cars." Steward proceeded to Chickamauga National Park, Georgia, "on a white people's car and the sky did not fall." The men were not completely bridled by the military's order to be peaceful. Numerous incidents occurred when the soldiers retaliated against racist acts of individuals or groups.[5]

Members of the Colored Regulars and their chaplains, Allen Allensworth, George W. Prioleau, and Steward, informed the colored press of their ambivalence about the impending crisis in the Caribbean. From Chickamauga, Steward wrote articles for *The Independent* and the Cleveland *Gazette*. On April 24, 1898, he and Prioleau, chaplain of the Ninth Cavalry, conducted religious services. They had no hymns; the soldiers' preoccupation with war made singing impractical despite the availability of regimental bands. After a prayer service, Steward read a part of the fortieth chapter of Isaiah: "comfort ye; comfort ye my people, saith your God." He chose this passage as it pertained to the "pardon of sin, the love of God, and eternal peace and bliss." Steward knew that many of the men were apprehensive about dying. Even some whom he viewed as Godless came to him and asked for the chapter he had read.[6]

Chaplain Steward mused about the form the war might take. He was not a pacifist, but he hoped that men would be spared from the awful jaws of battle. "If fight they must," he declared, they "will do their whole duty but it is a duty not to be coveted." Steward believed in the power of God's retribution. "It is much cheaper to do the right than the wrong thing. Had our nation walked in the highway of holiness, war would not come nigh her." In citing the main theme of his 1888 book, *The End of the World*, Steward saw the impending conflict as the fulfillment of scriptural prophecy to scatter the nations that delight in war. Contrary to those whites who thought blacks were cowards, and those of his own race who believed that war was not their business, Steward believed that war would "greatly help the American colored man of the South, and result in the further clearing of the national atmosphere." He believed that whites would recognize the patriotism of blacks and respect them as equal citizens.[7]

Despite the open racial bias in the South, some soldiers saw the coming of the war as a ripe opportunity for military advancement. Writing from Lakeland, Florida, on June 5, 1898, John E. Lewis, Tenth Cavalry, informed the editor of the Illinois *Record* that soldiers had an obligation to appeal to the people to enlist their sons instead of looking contemptuously at soldiers. Do this, urged Lewis, and "this regular army would be more of an honor to the race." The dishonor, however, was not caused by the race's lack of respect for soldiers. Instead it came from the government's refusal to commission black officers in the regular army. It was in this light that Steward was proud when Charles Young, a West Point graduate and professor of military science at Wilberforce University, was promoted from lieutenant to major in command of the Ninth Battalion of the Ohio National Guard. Steward, who was blinded to the military's institutional racism, saw Young's promotion as a positive sign. Major Young, he argued, was "a new colored soldier . . . who glories in his country and his flag." Steward happily went to Xenia, Ohio, to join in the public festivities surrounding Young's promotion.[8]

On June 14, 1898, an American invasion army of approximately sixteen thousand, including the four colored regiments, sailed for Cuba. Steward, who had volunteered to recruit in communities near Chickamauga, wanted to go to Cuba with the Twenty-fifth but the military ordered him to recruit in the Xenia area. Chaplain Prioleau remained stateside in Tampa, in charge of government property. Like Steward, Prioleau was kept stateside to recruit. His bitter letters complained about the blatant racism of southerners.[9] Black men were mistreated as recruiters, as southerners viewed them as outsiders bent on stirring up "their good Negroes." Other black men, unable to have their own as officers of the Colored Regulars, demanded black officers for the Negro Volunteers. In 1898 three volunteer units—Eighth Illinois, Twenty-third Kansas, and Third North Carolina—had complete rosters of black officers. Later, in the summer of 1898, Congress formed ten additional black volunteer regiments. "The Immunes," as they were known, were supposedly immune to yellow fever. The Seventh, Eighth, Ninth, and Tenth U.S.V. infantries had all black lieutenants. Thirty of their commissioned officers came from the Colored Regulars. It appears that the army was liberal, but actually it compromised. It was not political to commission black men in the regular army because it meant the dismissal of white officers.[10]

Like Prioleau, Steward wanted to go to Cuba. On July 5 he wrote to the War Department from his recruiting station in Dayton, Ohio, requesting to join his regiment "or to be placed on duty at . . . one of the hospitals where our wounded men are, until . . . I can get to my regiment." His request was heeded, and on August 2 he was ordered to proceed to Tampa to join his regiment. Unfortunately, the Twenty-fifth had left Cuba and was en route to Montauk Point, New York. On August 13 he was ordered to Montauk.[11]

On September 18 Steward spoke at Bridge Street Church at a peace jubilee sponsored by the Montauk Soldiers' Relief Association, which was under the leadership of his wife. Steward spoke of the soldiers' bravery, humor "and good cheer." Although he was speaking at a "peace" jubilee, he called for enlistments. "We will need an army of 100,000 for Cuba," he declared. Optimistically, he boasted that "Cuba will afford a field for Negro colonels and brigadier generals." Steward let his emotions outweigh logic. The military did not believe that there were enough intelligent black men to perform officers' duty. Racism, not lack of intelligence or talent, limited black commissioned officers to about one hundred and few achieved the lofty ranks envisioned by Steward.[12]

Steward was a patriot who believed in supporting the war effort. Although he was critical of racism both within and without the military, he profoundly believed that African Americans would benefit from the Spanish-American War. His patriotism was tempered by the reality of the nation's inadequate response to the sacrifice of men in Cuba and Puerto Rico. Within ten days of his Brooklyn speech, *The Independent* published Steward's sober essay, "A Plea For Patriotism." He was saddened that the war demoralized the nation despite the decisive victory. The war showed that the nation was unprepared to care adequately for the wounded. In contrast, the Red Cross received his praise.

Steward believed that the nation had an obligation to bring liberty and peace to the newly freed Cuba, Puerto Rico, and the Philippines. Again he naively believed that America was concerned with democracy.[13] Numerous letters to the black press dissented from Steward's view that the military offered opportunities. Many agreed with Chaplain Prioleau's assessment that American racism included the army. "Some say," he wrote in October 1898, "that [racism] is not in the army. No not so long as the Negro has no aspiration to command."[14]

Prioleau and Steward both saw an opportunity in the army to save souls and to educate men. Prioleau was more militant than his colleague in judging America's failures vis-à-vis equality for her black citizens. While Steward did not adopt a policy of "my country right or wrong," unlike Prioleau he had faith that his country would make the right decision regarding African Americans. It was this faith that compelled him to begin a lengthy campaign to get his son Frank, a Harvard law student, a commissioned rank. Steward convinced Frank to enlist, believing that a military record would benefit his future law career. Frank joined the Eighth U.S.V. but Steward, concerned that his son was only a private, wrote on August 12, 1898, to President McKinley, informing him about his son's linguistic and intellectual achievements. Undiplomatically, he suggested that McKinley remove a white lieutenant from the regiment to make room for Frank. The next day Steward wrote to the adjutant general, saying that it was "popular understanding that all the lieutenants . . . in the 8th immune . . . were to be colored." Convinced that his earlier letters led to Frank's promotion to corporal, Steward persisted in his efforts to make Frank a lieutenant. He bluntly informed the secretary of war that Frank had the support of the governor of Massachusetts and United States senators and congressmen. His white friends did not disappoint him. On January 4, 1899, after the resignation of the white lieutenant, Frank was appointed to a second lieutenancy. Two months later Frank was mustered out of service but was appointed on September 13 as captain in the Forty-ninth U.S.V.[15]

Steward did not realize how much his friendships helped him in obtaining Frank's commission. He honestly believed that the military only needed to be directed to intelligent men to increase the number of African Americans in the rank of line officers. Steward believed that the war was an opportunity for the race to show their patriotism and to help their government in the difficult process of reconstructing Cuba. On October 18, 1898, Steward informed the New York *Daily Tribune* that the government should recruit twenty thousand

Southern blacks to garrison Cuba. He was sure that these immunized recruits would enlist if they understood that their country wanted them. Certainly the opportunity for promotion would convince many of the government's sincerity. Steward's allegiance to the republic was shaken but not severed when Sam Hose was lynched in Georgia. He denounced mob spirit and urged the government to protect all its citizens.[16] But the government was not interested in protecting the rights of Southern blacks. Shamelessly, American racism would be extended to the Philippines, an action that would not go unnoticed by hundreds of blacks stationed in the archipelago.[17]

After a brief stay at Fort Logan, Colorado, the Twenty-fifth left in June 1899 for the Philippines. Steward did not accompany them immediately. During late 1898 and early 1899 Steward had resumed writing. The quietude of his recruiting duties provided him with ample time to write a novel, *Charleston Love Story*. The book depicted the lives of two southern sisters who married northerners. One was a minister and the other was a rogue who found God when his wife, Hortense Vanross, died. The novel did not describe race relations, but it clearly reflected Steward's observations of a city he had visited forty years earlier. His novel was one of the three hundred books exhibited in 1901 at the Buffalo Pan American Exposition's Negro Exhibit.[18]

The novel was not his only major literary work for 1899. On July 30, 1898, a noncommissioned officer in the Twenty-fifth U.S.I. had suggested that "leaders of our race [are needed] to make war records so that their names may go down in history as a reward for the price of our precious blood." Despite the bigotry of both the military and civilians, the black soldiers were proud of their exploits as Las Guasimas, El Caney, and San Juan Hill. The challenge of writing the history of the men was accepted by Edward A. Johnson, and his *History of Negro Soldiers in the Spanish-American War* was published in 1899.[19]

Johnson's story was of heroic men who would excite schoolboys' feelings of racial pride. Steward also accepted the challenge, but his account of the men was more accurate as he had partial access to the military archives. Steward brought considerable skills to the task. The week before Christmas 1898 he requested a four-month leave from service "and to be ordered to Cuba for about a month of this time . . . that I might gather the facts." He noted that Chaplain J. B. McCleary was also at Fort Logan and therefore his presence was not needed. The military granted him the leave on December 22 but refused permission to travel to Cuba. His nemesis, Colonel A. S. Burt, sought on February 13, 1899, to have Steward transferred to a fort in New

Mexico or Arizona. Steward, perhaps fearing that the transfer would interfere with his writing, informed the Bishops' Council of the AME church of Burt's intention. Benjamin W. Arnett, secretary of the council and an adviser to McKinley on race matters, informed the president of the importance of Steward's writing. Meanwhile, Steward had been assigned to Fort Apache, Arizona. The Reverend L. J. Coppin, representing the Ministers Association of the AME church in Philadelphia, asked McKinley to keep Steward at Fort Logan. In early March the army assigned and then revoked orders to send Steward to Arizona. During the confusion, Arnett on March 12 wrote to Secretary of War Russell Alger requesting that Steward be assigned to Wilberforce, Ohio, where Susan Steward was employed at Wilberforce University as a resident physician. Using political leverage, Arnett added that he had recently spoken with President McKinley, who expressed his support. "I hope," he concluded, "you will be able to grant this request in the interest of ten million people." Special orders no. 63, dated March 17, 1899, directed Steward to Wilberforce.[20]

He promptly began to write, even though he had not received any "definite instructions." A fast writer, he soon had "thirty thousand words nearly ready for the press." Fortunately Steward had no limit as to "the character of the work or the time [he] should occupy in writing." On May 31 he reported to the adjutant general that he had the history up "to the landing of the troops in Cuba and am now unravelling the many statements of the marches and battles immediately following." Again he requested to go to Cuba to see the battle areas, but the military still had no interest in sending him to the tropical island. On July 24 he requested "the names and records of the colored men appointed from ranks in the Regular Army to commissions in the Volunteer Army." The reply was negative. The adjutant general's office claimed that there was not sufficient clerical work to assist Steward. On September 14 he proudly reported that the four-hundred-page *Colored Regulars* was finished. The book, he noted, lacked the names of all the killed and wounded in the 24th Infantry as well as the names of all commissioned officers. He requested that this information be sent to him so that he could add it to the final revision. Happy with his accomplishment, he wrote that "the book cannot fail to be of inestimable value to the colored people of the land and is, I flatter myself, a substantial contribution to the literature of the Hispano-American War." It was not until 1904 that it was published by the AME Book Concern. Fittingly, as an expression of race pride and justification of racial development, it was published by a race organ. The manuscript, with its bold declaration of the prowess of the black soldier, was undoubtedly too militant for any other publisher at the turn of the century.[21]

The Colored Regulars' mission to show that whites did not possess a monopoly on either patriotism or fighting ability fulfilled one of the purposes of the American Negro Academy, "to aid, by publication, the dissemination of the truth and the vindication of the Negro race from vicious assaults." The reviews were full of racial pride. *The Christian Recorder* assessed it as telling "the true story. It shows that the Negro soldier cannot only fight in the ranks, but can also command." Another reviewer praised Steward for putting the information "where the white historian cannot lose it and where the black child cannot help finding it." *The AME Church Review* called for the book to be in every Negro's library, as "in this book we have the antidote to . . . pen murder." Others called for the adoption of the book as a school textbook. Judson W. Lyons, register of the treasury, praised *The Colored Regulars* for being "free from that ever present bane of our race authors—exaggeration."[22]

The Colored Regulars was used for political reasons by Emmett J. Scott, secretary to Booker T. Washington, who requested on March 8, 1907, that President Theodore Roosevelt "issue an order that six of the batteries of field artillery and not less than eighteen of the companies of the coast artillery by act of Congress, approved January 25, 1907, be recruited with colored men." Scott's request, suggested in 1889 by *New York Age* editor Timothy Thomas Fortune, championed the intelligence and bravery of the race, attributes emphasized in Steward's study.[23]

The army did not want Steward to remain in Ohio until *The Colored Regulars* was published. Instead the War Department in early October 1899 ordered him to San Francisco to await assignment to the Philippines. He bade farewell to Susan and two of his sons as he departed on October 11 for St. Paul, Minnesota, by way of Chicago. His train arrived in Minneapolis in time for him to join a festive crowd welcoming home the 13th Minnesota Volunteers from Asia.[24]

The American enthusiasm over victory in the Philippines would quickly be tempered by President McKinley's refusal to recognize Filipino independence. The treaty with Spain ceded the archipelago to the United States. Led by Emilio Aguinaldo, the islanders resisted American rule in a bloody conflict from 1899 to 1902. Seventy thousand soldiers, including members of the four Colored Regulars and the two colored volunteer regiments, the Forty-eighth and Forty-ninth, would occupy and pacify the Philippines. The presence of the colored troops would lead many to question their role as part of the occupying force. They were conflicted over their loyalties to the flag and the military as they saw in the mistreatment of the Filipinos a reflection of their own second-class status. Some deserted to join the rebels. Others developed friendships with Filipinos and acted as a buffer between them and racist American soldiers.[25]

Steward, who would not be a disinterested observer of American military, social, and educational policies, departed San Francisco on October 26. He spoke at a Thanksgiving morning service at a Manila YMCA. He greeted 1890 with these words, "I awake . . . thankful for health, vigor and peace of mind." From June to November he cared for the sick and distributed literature to soldiers. He lectured to the men against immorality and drunkenness and "had the pleasure to see men reclaimed."[26]

After a lengthy stay in Manila, Steward moved to the coastal city of Iba in Zimbales Province, fifty miles north of the capital. He was very active in the cultural, religious, and educational life of the Filipinos. He was also a keen observer of Filipino society. In late 1901 he informed readers of *The Colored American Magazine* about women smokers, education, and the archipelago's changing courtship and marriage customs. He viewed the absence of labor laws as "the curse of the orient," as young girls rolled "one thousand paper plagues . . . in [a] cigarette factory" for the equivalent of ten American cents.[27]

Steward shared many Victorian beliefs about the role of women in both the home and society. He had difficulty adjusting to the role of women in Filipino society and he was dismayed at the liberties taken by them. One night Steward was the guest of a lawyer and judicial candidate. He was received by the man's wife and her sister, daughters of a wealthy Spaniard. While discussing with the wife her husband's large sheep stock, she "suddenly . . . asked me how we caponized sheep in America; her sister took it up and the two explained that they were accustomed to mesh the testicles and that the sheep suffered greatly . . . and many of them died." The husband then returned to the room and joined in the conversation. Shocked, Steward wrote, "no one having the slightest thought that the subject was not highly proper. These were people of the highest respectability and there was no double meaning in their talk."[28]

Ironically, Steward felt closer to the Filipinos than he did to most Americans in the archipelago. American racism was rampant in the Philippines. Shortly after arriving in Manila, Steward wrote to *The Independent* that an American-owned restaurant discriminated against Filipinos and black soldiers. He warned that "a deep revulsion will set in as soon as the Filipinos come to understand what the word 'nigger' means." Many white soldiers publicly sang songs with words such as "all coons look alike to me." Steward complained when white soldiers neglected to salute him or "indulged in . . . vile cursing at [his] expense."[29]

Black soldiers informed friends and family of the spread of American racism to Asia. Sgt. Major John W. Galloway, Twenty-fourth U.S.I., wrote in 1899, "the whites have begun to establish their diabolical race hatred in all its home rancor in Manila." Galloway, who believed that Filipinos would have the same future as "the Negro in the South," reported that Filipinos were erroneously told that black soldiers would rape their women and plunder their graves, acts that many whites were guilty of during the occupation. The black soldiers and Filipinos had an affinity. Between white and black soldiers, Filipinos viewed the latter as "angels" and the former "as the devil." Steward agreed. "The great color question is dividing the world. Just as it is wicked to be *black* in America, I fear the day will dawn when it will be wicked to be *white*." Reiterating the theme of *The End of the World*, Steward declared that men of color who had "been kicked, cuffed and shot out of the white race" belonged "with the age to come."[30]

Steward's breeding and membership in the black aristocracy would not permit him to accept insults from white recruits. Fortunately, most of his time was spent with the black soldiers or Filipinos, who identified with him. Steward was concerned about the lack of religious instruction in the countryside, as the insurrection and reaction against the prewar power of Catholic priests left the area without religious leadership. He was concerned about the virtue of women due to the absence of a religious element. The people knew that he was a clergyman and they welcomed his presence. He even eased a woman's last moments by telling her that he was a *"padre"* so she could die in peace.[31]

The Spanish-American War and the Filipino resistance to American occupation brought the religious question to the surface. The Manila *Times* in early 1900 reported that the people were revolting against two powerful Spanish friars. Many priests, according to the Filipinos, were corrupt hypocrites who slept with the women. Concerned about the scarcity of religious figures in Zambales Province, Steward wrote a letter to Archbishop Chappelle, apostolic delegate in Manila, but was unable to have it delivered. He wrote, "I have visited all the pueblos of this province with the exception of three, and it pains my heart to see . . . the ever faithful sheep without the watchful shepherd." He was concerned about mothers who were trying to protect their daughters from temptations. He added that although he was an

AME preacher, he had much respect for the Catholic Church. This comment was different from his view expressed privately on December 31, 1899, when he wrote that the time was ripe for aggressive Protestant mission work. However, he warned that Filipinos would not convert if they did not have leadership roles in Protestant churches. He was happy that a Methodist mission was under the charge of a Filipino but he hoped that the Methodists would not "place over him a white American, whom he must obey and instruct at the same time."[32]

Steward not only served the religious needs of the people of Zambales Province but their educational needs as well. From November 1900 to January 21, 1902, he served as superintendent of schools for the province. He traveled widely, organizing schools, assisting teachers with curriculum development, and helping them to obtain books. Among other things, he recommended that teachers stop smoking in classrooms, that students learn English, and that rote memorization be eliminated. During his tenure as superintendent he organized forty-three schools.[33]

General orders no. 41, issued on March 30, 1900, established the department of public instruction. At first textbooks were warehoused Spanish texts that were deemed inferior by the American occupiers. Most were of religious nature, but they were better than nothing until books could be shipped from the United States. Americans were committed to changing the educational system in the pacified Philippines. The military governor's report recommended that English be the language of instruction, that industrial schools be established, that Americans teach English in the larger towns, and that a well-equipped normal school be established for training the natives to teach English. Other recommendations called for the construction of modern schools in larger towns and that all schools be "absolutely divorced from the Church." English was selected as the language of instruction, as it was believed that if the Filipinos learned English it would "prevent distrusts and misunderstandings."[34]

These recommendations met with Steward's approval. He traveled throughout Zambales to convince the local mayors and townspeople to adopt the American educational system. On November 22, 1900, he delivered an address in Iba on the importance of learning English. Filipinos were quick to accommodate the Americans, realizing that they could succeed economically with a knowledge of English and American mores. The next day Steward was informed by the ex-governor of the province that a boys' and girls' school would open on December 1. The boys were scheduled to attend classes in a

Theophilus Gould Steward, Chaplain, 25th U.S. Infantry, ca. 1900. Photograph courtesy of the Schomburg Center for Research in Black Culture, NYPL.

rented building while the girls' school would be in the home of a teacher. Steward considered the salaries of the teachers "ridiculously small." He promised in a November 23 letter to the superintendent of public instruction in Manila that he would labor "to have the pay increased as conditions improve." He requested that the superintendent forward to Iba books, specifically one hundred copies of *Lecciones de Lenguajie*, a similar number of *Baldwin's Readers*, copybooks, and "ink, pens, slates and pencils, inkstands, sponges, etc., according to the supply on hand." The next day he telegraphed the commanding military officers at Santa Cruz, Masniloc, and Botolen about the possibility of opening schools in those communities by December 1.[35]

The opening of school on December 1 was a festive day. The boys performed simple arithmetic exercises for the guests and sang, badly in his estimation, "Jesu Cristo ha unido." Committed to other schools, Steward left Iba two days later for Boloten, escorted by an armed mounted detachment. He was dismayed to hear the young boys sing "hello ma honey, hello ma baby, hello ma ragtime gal." Others, perhaps out of a misguided effort to please him, performed a minstrel dance. He was equally upset with the students' ability to memorize without understanding what the words meant.[36]

As an American and a school superintendent, Steward was viewed as an authoritarian figure. On December 7, the teacher of the girls' school in Botolen inquired if it was all right to engage in panguinjue, a type of gambling done by women when school was not in session, on Sundays, or on feast days. Steward did not know what to say, so he said nothing. A week later, he visited the boys' school in San Felipe, which he described as "the best I had seen so far." He was surprised to enter a classroom where the teacher had been absent for over an hour to find the class orderly.[37]

Steward's superintendency ended on January 21, 1902, when a civil commission act terminated military control over the Philippines. His last proposal was the recommendation of the establishment of an American high school with emphasis on natural science and advanced mathematics. He requested the residents of Iba to establish a newspaper devoted to agriculture, forestry, education, and politics. He suggested that the local officials establish sawmills and rice hulling machines to diversify employment.[38]

Steward's educational efforts attracted attention. Colonel Andrew W. Burt informed the adjutant general, Third District, Department of Northern Luzon, on June 6, 1901 that it was not Steward's fault that Zambales Province lagged behind other provinces in teaching American subjects, as there were only two qualified teachers in the province. A more positive assessment of Steward's effectiveness came from a soldier who observed that the chaplain accomplished much as he "got right down to work, and with his knowledge of Spanish, instilled in them ideas which to this day [January 15, 1902] carry them a long way in school." Steward's rapport with the people was noted by the correspondent's observation that two Filipinos attended a church service with Americans, as "they had been earlier pupils of his and they naturally felt they must attend all meetings he conducted."[39]

To change the educational system from a Spanish one to an American-style system, the United States decided to send Americans to the Pacific islands. Civil Governor William H. Taft stated on July 4, 1901, that one thousand Americans would be sent to the Philippines within three months to teach English to pupils and to Filipino teachers.[40] One of the American teachers was Steward's son, Gustavus Adolphus. Dock, as he was commonly known, had wanted to go to Africa to be a missionary. "But this dream," he wrote in 1933, "was shattered by my anxious parents who considered my nineteen years had not given me sufficient experience or wisdom to dispose intelligently of my life. Through the intercession of my father . . . I got a small school at Agno, a provincial coast town of Zambales." The sending of Dock to the Philippines was typical of Steward's control over his sons. It is likely that Steward did not want his son to go to Africa because he thought it would be similar to his unpleasant experience in Haiti. Steward's absolute control over Dock was revealed by a letter to him on his twenty-first birthday. The complete letter was succinct: "Gustavus Adolphus Steward today this name takes its place among the names of *men*. You are now responsible for yourself. Let your name stand for truth as God gives you to see it; and for righteousness without compromise for yourself and with charity for others."[41]

Steward's involvement in the education of Filipinos reflected his desire to serve his country. Even though the war raised contradictions for him and other black men, he did not show revulsion toward assisting white Americans in oppressing Filipinos through educational "reforms." Nor was he a bootlicker who felt no sympathy for the rebels. Although Steward considered the guerrillas "nothing more than murderers," a common view among military men, he was impressed with the intelligence and refinement of Don Pedro A. Paterno, president of Aguinaldo's cabinet. After Aguinaldo was captured on March 28, 1901, Steward briefly spoke with the rebel leader, who gave him two statements. "No, he didn't suffer in the revolution," and as to the future of the Philippines, he said that it was "in the hands of the American people." Steward was very much impressed with the insurgent's patriotism.[42]

Steward spent the summer of 1901 in the United States. During this time he lectured on the Philippines in south New Jersey, Philadelphia, Washington, and Wilberforce, Ohio. On September 24, after a pleasant and restful vacation, he left Ohio for San Francisco where he sailed on October 1 aboard the transport *Hancock*. Five weeks later he was back in Iba. Steward wrote many observations of Filipino life during his last six months in Asia. Most of his thoughts were not for public consumption and represented his frank appraisal of the people and their customs. He viewed the people as "hospitable to a fault . . . [who have] a decided fondness for colored Americans, many of whom . . . have married handsome Filipino belles."[43]

In an unpublished essay, probably written in 1902, he noted that, like William H. Taft, he had previously believed that there were tribal differences among the Filipinos. He changed his view and concluded that his three years of close observation convinced him that tribal animosities were nonexistent. "In their army, in their journals, in their social gatherings, in their churches no mention is made of the different so-called tribes." In contrast to official policy, he added that it was gratuitous to assert that Americans were needed to "prevent the people from rushing at one another's throats." In a conversation with the wife of an American supporter, Steward learned that 90 percent of the Filipinos wanted independence. While he believed that there would not be a mass uprising against American occupation, he properly noted that Filipinos "do not see in American domination the realization of their ideals and there is likely to be discontent." He asked his nation to show its greatness by guiding the Filipinos toward independence. He observed that throughout the world people of Asian and African blood were uniting around the issue of color. Interestingly, the widow of Jefferson Davis, the Confederacy's only president, thought it foolish for America to remain in the Philippines and "add several millions of Negroes to our population when we already have eight million . . . in the United States." The outspoken Mrs. Davis believed that since America had not solved its own race problem, it would be best to leave the Filipinos to themselves.[44]

Steward did not want to have American culture transferred wholesale to Asia. He wrote a six-page essay, "Venerable names in the Philippines," in which he criticized the American occupation force for replacing Spanish and aboriginal names with those of obscure American officers. He had no objection to applying American names to those institutions created by Americans, but he considered it absurd to change the venerable names of provinces, streets, and buildings in a wave of Americanization.[45]

Despite his criticism of some aspects of the Filipino culture, Steward saw in the Pacific Islands a potential haven for the oppressed of his race. In March 1902 the New York *Sun* had printed an essay by Steward that claimed the archipelago was a "veritable Eldorado for the American Negro." He predicted that thousands would go there once they had knowledge of its favorable conditions. A supporting view of emigration came from the pen of Timothy Thomas Fortune. Fortune was appointed a commissioner to the Philippines, where he worked from February 17 to May 10, 1903. His main duty there was to examine the colonization possibility. The following year, Fortune had three articles on the Philippines published in *The Voice of the Negro*. He noted that the approximately four hundred Afro-Americans working there as civil servants or owners of small businesses had cordial relationships with Filipinos. A number of soldiers remained in the islands after their discharge, preferring life there to the certain bigotry in the land of their birth. It was ironic that both Steward and Fortune, opponents of African emigration, supported an exodus to South Asia. A dissenting view was expressed by a contributor to *The Voice of the Negro*, who argued that it would be wrong for "the emigrants . . . to . . . ally [themselves] . . . with another people" who would bring disadvantages of illiteracy and thriftlessness. Despite Steward's and Fortune's declarations, few sought to make the arduous journey to take advantage of what Sgt. Major T. Clay Smith, 24th Infantry, considered "the best opportunities of the century."[46]

The desire of black soldiers to remain in Asia after their discharge alarmed William Howard Taft, civil governor of the Philippines. He believed that the soldiers "got along fairly well with the natives . . . too well with the . . . women," which led to "demoralization in the towns where they have been stationed." Taft managed to have the black troopers withdrawn from the islands in 1901 "out of their regular turn."[47]

Steward left Manila on July 7, 1902. Always mindful of race, on the eve of his departure Steward noted that "the presence of the so-called *colored man* is the acid test of American culture." He was returning to the land of his birth where the forces of bigotry were rapidly spreading southern racism northward. Entering San Francisco Bay on August 13, the regimental band played "Hail, Columbia, Happy Land." The song stirred in him mixed feelings. "I had never liked either the words or the tune before, but I confess it awakened a thrill of gladness . . . as I heard it after a siege of over forty days on ship board." But he was coming back to a nation that denied some of its citizens the franchise and lynched scores every year. "After all is Columbia altogether a happy land

144

to me? Ought Columbia with its race phobia be in all respects a happy land to me?" He left it up to his readers to judge. Steward, however, admitted his conflict in living in a discriminatory nation: "keenly sensible as I am to the ills which my people have suffered here, I nevertheless appreciate the opportunities into which they have been thrown." Despite America's race chauvinism Steward admitted that his race had been "*pitched* into a civilization stimulating to the highest development."[48]

It was this faith in the potential goodness of his country that separated him from the radicals who saw no possibility of a color-blind nation where all people would be respected. Soon he would be at Fort Niobrara, Nebraska, where he would be united with his wife and his sixteen-year-old son Walter.

ELEVEN

Fort Niobrara and the End of Chaplaincy

In 1898 the men of the Twenty-fifth left the United States to defend the flag. They returned home four years later as unfortunate instruments in America's imperialistic ventures in Asia and the Caribbean. Those who saw the spread of American racism to the Philippines returned mindful of the rising tide of racism in this nation. The beginning of the new century led to a continuation of lynching and disfranchisement. Insults were hurled at both Theodore Roosevelt and Booker T. Washington when the president invited the educator to dine at the White House in 1901. "The President of the United States has committed a crime against civilization, and his nigger guest has done his race a wrong which cannot soon be erased," declared the Memphis *Scimitar*.[1]

Chaplain Steward and the recruits were well aware of American racism, but their loyalties were to the flag and the nation regardless of their personal feelings. Those who could not resolve the conflict of serving a government that could not protect its own citizens left the employ of the army. Others, like Steward, remained, believing that their presence would lead to the larger society judging them by their character. During the next few years Steward's faith in the goodness of the military would be tested.

Meanwhile, the regiment traveled by train from San Francisco to Nebraska. Fort Niobrara, which had been in intermittent operation since 1880, had been vacant for several years until the arrival of the Twenty-fifth on August 27, 1902. The men spent their first few weeks clearing the fort of snakes and making the facilities livable. Compared to the lush greenery of the Philippines, and even compared to Montana with its good hunting and fishing areas, Fort Niobrara was a dreary place. Steward continued the pattern he had established at Fort Missoula of interacting with the recruits. He organized in October 1902 a YMCA chapter and lectured before its membership the following month on the evils of gambling. In December he organized an afternoon and evening class for the soldiers, teaching them Spanish, American history, civil government, and patriotism. In February 1906, after the number of children at the garrison increased, he offered them a day school. He did not neglect the nearby racially mixed community of Valentine, which had his service as a guest preacher.[2]

Providing a religious atmosphere was Steward's main duty. In this he had the support of the officers and the faithful assistance of his wife. In contrast to Montana, Steward now had an easy time bringing the men to religious services. His success led to overcrowding in the seventy-four-seat chapel. The surplus were placed in the adjoining schoolroom.[3]

At the end of October, Sunday evening services averaged over one hundred in attendance. Susan Steward's contributions as an organ player and musical director contributed to the fine services. Her long-standing interest in the African Methodist Episcopal church's South African mission work was shared with the soldiers, who by September 1903 contributed $40 to Bishop Levi J. Coppin's work in that area. On the surface, religious work at Fort Niobrara appeared to be of the highest order. As many as 146 attended service in November, with the average for the month 99. But the strong religious interest declined as winter approached. Several explanations account for the falling off in attendance. The longer the men were removed from the battles of the Philippines, the less they thought about their own mortality. Perhaps more important was the garrison's prohibition against beer and wine sales. In 1901 Congress, persuaded by the Women's Christian Temperance Union, forbade the sale of alcoholic beverages at base canteens. This forced men to seek their liquid pleasures at off-base saloons that doubled as gambling dens or houses of prostitution. Despite numerous editorials, memos from officers, and Secretary of War William H. Taft's 1905 comment that anticanteen law increased drunkenness, Congress refused during Steward's chaplaincy to abandon the prohibitionists.[4]

Steward's strong prohibitionist views prevented him from supporting those chaplains and officers who supported a revocation of the law. His puritanical views allowed him only to tell the men to stop sinning. While it was true that white soldiers had a higher admission rate to army hospitals for alcoholism, foremost in Steward's mind were the moral standards of African-American men, whose presence in the military reflected well or badly on the race as a whole.[5]

The inadequate facilities hampered Steward's YMCA work. The national office of the Y was unwilling to build better facilities at Fort Niobrara, as the garrison was scheduled for closing in the near future. Steward complained that the lack of space for a library and reading room undermined his religious efforts. Throughout 1903 Steward worked closely with the guardhouse prisoners, who were required to attend religious services. He was sensitive to their presence and conducted the service "as not to arouse their ill feelings." In December he read to the prisoners *Letters From a Selfmade Merchant To His Sons*. Like tending his garden in Montana, this effort endeared him to the men.[6]

Steward enjoyed the outdoor life. Far from being an effete intellectual, Steward, despite his advancing age, was physically active. In Montana his masculinity was expressed in his hunting trips. In Nebraska Steward accompanied the regiment on a 109-mile march from Fort Niobrara to Norfolk. The sixteen-day trip provided the regiment's baseball team with opportunities to play local teams. The regimental band entertained the local citizens at well-attended concerts. Chaplain Steward "rode the distance on horseback, slept in a tent every night," and came to a fire only to warm his feet, despite the presence of frost. At Norfolk the troops boarded a train for Fort Riley, Kansas, where they had three weeks of maneuvers.[7]

The cordial reception the troops received from the local residents was indicative of the pleasant relationship they had with the people of Valentine. Race relations were not, however, favorable throughout the entire state. The color line was drawn on November 9, 1903, "when all the best hotels refused to entertain delegates to the National Freedmen's Aid and Southern Educational Society." Later the Ku Klux Klan found strong sympathy and support in the state.[8]

After returning from maneuvers, Steward used the intimacy gained on the trip to get closer to the men. He and his wife put a special effort into making their first Nebraska Christmas memorable. The garrison's Christmas tree had gifts for the children beneath it, a contribution from Grace Dodge, a friend of Sarah Garnet, Steward's sister-in-law.

The joys of the holidays turned to grief for the Steward household. Several months earlier Walter had accompanied his brother Benjamin, a Chicago sanitary beef inspector, on his rounds of refrigerated lockers. Walter returned with what everyone thought was just a bad cold. Then on January 13, 1904, he suddenly died. Steward was devastated by the passing of his youngest son. He wrote, "to live is to suffer. We who were left looked at one another and asked in a muffled speech: 'what does it mean?' and the answer is not yet." His unpublished papers contain a eulogy to "Our Walter."

> Bright, cheerful, helpful and free,
> Singing, laughing, whistling with glee,
> Scattering smiles as he passed along,
> Gladdening all by his joyous song,
> A fountain of love, a gush of light,
> A hope incarnate, a flash of truth,
> A gift from Heaven. A sparkle of youth.[9]

The death of Walter profoundly affected Steward's work. Normally stoic, he admitted the impact of his son's death on his chaplain's duties. His February 1904 report noted "the interruption occasioned by death in my family caused some falling off but the interest is again reviving." Throughout the spring he increased his work among the prisoners who attended the morning service. To boost their morale, he sometimes permitted a prisoner to play the organ. His interest in the prisoners had a positive effect. In his report for April, Steward wrote that two paroled men continued to attend services and that several "continued . . . to come to morning service voluntarily" after completing their sentences.[10]

Steward was a conscientious chaplain who sought ways to bring the men into a moral life. Such diligence in his view warranted a promotion. He had held the rank of captain since his appointment in 1891. In early 1903, anticipating that Congress would pass a bill promoting qualified chaplains to the rank of major, Steward requested a promotion. He obtained endorsements from the regiment's officers and included in his request a March 13, 1895, resolution from the Presbyterian church of Missoula praising him for serving as a substitute pastor.[11]

On April 21, 1904, Congress passed an act to promote up to fifteen chaplains to the grade of major, providing they had at least ten years' service. Steward formally applied for promotion on May 30, fully expecting no problems. He was shocked to learn several weeks later that the judge advocate general had decided "that there was nothing of record" to prove that he was "worthy of special distinction for exceptional efficiency." Upon hearing about his father's setback, Frank Steward, now a Pittsburgh attorney, took the initiative to inform President Theodore Roosevelt that Steward had been unfairly denied promotion. Frank informed the president of his father's educational work in the Philippines and "his familiarity with the Spanish tongue . . . enabled him to do much towards reassuring the Filipinos of our proper purposes in those islands," which were not part of his official record. Frank called on the president to promote his father because he was "entirely fit and worthy regardless of race." But Roosevelt did not intervene. Steward did not give up his quest for advancement. In mid-July 1904 he forwarded to the military secretary in Washington endorsements from the regimental officers and from several retired officers who knew of his work in Montana and the Philippines. A year later he applied again for a promotion. He again was turned down.[12]

Ironically, shortly before the army rejected his first application for promotion, Steward was in Chicago attending the quadrennial meeting of the AME church. It was the first gathering of the African Methodists that he attended since the raucous meeting in Indianapolis in 1888. Steward's paper, "The Army as a Trained Force," was read by his cousin Benjamin F. Lee, since he was suffering from a severe cold. The paper stressed the army as a place where the African race could achieve equality.

Steward returned to Nebraska in late May. He was pleased with the men's religious interest but he knew that they were capable of being easily influenced by their peers and the local prostitutes. Both Steward and Colonel R. W. Hoyt, the garrison's commander, knew that the men generally behaved themselves when they had positive alternatives to gambling, liquor, and sex. One such alternative came on July 1, 1905, when the regiment celebrated the seventh anniversary of the battles of El Caney and San Juan, pivotal engagements in the Spanish-American War. Nearly one hundred veterans were present. There was much good will in the garrison. Perhaps because of the rekindled race pride created by the celebration, the men's good behavior continued for the rest of the year. During the afternoon of New Year's Eve, Steward joined a Valentine minister to begin a " 'rescue' movement in behalf . . . of the colored people of [Valentine to arouse] the good and right thinking to exert themselves in the interest of those who have gone astray." Some of these were camp followers who provided the soldiers with liquor and women. The closing of two houses that sold illegal liquor and the arrival of a young soldier who was a licensed preacher in early 1906 aided Steward's efforts. Happily, Steward preached to 105 on February 11 and to 200 on April 15, Easter Sunday.[13]

In May the War Department ordered the garrison to abandon the fort and relocate to Texas. While the news had been expected for some time, it shocked

Valentine's officials, who considered the men of the Twenty-fifth better disciplined than the white troops who had served the region.[14]

No one wanted to go to Texas, a state described by Steward as "the maelstrom for colored regulars." During maneuvers at Fort Riley, Kansas, in 1903, Steward had been assaulted with an "uncivil and ribald speech by a . . . Texas militiaman." Other men in the regiment had had similar unpleasant experiences. On June 30, 1906, Steward informed the regiment's adjutant officer about his fears. "The introduction of the Negro soldier . . . to . . . the South . . . might serve . . . as an aggravation and might be the occasion of serious trouble."[15]

Nevertheless, the men were assigned to forts Brown, Bliss, and McIntosh. Normally the chaplain would have gone to Fort Bliss, regimental headquarters, but the altitude of four thousand feet was adverse to his health. He was assigned instead to Fort McIntosh. En route, Steward reported that the officers prepared meals for the enlisted men to avoid confrontations at public eating houses. "The signs of hostility were everywhere evident," he noted. A delay at one of the stations gave him an opportunity to counsel the noncommissioned officers "to use all sorts of patience and circumspection in order to avoid occasions for offense."[16]

Many residents of Brownsville, a Rio Grande River town, openly expressed their distaste for the black infantry even before their arrival on July 25. There were soon several racial incidents that foreshadowed the explosion on August 13. A white woman was standing on the sidewalk talking with a Mr. Tate, a customs official, when two soldiers walked near them. A private inadvertently brushed the woman's dress, which prompted Tate to knock him down with the butt of his revolver and threaten to shoot him if he did not learn to respect white women. Black men as rapists of white women was a prevailing stereotype in 1906. Ironically, white women in Montana freely traveled in the wilderness areas without any fear of soldiers molesting them.[17]

It is not clear if the incident between Tate and the soldier precipitated ten minutes of terror that evening, when shooting led to the death of a bartender and the wounding of the chief of the police. Although all soldiers were accounted for and no ammunition was missing, suspicion was directed at Fort Brown. Outraged citizens demanded the next day that Major C. W. Penrose, the fort's commander, produce the names of the guilty within twenty-four hours. On August 16 over a hundred armed men threatened to shoot any soldiers who left the fort. On August 17 a committee of citizens demanded that white troops replace the men of the Twenty-fifth. A second appeal came the next day, as town officials indicated that people were frightened by the soldiers' presence. The colorphobia led to the army ordering the troops out of Fort Brown on August 20 for reassignment to Fort Reno, Oklahoma. They were replaced by a company of white soldiers from the Twenty-sixth Infantry.[18]

Accommodating the racism of the white citizens, the military sent Lt. Colonel Lovering, inspector general of the Southwestern Division, and General E. A. Garlington, inspector general of the army, to conduct an inquiry. The soldiers refused to testify against their comrades, which led the army to believe that some were covering up for guilty friends. The military charged twelve men with murder and conspiracy to commit murder and placed them in the stockade at Fort Sam Houston near San Antonio. Steward spoke to the accused on August 30. He reported, "I found them . . . manifesting no signs of consciousness of evil doing. They are . . . men who have borne good reputations and as I know them personally, I feel very strongly that they are not likely to be found guilty." He felt so confident about their innocence that he had his vacationing wife hand-deliver a letter to the New York *Tribune* stating this fact.[19]

Booker T. Washington, an adviser to President Theodore Roosevelt on racial matters, on November 10 wrote a confidential letter to Steward requesting information "that will help me to see that justice is done." He promised to protect Steward with confidentiality. Sixteen days later Roosevelt, angered that not one soldier broke the "conspiracy of silence," dishonorably discharged 167 men. With a stroke of a pen he removed from active service six former Medal of Honor winners and thirteen soldiers who had received citations for bravery during the Spanish-American War.[20]

Steward did not publicly respond to the decision. He wrote in his autobiography that not a single officer believed the men were guilty, but they could not criticize their commander-in-chief. Steward never condemned Roosevelt, not even after his discharge from service, because he considered himself an inactive member of the military for the rest of his life. Others, however, were outraged by Roosevelt's decision. On November 15 the 160,000-member Negro Baptist Association of North Carolina assailed the Rough Rider in a strongly worded resolution. The African-American press condemned Roosevelt for his act, which they viewed as racist. Ironically, Roosevelt had humiliated a regiment that had saved his life during the campaign of San Juan Hill in 1896. His decision was not corrected until 1972 when the secretary of the army changed their discharges to honorable.[21]

Steward's health was deteriorating. He had been admitted to a military hospital on October 5, suffering from neurasthenia characterized by fatigue, loss of energy and memory, and feelings of inadequacy, symptoms attributed to his concern about the fate of the soldiers under investigation. On October 22 he was granted a three-month leave to visit his brothers Stephen and William in Bridgeton. On January 10, 1907, Dr. W. T. Good, who had been treating Steward since December 10, informed the army that Steward was unable to travel "or follow his usual vocation." On January 12, writing from New Jersey, Steward requested that the army send him to Wilberforce, Ohio, on his impending retirement. En route to joining his regiment, Steward wrote from Pittsburgh that his health had improved but since he still had six weeks of leave due to him, and his retirement was set for April 17, he wished to avoid the taxing trip to Laredo. On February 1 the War Department ordered him to proceed to Wilberforce to await retirement. Steward was removed from active duty on April 17, his sixty-fourth birthday.[22]

Steward's sixteen years in the chaplaincy were characterized by a devotion to race and patriotism. Despite his own problems with bias in the military, he believed that the army offered opportunities for racial advancement. He was so enamored with military life that he suggested in 1905 that military education be taught in every school and that every town organize battalions "composed of boys and young men." He believed that military education would prepare men mentally and physically to resist their enemies. He believed that character building resulted from hardship, discipline, and sacrifice, attributes acquired in the military. Many of these same traits motivated Booker T. Washington to propose industrial education for the nation's African-American youth. While Steward was not a personal follower of Washington's accommodationist philosophy, particularly his willingness to blame his own people for their misfortune, they shared the same respect for discipline and sacrifice. Steward viewed industrial education as neither "fundamental nor constructive." He attacked the supporters of industrial education as ignorant of history if they believed that people or races could develop "without passing through the fires that harden and toughen." Steward argued that "the primary need of the American Negro . . . is military education." The leading black thinkers agreed that African Americans needed to be brought into a higher civilization, but they could not agree if the vehicle should be industrial, military, or higher education. All agreed with W. E. B. Du Bois's assertion that "unless we conquer our present vices they will conquer us." Although Steward advocated military education, his own children had received an outstanding classical education and he was a member of the American Negro Academy, which called on graduates of higher education to be "a reforming force for the world's betterment." Despite his self-declared aversion to industrial education, Steward did not object when his son Gustavus later sought employment at Tuskegee Institute, the nation's leading industrial education school.[23]

Steward's advocacy of military education was a reflection of his love of country and all its symbols. The American flag, he noted in early 1906, "stands as the symbol of our liberty and independence, peaceful business and democracy. It means now that the 'door of hope' shall never be closed to any honest boy growing up in our land." Although many African Americans did not share in the nation's liberty, Steward viewed the American flag as "the banner of hope and flag of the free."[24] The Brownsville affray, with all its overt racism, did not dim his opinion about the flag or American principles.

Steward's departure from the military was a loss to young recruits. He represented to them the best and the brightest of the race. Many were inspired by his kindness and concern and appreciated his efforts to extol their bravery and patriotism. He was fortunate in having at forts Missoula and Niobrara the support of commanding officers who, unlike some other garrisons' commanders, did not discourage the men from attending chapel services. Some officers believed that war and Christianity were incompatible. Steward had the support of two loving wives who provided the men with warm smiles and cheerful voices. Susan's musical talents added to the wholesome atmosphere of church services. Although he did not have deacons, stewards, or Sunday school teachers to assist him, he performed his duties with devotion. He labored among the soldiers to bring a moral order to their lives. His endeavors were not always successful, but he constantly moved forward with the knowledge that he was doing the work of God.

Steward chose not to return to the AME itineracy. Perhaps he was tired of moving around the country or maybe he was unwilling to resume his sometimes fractious relationship with the bishops. In a sense, his life was in pieces. His first wife, parents, and three sons were dead. His surviving sons were scattered from Ohio to Massachusetts. Steward decided to join his wife as a faculty member of Wilberforce University, the institution he nearly became president of in 1884. In moving onward he was practicing his motto: "save the pieces; never despair."[25]

TWELVE

Educator and Traveler

To those who worried that even a sedentary university life would be too taxing for the sickly Steward, the former chaplain complained that some think "I should now wholly retire, drink hemlock, or take chloroform, or else quietly await the summons to lie down amid pleasant dream." He vowed to continue to enjoy life and work hard, traits that had their origin in his Gouldtown youth. "When I keep still," he wrote, "I get sick. How delightful it is to work until one is really tired and then fall into bed and sleep like a log." To his concerned friends, he added, "I am very busy, have enough work for three men today and while strength lasts I shall continue to work with my might." He vowed to "live, labor and enjoy; and to preach Jesus by exhibiting the peace and joy of His service, and be ready to give the helping and the glad hand of my fellowmen."[1]

Steward had difficulty adjusting to his civilian role. For the past sixteen years he had proudly worn the uniform of the U.S. Army chaplaincy corps. He found it expedient to duplicate the garrison's life of discipline at Wilberforce.[2] It upset him to be referred to as "ex-chaplain" because he was "still reporting [his] address regularly to the Adjutant General . . . and drawing [his] monthly pay as chaplain . . . retired." He still considered himself under the army's jurisdiction. "Indeed," he added, "I expect to die in the army." As late as 1913 he still wore his military uniform.[3]

Steward arrived at Wilberforce University in the middle of the spring term and was not obligated to teach until the fall. His strong interest in the affairs of the AME church motivated him to offer a practical but controversial suggestion shortly after his discharge from the military. He proposed that one of the bishops be given full pay to write the history of African Methodism, to be available for the 1916 centennial of the AME's quadrennial conferences. Despite his assertion that the writing be done by a bishop, Steward's suggestion that the writer "have the historian's interest . . . scholarship and patience" indicated to some that he had himself in mind for the prodigious and prestigious undertaking.[4]

This assumption had some merit. Steward had employed this technique to obtain a missionary position to Haiti in 1873 and it nearly won him the presidency of Wilberforce in 1884. There was no one in the church who had written a scholarly work comparable to Steward's *The Colored Regulars*. William J. Laws, president of Paul Quinn College, an AME institution in Waco, Texas, immediately suggested that the project be adopted and turned it over to Steward, who "ranks with the greatest writers of the age." The selection of Steward, argued Laws, "would crown our church with historic glory; to fail, historic death." The trial balloon was punctured by the Reverend R. C. Ramson's declaration that Steward had been away from the AME church too long to write an effective history. He recommended that the honor go to Dr. J. T. Jenifer. Later, Bishop Henry M. Turner, who often clashed with Steward, was selected to write the history.[5]

After a summer reunion with the Gouldtown clan, Steward settled down to his new position in academia. Wilberforce University, founded in 1856, was the church's flagship educational institution. Located in southwestern Ohio, three miles from Xenia, a town with a nearly 30 percent black population, Wilberforce had a small campus with four hundred students.[6] Despite its tranquil environment, Wilberforce had both administrative and student problems, a situation shared by many of the nation's African-American colleges and universities as students during the next two decades would rebel against paternalistic administrations and/or outdated curricula.[7]

Steward took an active role in teaching and administration. At various times he taught political economy, Spanish, biblical theology, anthropology, Christian sociology, elocution, and history. From 1908 to 1918 he served as vice president, and throughout the years he served on the committee of lectures, religious life and affairs, and admissions. Ironically, he was never a member of the military life committee.

Steward's academic life began on a controversial note. He informed the *Christian Recorder* at the beginning of the fall 1907 term that the faculty did not receive their salaries on time and that the teaching conditions were deplorable. He added in a later report that he had to spend $100 of his own money to "fit up my history room." His frank declarations embarrassed the university but it led to the faculty receiving their salary in full for the period 1908-1912. But by 1914 the situation was so intolerable that President William S. Scarborough reported, "our teachers for two years have not been fully paid up due to the necessity of paying old debts out of current funds." He recommended the formation of endowed chairs so that the faculty would "have a certainty of their salary." Besides the salary issue, Steward was critical of the college's subordination to the preparatory and normal students. At that time the commencement oration was delivered by a preparatory student. Steward and his supporters gave dignity to the college students by separating their commencement from the others. As a distinguished professor, Steward lectured during the 1909-1910 academic year on "The Ocean Paths." In 1913 he gave the Baccalaureate Address, "The Virility of the American Negro." Two years later he delivered the Baccalaureate Sermon, and in 1922 he addressed the graduates of Payne Theological Seminary, the university's theological school.[8]

Today many of the historically black colleges are viewed as important alternatives to white universities. Studies have indicated that African-American students perform better in the nurturing environment provided by these institutions.[9] This was not true at the turn of the century, when students at Fisk, Hampton, Howard, and Wilberforce, to name a few, felt smothered by the paternalism of their faculty. Acting in loco parentis, university officials took pains to keep students away from real or imagined temptations. Students could not hold hands on campus. Undergraduates had to maintain a daily account of their activities "in such a way as to afford a full exhibit of [their] habits." Only seniors were permitted to visit families off campus and only if a short distance away. Hours for socializing were strictly regulated, and card-playing, smoking, drinking, and sexual misconduct were grounds for dismissal.[10]

The rigid control was directly connected to the administration's racist contention that students, particularly men, had no control over their sexual impulses. They may not have agreed with the language, but they agreed with the message of William Hannibal Thomas, a self-described man of "mixed blood," who wrote that "the chief and overpowering element in the [Negro's] makeup is an imperious sexual impulse, which, aroused at the slightest incentive, sweeps aside all restraints in the pursuit of physical gratification." Steward's observation of young recruits in the West and the Philippines caused him to agree in principle with Thomas's conclusion that "the pursuit of physical gratification . . . is the chief hindrance to [the race's] social uplifting."[11]

The rigidity of the administrators led to student strikes at Wilberforce in 1920, at Fisk in 1925, and at Hampton in 1927. President Scarborough and other university administrators were forced to repeal the rigid regulations that denied to students many social privileges and adult responsibilites.[12]

Both before and after Wilberforce's student strike, Steward maintained a rigidity that typified his upbringing and, to a lesser degree, his class status. Steward was a compelling speaker who was fascinated with the art of debating. He adamantly believed that a debating club should be a permanent part of Wilberforce's offerings. With the help of Professors Finch and Thomas, he organized a debating club shortly after his arrival. Despite his general support for women's rights, Steward at times held fast to sexual exclusiveness. In an undated note he wrote that even though some schools permitted women to engage in debating societies, Steward frowned on coed debating as nothing more than "literary diversion." A coed debating team was in his estimation akin to a coed basketball team; amusing to watch but not to be taken seriously. Somewhat illogically, he stated that even though some women were highly intelligent, "the serious work of college debate as now carried on must be left to the young men of the college."[13] This view was indicative of his attitude toward women. Although he often supported the rights of women, he normally supported their exclusion from male activities, particularly those of a cerebral nature.

Steward sought to inspire his students. He lectured that "to narrate anything well the first thing necessary is to feel that the thing is worth telling." He added, "unless we are deeply interested ourselves we cannot interest others." He believed that a teacher had the responsibility to keep a roll of honor "for the pupils are anxious to have a good name." Some years earlier, in 1884, he said that students should not be given readings containing "*love stuff*." This belief was not altered decades later when he taught older students. He urged them to read at night instead of running around the streets. He urged them to pay attention to their experiences as they would become in later years valuable lessons to share with others.[14]

Steward followed his own suggestion and sought to create in the minds of his students "a complete picture of each event, scene or moment" that gave life to history. Among the history courses he taught, he was especially happy with "The History of African Peoples in the Western World." Like many of his contemporaries, he was not a nationalist who identified with African culture. Nevertheless, he was proud of his ancestry. He was thrilled by the publication in 1922 of Carter G. Woodson's *The Negro in Our History*. Woodson was director of the Association for the Study of Negro Life and History, founded in 1915, and editor of *The Journal of Negro History*. Steward was immensely impressed with Woodson's scholarship. "Enfin!" he wrote to Woodson, "we have a *book*. A real text book—language, arrangement and reliability, such as to commend it. You are to be congratulated and you have made us all debtors." In 1916, when *The Journal of Negro History*'s first issue reached him, Steward praised the editor for his "fine publication."[15]

Steward's interest in using Woodson's book was indicative of his desire to expose his students to diverse views. Perhaps President Scarborough had Steward in mind when he wrote in his 1914 annual report, "we expect freshness of material offered by teachers . . . those who can make their students anxious to learn and to enter upon special lines of research and investigation."[16]

Steward displayed his concern for Wilberforce students by establishing in 1910 the Walter Hall Steward Memorial Fund by contributing $1,309.84. The interest provided a first scholarship of $50. Scholarships were limited "to members of the senior college class, by vote of the college faculty."[17] Wilberforce students appreciated Steward's scholarship and exemplary teaching. In 1922 A. E. Morris, senior class poet at Payne Theological Seminary, wrote in the yearbook, "then under [T. H.] Jackson, of Homiletical fame we set about to gain a name; and T. G. Stewart [sic] that author of books so fine we attempted to learn line by line."[18]

Indeed, had events transpired differently, Steward's reputation as a scholar could have placed him among the major historians of the Reconstruction. James R. L. Diggs, president of Virginia Theological Seminary and College, declared in a 1909 letter to W. E. B. DuBois, that "the educated Negro owes the world a history of Reconstruction." Diggs was outraged by William A. Dunning's interpretation of Reconstruction as a period of corruption, incompetency, and "Negro misrule." He suggested that a ten-volume study be written by Reconstruction participants like John R. Lynch, Robert Smalls, and Theophilus Steward. While DuBois replied that he agreed with Diggs and planned to devote time to his request (*Black Reconstruction* appeared in 1935), Steward's thoughts about that era remained in his private papers.[19]

His observations on America would have to wait, for in the summer of 1909, Theophilus and Susan Steward left for Europe aboard the *Caledonia* in New York.[20] They arrived in Great Britain on August 1. Steward found very liberal race relations in London. He noticed on Tottenham Court Road "a smart looking black man moving rapidly along with a well dressed white girl by his side attracting no attention. He also saw a white man with an African woman. He was amazed to see so many mixed couples, especially "colored men and white women . . . another striking illustration of the social liberty enjoyed."[21]

The mixing of the races was prominent in Paris too. He noticed in St. Etienne only one distinctively black person, but there were many who he thought would "be classed as colored in the United States." He judged that France had no color prejudice, and that there was perhaps only a slight bias in England and Scotland. His views, of course, were based on fleeting impressions. An American who had lived in Paris for nine months wrote in 1907, two years before Steward's arrival, that the French despised "black people," and that the local papers referred to the king of Cambodia as "the ginger bread colored King." According to this writer, the French often made laughing remarks about interracial couples.[22]

The Stewards did not encounter any direct racial discourtesies in Europe, however. On August 12, while in Edinburgh, they received an invitation "to dine, and also to make a call in the evening." Steward was fond of English civilization, which he considered to be "an admirable thing. Everywhere one meets with courteous civility."[23]

Steward's goal was to obtain lecture notes on European architecture and battlefields, and to observe human nature. Men in London, he noted, "are serving as horses. They pulled carts and performed as beasts of burden in many ways." Still, the British were civil and courteous; not so the French. He classified the leaving of England during the channel crossing as going "from comfort to chaos." He stereotyped the French as rude.[24]

Interestingly, Steward, who was a prohibitionist, offered a sympathetic view on the role of wine in French culture. He believed that the "use of wine accounts in part for the French levity," and that it made them "so brilliant, so scientific, so industrious, so patriotic, so affable, so fickle." He even drank some Bordeaux while en route from St. Germains to St. Etienne. He wrote that he could not detect any of the "bite of the serpent or the sting of the adder," but he admitted, "I never realized before so fully the force of the saying 'wine is a nocker and whosoever is deceived thereby is not wise.' "[25]

Steward was a believer in the equalizing potentials of capitalism, but he looked favorably on France's ability to provide for the public good. He was impressed that the wealth was distributed more equally there than in Great Britain. He was highly impressed with the historic sights in Italy. The Stewards visited Rome, Florence, and Naples. The Italians did not impress him. They were more "brusque, less tactful and less agreeable than the French and perhaps not so quick mentally." He characterized train passengers in Naples as "that lowbrowed murderous looking class, so prevalent in lower Italy." Most Italians reminded him of "garlic and the dagger."[26]

The Stewards left Naples on September 29, after nearly nine happy weeks in Europe. They continued their official duties at Wilberforce, he as professor and vice president and she as resident physician. On March 12, 1910, Theophilus left Susan in Ohio and attended the fiftieth wedding anniversary of his sister, Mary Steward Gould, in New Jersey. The trip gave him a chance to visit with his numerous relatives in the Bridgeton area.[27]

His devotion to family was evident by letters received from his sons. On April 17, 1910, Steward celebrated his sixty-seventh birthday. T. B., as Theophilus Bolden Steward was known, wrote a birthday note to his father: "I rejoice in the knowledge that thru various conditions you are yet alive, in spirit and in health, possessed of a sufficiency of the comforts of life." T. B. expressed joy that the family was in good health and reasonably successful. "You find yourself at 67, well settled and well satisfied, and we find ourselves unconsciously following your examples and advice." With profound love and respect he added, "this day I always celebrate as my Thanksgiving Day." On his father's sixty-ninth birthday, T. B. wrote, "indeed I am very grateful to God for all that He has done for us all. In many respects we have seemed to have had special dispensations."[28]

Despite his advancing age, Steward in 1911 traveled to England. He accompanied his wife and sister-in-law Sarah Garnet to the First Universal Race Congress's conference in London, July 26-29. Susan Steward presented a paper on "Colored American Women."[29] The Council of Bishops of the AME church commissioned Steward to represent the church at the London meeting. The congress was described by W. E. B. Du Bois, a delegate, as the greatest idea of the twentieth century because "the chief outcome of the Congress will be human contact . . . the spiritual contact which will fun round the world."[30] Steward attended many of the sessions and offered from the floor his opinions on anthropology. During these discussions on race he noticed "a tendency to confound differences with inequality."[31]

On returning to the Brooklyn home of Sarah Garnet, a reception was given on September 9 by the Equal Suffrage League. Dr. Steward entertained the large gathering with a reading of her conference paper. Du Bois, too, presented an account of his impressions of the congress to the crowd. Two days after the festivities, a gloom was cast over the Stewards. Sarah Garnet died unexpectedly. Du Bois was among the dignitaries who delivered a eulogy.[32]

The saddened Stewards returned to Ohio and settled themselves into their positions. On November 5, Steward wrote to the governor general of Algeria.

Steward's letter is not extant, but as gleaned from Count Meynier's reply, Steward evidently wanted to know how one could join the French army. Meynier answered that he had previous experience with "colored troops . . . in our African colonies" and respected them. But he was unable by French law to accept non-Frenchmen. Steward was apparently writing on behalf of some Americans, perhaps U.S. army veterans.[33]

Perhaps these unidentified men wanted to join the French army as a response to America's color-consciousness. In a note sent to a Xenia, Ohio, newspaper Steward requested help from anyone who had witnessed a discriminatory act against his wife in the Candy Kitchen on East Main Street during the afternoon of December 21. He wanted witnesses who heard the proprietor's answer to his question, "did you refuse to sell my wife a glass of soda." It dismayed him that they were victims of discrimination.[34] During the early twentieth century, racism was fairly common in Ohio.[35] An angry Ohio legislature sought to outlaw intermarriage after Jack Johnson married a white woman. The bill passed the lower house in March 1913 by a vote of 63 to 33. William S. Scarborough and approximately fifty other couples would have to break up their marriages if they wanted to continue to reside in the state. Fortunately for them justice prevailed; the senate did not approve the bill.[36]

The raising of the color question perplexed Steward. His love of country and his patriotism were unmatched by any of his contemporaries. In Du Bois's famous observation, Steward did not want to "bleach his Negro soul in a flood of white Americanisms, for he knows that Negro blood has a message for the world."[37] Steward and other blacks had to "wrestle with the problem of a dual identity; struggling to excell as both learned professional and racial leader[s], as . . . American[s], but . . . who could never transcend the restraints and responsibilities of [their] blackness."[38]

Steward also strove to show the doubting world—which in some instances included members of his own race—that African Americans were equal, if not superior, to Europeans and white Americans. His essay "Some Glimpses of Antebellum Negro Literature" touted the literary skills of Phillis Wheatley, Benjamin Banneker, Solomon Northrup, Austin Steward, and Frederick Douglass.[39]

In an earlier undated essay, Steward declared that one would have "to give the term literature a broad significance and place it in a juxtaposition with oratory and agitation." He believed it wrong to "narrow the term to its classic acceptation," as that would give people very little to examine. In his broader sense of literature, Steward praised the accomplishments of Richard Allen,

Frederick Douglass, George W. Williams, and William Wells Brown. Steward admired the literary tone of Douglass's *My Bondage and Freedom* for its "aspiration of a soul for liberty and justice." In contrast, Steward dismissed Booker T. Washington's *Up From Slavery* as "the aspiration of a man anxious to add to the material comfort of his fellow by teaching them how to work." He did not care for Washington's liberal use of "old darky" and "nigger" in his speeches. Steward criticized the Tuskegee Wizard for not making "a single moral protest against wrong." Steward added that Washington speaks of the lynching horror "as one might speak of the evil habit of smoking cigarettes." Washington, he asserted, had not yet learned "the words justice and liberty . . . [nor] does . . . he embody the ideas, sentiments and feelings of the American Negro of the present nor does he in any sense represent the future that the Negro seeks." Like fellow intellectuals Monroe Trotter, W. E. B. Du Bois, and the Reverend Francis J. Grimké, Steward was critical of Washington's refusal to condemn racism. Washington, of course, further alienated intellectuals by accusing them of knowing books but not men. He castigated them for understanding theories but not understanding things. Worse in his estimation was the intellectuals' failure to understand "the actual needs of the masses of the colored people in the South."[40]

Steward's interest in literature went beyond that of an observer. He was a prolific writer who freely presented his views in newspapers, magazines, and journals. In late 1912 or early 1913 he collaborated with his brother William, a gifted essayist in his own right, on a genealogical study of their family. *Gouldtown, A Very Remarkable Settlement of Ancient Date* was praised by the local New Jersey papers, but *The Journal of Negro History* faulted the writing as "dry Isaac begat Jacob passages" and *The Crisis* described it as a true fairy tale "set down gravely, sedately, and completely." Still, the book gained wide acceptance by the vast Gouldtown community. Steward's grandnephew Garfield W. Steward, a civil rights attorney in San Francisco, considers *Gouldtown* "an inspiration" because "it meant . . . somebody important thought these kids could do something, could go to college, could *make* something of themselves, that their promise was worth the effort it takes to have a career. It's something the Goulds still cherish."[41]

The success of *Gouldtown* encouraged Steward to publish his ambitious study of the Haitian revolution. Despite his brief and traumatic experience in 1873, Haiti represented to Steward the triumph of the African spirit over prejudice and physical obstacles.[42] He sought to "depict the revolution and to follow to some extent the results occurring in the history of the Black

Republic." He believed that the story of the uprising would be particularly "instructive and encouraging to the American colored man . . . [for] the Haitian Revolution . . . is the special heritage of the Negro race." Steward believed that oppressed peoples, including those in the United States, had the right to fight for liberty. Steward, despite his research for *The Colored Regulars*, was not a trained historian. His examination of Haiti was limited to secondary sources as he did not have access to the archives in Haiti or France. His research relied on Haitian writers, newspapers, journals, missionaries, and American diplomats such as John Mercer Langston and Frederick Douglass, and his own recollections.[43]

Coincidentally, Theodore Lothrop Stoddard's *The French Revolution in San Domingo* was also published in 1914. Stoddard lamented the annihilation of the white population in Haiti because it led to "the progress of black supremacy."[44] Mainstream historical journals reviewed *The French Revolution in San Domingo* while ignoring Steward's study.

The historical establishment ignored Steward's study for racial reasons. White reviewers did not share his pride in the accomplishment of the Haitian people. Although his book was published by a reputable white publisher, and it was not a polemic study, it attracted the attention of only the so-called race journals. *The AME Review*, a journal that Steward had contributed to since its founding in 1884, praised *The Haitian Revolution* and panned *The French Revolution in San Domingo*. Jessie Fauset, in the inaugural issue of *The Journal of Negro History*, noted that Steward's book "combines the unusual advantage of being very readable and at the same time historically dependable."[45]

The Haitian Revolution remained popular for many years. It was used as a history textbook at Wilberforce University, and for some years it was listed in *The Crisis*'s selected reading list. Ironically, it escaped the attention of C. L. R. James's major study, *The Black Jacobins*. In contrast, Du Bois cited it and Steward's American Negro Academy lecture on the role of Haitians in the 1779 Savannah siege in *The Gift of Black Folk*.[46]

Perhaps to instill interest in *Gouldtown* and *The Haitian Revolution*, Steward suggested in early 1915 that readers of *The Crisis* support "The Buy a Book Movement." Support for this movement would benefit black authors, who normally wrote for white readers. Steward deplored the fact that he and others had to "remain chained hard and fast to one subject, the only one upon which the white people of this country will hear us." He called upon authors properly to interpret African American social life because readers would buy more books. He challenged readers to buy one million books. *The Crisis* supported his proposal and noted that its adoption would increase their sale of "Negro literature each month" from $100 to $1,000.[47] Steward's proposal, which would bear fruition during the following decade of the Harlem Renaissance, had been suggested in 1913 in William H. Ferris's two-volume *The African Abroad*. Ferris, who later became associated with Marcus Garvey's Universal Negro Improvement Assocation, called on "colored men [to] write as colored men and not as white men [because] in assimilating the culture and traditions of Anglo-Saxons they . . . [lost] their rich and luxuriant African heritage."[48]

Steward's interest in making his people more appreciative of literature suggests a concern for their intellectual development and the freeing of writers from artificial restraints that hindered the true expression of their cultural identity. He was no less diligent in protecting the image of African-American men. "To relieve the wretched was his pride."[49] By upbringing, class, and racial consciousness, Steward felt compelled to speak out against injustice. Lynching was a social problem that white America sought to ignore. Many white Southerners believed it their right as men to protect their way of life, not to mention "their" women, from the brute Negro. Lynchings were rampant on the eve of World War I, a war that America would soon join in order "to make the world safe for democracy." Steward, like Ida Wells-Barnett, former congressman George H. White, and the NAACP, condemned the lynch mobs. He was particularly angered after viewing in *The Crisis* a drawing of a lynching of five men in Lee County, Georgia. Steward informed editor Du Bois that *The Crisis* should reprint the hideous illustration and add a caption: "the glory of the land of the free!" "What greater freedom," he stated sarcastically, "can be found anywhere on earth the freedom to kill people; a kind of game license that never expires."[50] This assessment of the land he loved was difficult for him. He wanted to believe that his country was capable of obliterating racial differences. But he could not remain silent.

Under no circumstances could he adopt a "my country, right or wrong" approach to patriotism. He believed in the greatness of the nation and he wanted to see the day come when America would recognize the contributions of all its citizens and amply reward them with equality and justice. Like many of his contemporaries, he became an active participant in the discussion of the African American's role in World War I. Some radicals, like A. Philip Randolph and Chandler Owens, coeditors of *The Messenger*, self-proclaimed as "the most radical Negro magazine in America," deemed it slavish to fight for a government that would not protect their basic rights of citizenship. "We would rather fight to make Georgia safe for the Negro," declared *The Messenger*. The majority of Americans of African descent eschewed this radicalism and displayed their patriotism by buying Liberty Bonds. Nearly 200,000 served in the military, despite the army's unwillingness to make them officers to protect them from hostile mobs in southern states. They volunteered out of patriotism even though the military segregated them in training and often assigned them to tedious and dangerous work details. Their poor training and inadequate housing did not prevent them from demonstrating an ability to fight when the French military, unlike its American counterpart, gave them an opportunity. Their heroic efforts on the battlefield made them recipients of French gratitude and medals.[51]

Race leaders differed on their sentiments toward the European conflict. Even before the breakout of hostilities in Europe, *The AME Review* reminded its readers that "the Negroes of the United States are better housed and fed under the stars and stripes than are the members of this race anywhere else in the world."[52] The *Review* implied that the race had a duty to fight for America. But others did not agree. It was not without irony that Booker T. Washington in August 1914 canceled a European speaking engagement. He notified the tour organizer, John Hobbs Harris, that he could not travel until Europeans tired of butchering one another. With strong words, he added, "the more I see of the action of . . . Europe the more I am inclined to be proud of the Negro race." He confided to journalist Robert Ezra Park that he could not leave the country "until white people [in Europe] get a little more civilized. I really think it would be worthwhile to consider sending a group of black missionaries to Europe to see if something can be done for the white heathen."[53] For financial and political reasons, Washington could not publicly assess white Americans with such heat.

Steward supported the idea of American intervention into the war. His own problems with a military promotion twelve years earlier did not prevent him in 1916 from informing the War Department of his willingness to recruit "a large body of colored men for the army" if America was drawn into the conflict. In an unpublished essay, "How The Colored Man Sees The War," Steward announced that "Sambo is ready" to fight even though the government was low in recognizing his patriotism.[54]

Steward unstintingly agreed with Du Bois's call for the race to "close ranks" with the government as the defeat of Germany was urgent. Later, both were in agreement that if America was also the black man's country, he had to fight for his rights at home and fight in France, "to show the world again what the loyalty and bravery of black men means."[55] During the late summer of 1918 Du Bois was offered a military commission. He had to decline it after receiving criticism from his own people, who viewed it as a reward for his support of the war. Steward, who had constantly called for men of intelligence to join the army, urged Du Bois to remain with *The Crisis* where his sound editorial leadership was needed. His friend's words represented a "sound philosophy, a rational philosophy, and sound sympathy with the forlorn conditions under which the darker races labor."[56]

Thousands of African Americans, who harbored no personal animosity against the kaiser or the Austrians, supported America's entry into the war in early 1917 out of the belief that their patriotism would be rewarded. This attitude was attacked. William H. Crogman, president of Clark University and one of the founders of the American Negro Academy twenty years earlier, wrote to Francis J. Grimké that his family's own connection with the "man devouring conflict" was his son's commission in the officers' Dental Reserve Corps. "They tell us it is a war for 'democracy.' This war is largely a war for commercial supremacy with Africa as the chief prize." Taking a page from Steward's *The End of the World*, Crogman concluded that "God is riding upon the storm, and that some good is to come out of it from the darker races." Grimké agreed. "It makes no difference to the colored man," he recorded in his journal, whether Uncle Sam or the kaiser was victorious. It angered him that there were then 100,000 blacks in the military when the nation's capital was segregated. The war in Grimké's estimation was a conflict over white supremacy. The editor of the Cleveland *Gazette*, angered by Du Bois's July 1918 editorial "Close Ranks," demanded that he be fired as editor of *The Crisis*.[57]

Steward was not willing to address either the causes of the war or the widespread belief that it was a war between greedy capitalists. Instead, recalling the horror of the Spanish-American conflict, he called the war "a hungry monster that crushes men's bones." The massive loss of property and lives were necessary, in his estimation, because it was God's message to His errant people to heed His call for peace.[58]

Angered that Woodrow Wilson's call to "make the world safe for democracy" did not include them, a number of black intellectuals were ambivalent about Armistice Day, November 11, 1918. The war had ended and their loved ones were returning home, but they returned to a land that greeted them with race riots of such intensity that 1919 was known as "red summer."

Du Bois, stung by criticism of his "Close Ranks" editorial, wrote a bitter denunciation of American racism, concluding with the observation that America wanted Negroes to act like "dogs, monkeys and whores."[59] A month earlier, the Reverend Francis J. Grimké spoke to returning soldiers. "You know that the mean, contemptible spirit of race prejudice that curses this land is not the spirit of other lands." He urged them to continue to fight American injustice, for "I know nothing that sets forth this cursed American prejudice in a more odious, excrable light than the treatment of our colored soldiers." His reference was to a segregated army.[60]

Despite his support for the war, Steward was not silent when it came to the mistreatment of his fellow African Americans. He bluntly assessed American racism in 1919 as a mandate: "thou shalt never fail to observe the distinction between white people and colored people, either by confounding their persons or by equalizing their rights." He considered this mandate one that white Americans "exalted above the Decalogue, and above Christ." Steward believed that whites needed to eliminate racial prejudice so that men would accept Jesus Christ and redeem humanity. Their failure to do this would lead to a destruction of civilization.[61]

Steward wanted to see his native land change for the better. He wanted the color line eliminated. He believed that "behind every human form and face" there was "a man and a brother." He believed that people of diverse backgrounds, languages, customs, and philosophies would get along if they had something in common. This commonality he believed would be achieved through acceptance of Americanization, a concept that began in 1914 when the mayor of Cleveland hosted a reception for newly naturalized citizens to impress upon them pride in their citizenship. This policy was quickly adopted by mayors of major cities with large immigrant populations.[62] Many leading politicians, scholars, and social welfare activists supported Americanization; they saw it as a way for immigrants to retain their cultural "quaintness" while rapidly learning English to integrate into American society. It was hoped that this would lessen their ties to the old country.[63]

Americanization was supported by many leading African Americans. In 1920, Emmett J. Scott, Booker T. Washington's former private secretary; Eugene K. Jones, executive director of the National Urban League; Alice Dunbar-Nelson, widow of Paul Laurence Dunbar; and others helped Robert L. Vann organize *The Competitor*. Besides Steward and his son, T. B. Steward, the thirty contributing editors included James W. Johnson, NAACP field secretary; Archibald H. Grimké, U.S. minister to Santo Domingo; Jesse E.

Theophilus Gould Steward, ca. 1920. Photograph courtesy of the Schomburg Center for Research in Black Culture, NYPL.

Moorland, internal secretary, YMCA; Robert R. Moton, principal of Tuskegee Institute; Kelly Miller, dean of Howard University; William S. Scarborough, president of Wilberforce University; Robert H. Terrell, municipal judge in Washington; Mary Church Terrell, former president of the National Federation of Colored Women's Clubs; Bert Williams, comedian; Richard R. Wright, Jr., editor of the *Christian Recorder*; and Colonel Charles A. Young, retired U.S. Army. *The Competitor's* inaugural issue in January 1920 flatly declared that the publication was for the black, "who is reading more. He is beginning to see the folly of being a special American. He is thinking less of color and more of his country. The Negro," asserted the editor, "wants to be swallowed up in the great scheme of Americanization." *The Competitor* declared itself not the bearer of "the burning torch of the Bolshevist, anarchist or blind radicals, nor will it tolerate a cringing coward who declines to defend his honor or his home against any invading foe."[64]

Steward believed in equality of opportunity but he did not necessarily advocate social integration. He emphasized that cultivated blacks were superior to whites in their cultural tastes, choice of associates, and personal dignity. In *The Competitor* he described "social equality in the society sense [as] an absurdity." While "white friends" call for "the colored man [to have] equal rights before the law . . . at the ballot box . . . that the colored man be made a full citizen . . . [yet] at the same time they stand firmly on the ground that he should continue to be a social outlaw." He believed that true equality would depend in part on whites acknowledging that blacks could obtain prominence in business, literature, politics, and the military. Steward declared that whites had to understand that true democracy meant complete integration and not the phony pretense that the races could mingle together at a charitable fund-raiser but not dine together in the privacy of their homes. Bluntly he asserted that whites want democracy, "but not with the NEGRO in it." Steward warned that violence might bring democracy but, like others, he was opposed to violence for social change. He called upon white Americans to "ameliorate the condition brought on by slavery and race discrimination" or the United States would never honor her stated commitment to liberty and justice for all her citizens.[65]

For some, Americanization meant not only the rejection of southern and eastern European traditions but also an attempt at "a renewal of the Anglo-Saxon cult; the worship of the Nordic totem, the disfranchisement of [all non-Anglo-Saxons], the world rule of Nordic whites through brute force." Many others agreed with Du Bois, who assessed Americanization as nothing more than a paternalistic approach to the race problem.[66] They feared that "the Negro can be used to advantage or he can be the means of degrading" white Americans. Many whites adopted a page from the speeches of Booker T. Washington and urged that African Americans be more law abiding and religious so that whites would find them acceptable. Whites, on the other hand, were rarely counseled to alter their vicious racist behavior.[67]

Steward debated with himself the correct way to refer to people of African descent. While he believed that it was admissible to use "colored," "Negro," or "Afro-American," he preferred simply "American." Steward acknowledged that many did not identify with the African in "Afro." He considered "Negro" a name without an ethnographic basis. Although he admitted that Chinese, Jews, Japanese, and Native Americans, commonly called "Indians," technically could be called "Negroes," too, since they were excluded from white American social life, the possibility existed that all the groups save the Africans could eventually enter into the mainstream of American culture and life. While expressing support for Americanization, Steward did not believe that his people were necessarily improving themselves culturally by integrating with whites. He and other blacks were indifferent about "social home intercourse with the whites." In contrast, "the colored man's demand restricts itself to open public privileges. He objects to being denied a place at a public pie counter, at a public hotel . . . but entrance into private homes does not enter his thoughts; his own visiting circle is usually more varied and satisfying than that of the American white of his class." Clearly he was not a fawning integrationist. Integration for Steward and many others meant opportunities to use their talents in a world that constantly frowned on their presence and sought to exclude them merely because of race and color.[68]

As the second decade of the twentieth century came to a close, Steward was in good health. His mental faculties were strong. Financially, he was secure, with property holdings in Ohio and New Jersey. His surviving sons were successful in their occupations. He was, however, lonely. Susan, his wife of twenty-one years, died on March 17, 1918. Once again he made the sad trip east to bury a wife. Theophilus Bolden and William S. Scarborough accompanied the grieving husband to Brooklyn, where eulogies were provided by Scarborough, Du Bois, and Dr. Helen S. Lassen, a white classmate of Susan's a half-century earlier at the New York Medical College for Women. Hallie Q. Brown memorialized Susan as a woman who was true to the cause of justice. "She could strike . . . hard in what she believed to be a righteous cause. With her it was justice on the one side, and injustice on the other."[69]

Like many others who influenced Steward's life, Susan remained in the shadows. This is partly explained by his overpowering personality, her avoidance of the limelight, and the loss or destruction of her correspondence. Steward barely mentions her in his autobiography, a fate that other family members shared.

With the exception of parts of two years while he was in the Philippines, Steward was never separated from Susan for more than a few weeks. But instead of despairing, he picked up the pieces and moved forward.

THIRTEEN

The Last Years

Steward kept busy. He taught and tended his garden. He made an annual journey to Gouldtown to see his still large but rapidly declining family of brothers, sisters, aunts, uncles, and cousins. He wrote occasional essays. Stewards did not retire from life's chores. They worked until they died. "It is a glorious thing," T. B. wrote to his father, "to be able to crown a life of labor with a time of ease, unworried as to what may happen either now or hereafter. It is indeed worth a life time to have lived well, to have done and still be able to do something."[1]

"To do something" was characteristic of Theophilus Steward. He was taught to make something of his life and to spread his success among those in need. As a believer in the goals of the National Association for the Advancement of Colored People, he forwarded in early 1920 a check for $150 in "appreciation of the[ir] work." In 1923 he donated $500 to the Bridgeton Hospital Association.

From 1920 to 1922 Steward was busy with publications. He submitted six articles and one poem, all pertaining to theology, to the *AME Review*. This was his first writing on theology in some years. One article revised the theme of *The End of the World*. Citing Lothrop Stoddard's *The Rising Tide of Color*, Steward emphasized that this author too predicted that out of the ashes of the last war would come an organized resistance to colonization. Reiterating his earlier view, Steward noted that even if white nations succumbed to Bolshevism or other perils, "civilization will not flee the earth [as] the Lord's vineyards will simply pass into other hands."[2] His poem "The Coming of the Prince" showed that while man slaughtered millions on the battlefield of Europe, God is supreme and on Judgment Day the true believers will proclaim their heavenly king.[3]

He also addressed the issue of humans possessing the ability to see spirits. He concluded that angels were God's special messengers. Although he had no hard evidence, he believed that the spirits of the dead communicated with Jesus and that through "the intermediation of Jesus . . . their wishes may be known

. . . to those on earth . . . while our same desires and sympathies may be carried to them." As a little boy, Steward was convinced that he had visited with his bedridden mother in the garden. He believed that his mother was in the garden with him and that God sent her spirit back to her sick body.[4]

African Methodists, like other Christians, believe in the afterlife, but few accepted the possibility that spirits communicated with friends or family. Steward never accepted the pure dogma of religion. In 1922 he wrote in his notebook his frank assessment of the AME church. He did not believe that it represented "the highest possible form of human organization," nor was it "the perfect incarnation of either the Christ teaching or the Christ spirit." He was critical that the church did not publish very much and what was published he deemed "poor." Recalling the church's lack of support for him in Haiti, he criticized the missionary work as "weak, halting and wasteful, except as it has been carried on definitely by our women." He praised the educational work of the bishops but considered the role of the educational secretary useless.[5]

Sometime during the summer of 1922 Steward vacationed in the East, where he twice occupied the pulpit in a white Methodist Episcopal church. He who in earlier years had called for greater congregation participation, criticized the M. E. church for adhering "rigidly to a very simple form or order of worship." He was perturbed by the absence of "real worship" and reiterated his view of 1906 that white churches so revised and edited the Bible that they rendered religious worship ineffectual.[6]

Late in 1921 the AME Book Concern published his autobiography, *From 1864 to 1914: Fifty Years in the Gospel Ministry.* It was not clear why Steward limited his account to fifty years, nor does he explain why he considered 1914 the end of his ministry. Technically his involvement with the ministry as a practicing preached ended with his retirement from the chaplaincy in 1907. The autobiography was well received by the African-American press. The *Christian Recorder* urged young readers to examine the book for church history. *The Crisis's* reviewer considered it "a good commentary for nearly three quarters of a century on the happenings among colored people in the United States."[7]

In 1922, flushed by the success of his autobiography, Steward broke ranks with his usual reserve and happily engaged in a public celebration of his seventy-ninth birthday. The festive event, held on April 17 at Emory Hall on the Wilberforce University campus, was crowded with family and friends. Later that year, he traveled back to Bridgeton. He had a happy visit to Bridge Street Church, where some remembered him as their pastor nearly fifty years earlier.

The trip rejuvenated him, and so he visited Gustavus in Columbus for Christmas.[8]

Despite his by now frequent ill health, Steward continued his teaching, reading, writing, and activism. In early 1923, A. Laurence Lowell, president of Harvard, created racial tension when the institution limited dormitory space to white students only. Frank Steward and others bitterly criticized this action in the Pittsburgh *Courier*. Roscoe Conklin Bruce, a 1902 graduate of Harvard, was outraged by the dormitory policy, which excluded his son. Steward wrote to Frank that even though Lowell was under severe criticism, he was safe, as "the great volume of American sentiment is with him silently. They will say nothing," he predicted, "but they will stand pat. Look at the KKK. I am having a picture copied of fetish worship and I intend to put this out as the original ku klux."[9]

Steward embroiled himself in a controversy with Harvard professor William McDougall, author of *Is America Safe For Democracy?* Steward objected to the statement, "almost all the negroes of this country who have shown any marked capacity of any kind have had an evident mixture of white blood." Although McDougall was quoting *The Neighbor* by N. S. Shaler, Steward challenged, "how is it possible to perform so broad and so personal a survey, as would make the basis of such wholesale prediction?" He provided a long list of notables who were not mulattoes to prove that white blood was not needed for success.[10]

It was interesting that Steward, who was fair in complexion and had relatives who passed for white, strongly defended the capabilities of his darker brothers. For one who found much to admire in European culture, he was quick to denounce the cult of whiteness. He told Frank that Negroes would not develop more until they "drop the white fetish." He boldly stated that whites had failed to lead "and their overthrow is nigh." He noted that "Europe is going to the bow-wows; and America will follow." He urged Negroes to give up their fascination with whites "and hold on to GOD." Steward, of course, was not advocating a black nationalist dogma of racial separation. Although he did not accept the racial viewpoints of Marcus Garvey or believe that African Americans should emigrate to Africa, Steward did at times advocate a "race first" philosophy that described Garvey's Universal Negro Improvement Association. The difference between the two men was Steward's belief that his people needed to develop personal character and conduct so that they could take their place next to whites as equals. Unlike Garvey, he did not believe that the future of the race depended on separation. Instead, he argued

From left to right: Charles Steward, Benjamin Steward, Adah Steward (wife of Frank), Frank Steward, Theophilus Steward, Theophilus Bolden Steward. Probably photographed by Gustavus Steward, Wilberforce, Ohio, 1922. Photograph courtesy of the Schomburg Center for Research in Black Culture, NYPL.

that Negroes should not delude themselves in believing that whites were innately superior, a fact that many white supremacists preached.[11]

Steward in 1923 was disillusioned with America's failure to do right by her African-American citizens. Woodrow Wilson had failed to make America a color-blind society. To the contrary, he instilled segregation in government buildings and did little to convince African Americans that the government was interested in protecting their rights. Warren G. Harding offered little hope that his administration would end lynching, disfranchisement, and other restrictions to the rights of African Americans.[12] When Steward read that the black American resident minister and his wife in Haiti were closely watched by a white military attaché, he informed Frank, "That settles it. I shall not go to Haiti, if I ever go, on a government ship."

Steward freely spoke his mind. A controversy developed when a veterans hospital opened on April 1, 1923, in Tuskegee, Alabama. It was rumored that the staff would consist of white doctors and nurses with black nursemaids for the white nurses. This was too much for those who did not understand why a "Negro hospital" needed a white staff. Ironically, Du Bois and others who denounced official segregation were advocating that a hospital for black veterans be staffed by blacks only. Du Bois, however, was concerned about the quality of care the soldiers would receive from an indifferent if not racist white staff. He bluntly stated that white nurses would refuse to "touch colored patients." That would be the role of the black nurses. He exclaimed bitterly, "human hatred, meanness and cupidity [have] gone stark mad! Separating races in hospitals and graveyards and fighting to put white men over a Negro hospital! Giving nurses black *maids* to do the work while the white 'ladies' eat with the interns, dance at the balls and flirt with the doctors and black men die!" Despite his hyperbole, Du Bois had a point. The New Negroes wanted power and control over their own destiny. Steward informed Du Bois in the fall, "look out for the crackers in that Tuskegee hospital. If they win their point it will soon degenerate into a slaughter house and a brothel." He urged Du Bois to tell the truth. "Justice will win," because slaveholders no longer rule the country.[13]

On April 17, 1923, Steward reached the age of eighty. He confided to his journal his thoughts "On Being Fourscore." "I cannot say," he confessed, "that I have lived in all good convenience as St. Paul could declare of himself before the Jewish Council." He recalled his friendships with Charles Sumner, William Lloyd Garrison, Henry Ward Beecher, Fred Douglass, Henry H. Garnet, and William Howard Day, all men of action and unyielding principles. They were men who behaved exactly the way he did—forthrightly and guided by a strong sense of moral outrage against injustice. He was especially proud that he had "marched in Lincoln's funeral procession" and had campaigned for Ulysses S. Grant in 1868 and 1872.[14]

Steward delivered a series of lectures at Wilberforce to a group of young ministers. The lectures inspired the dean of women. She was happy that he still possessed a strong speaking voice and presence despite his age and infirmities. "Nature . . . did much for you . . . [but] much, very much is due [to your willingness] to develop the excellencies with which you were endowed." She expressed hope that the young men would learn from Steward "how much study and scholarship have always meant to you. Too many of our ministers," she lamented, "are content with a smattering of knowledge, making up in bluster for what they lack in brain power." She asked Steward to continue to inform the youth to "realize that to be great preachers they must be great men." She urged him to use himself as an example of one who is "great in spirit, big hearted, broad minded, unselfish, courageous, true to the highest ideals of manhood; loving Christ, and like him, going about doing good work."[15] In a true Christian sense, her letter was one of deep love and respect.

In the summer of 1923 he made his annual trek to Gouldtown. Afterward, Charles wrote a moving letter to the man he loved, respected and, especially, feared. Charles's reference in his salutation to "Chaplain T. G. Steward" suggests how timid his sons were with him. Charles confessed that all the sons loved him, but that "[we] cannot warmly express it . . . due to the stoical training which you gave [us]." Charles admitted that it was hard for him to express his love and pride but he decided to express his feelings "for fear that our reserve diffidence might be misunderstood or misinterpreted as a lack of feelings." Charles invited his father to spend some time with him in Boston, but Steward declined.[16]

Steward greeted the new year 1924 with the purchase of a new car, which both pleased and astonished his family as he was known to be frugal. William warned him to get a "sober driver" and Frank reminded him to place alcohol in the radiator to prevent freezing in winter.[17]

January 11 was a normal day for Steward. He ate breakfast and went to teach his classes at nearby Payne Theological Seminary. Not feeling well, he left campus and went to the home of Bishop Benjamin F. Lee. His condition rapidly declined and he died at 4 p.m. The shocked campus held services for their esteemed colleague and professor. President John A. Gregg preached the funeral sermon, taken from Job 5:26, "thou shalt come to thy grave in a full age, like a shock of corn cometh in his season." He was praised by *The Christian Recorder* as one of African Methodism's greatest preachers. *The Journal of Negro History* considered his death a blow to "the cause of writing and popularizing [of] the history of the Negro."[18] His body was brought to Gouldtown, where D. M. Baxter, business manager of *The Christian Recorder*, told the hushed gathering that "the church has lost a great man, Wilberforce a splendid teacher and the race an advocate."[19]

Theophilus Steward died doing what he liked best. His mind was active, he prodded students to think, and age did not deter him from speaking out on behalf of his race. His active teaching at the age of eighty was a reflection of his motto: "labor on till the close of the day."[20] Steward is buried beneath an obelisk in the family plot, surrounded by ancestors and family. On the impressive monument that dominates the small cemetery are inscribed words that aptly described Theophilus Gould Steward: "minister, teacher, author Christlike in words and ways."

Notes

CHAPTER ONE

1. William Steward and T. G. Steward, *Gouldtown, a Very Remarkable Settlement of Ancient Date* (Philadelphia: Lippincott, 1913), 49-50; T. G. Steward, *Memoirs of Mrs. Rebecca Steward* (Philadelphia: AME Publication Department, 1877), 13; Richard R. Wright, Jr., "The Economic Conditions of Negroes in the North, III, Negro Communities in New Jersey," *Southern Workman* 37 (July 1908): 386; Giles R. Wright, *Afro-Americans in New Jersey: A Short History* (Trenton: New Jersey Historical Commission, 1980), 14.
2. Steward, *Gouldtown*, 50.
3. Wright, "Negro Communities in New Jersey," 387-88; "The Lees From Gouldtown," *The Negro History Bulletin* 10 (February 1947): 99-100.
4. Wright, *Afro-Americans in New Jersey*, 39-41; Edythe Ann Quinn, " 'The Hills' in the Mid-Nineteenth Century: The History of a Rural Afro-American Community in Westchester County, New York," *Afro-Americans in New York Life and History* 14 (July 1990): 35-50.
5. Clement Alexander Price, ed., *Freedom Not Distant: A Documentary History of Afro-Americans in New Jersey* (Newark: New Jersey Historical Society, 1980), 134-35.
6. Steward, *Gouldtown*, 4, 13, 14, 17, 160-62.
7. Steward, *Memoirs of Rebecca Steward*, 18-19.
8. Steward, *Gouldtown*, 94-95; T. G. Steward, "James Steward," *The Freeman*, February 9, 1889, 1; T. G. Steward, *Journal of Reverend T. G. Steward*, n.d., T. G. Steward Papers; T. G. Steward, *From 1864 to 1914: Fifty Years in the Gospel Ministry* (Philadelphia: AME Book Concern, 1921), v.
9. Steward, *Memoirs of Rebecca Steward*, 14, 15, 16, 19.
10. Ibid., 48. M. A. Broadstone, *History of Greene County, Ohio*, 2 vols. (Indianapolis: B. F. Bowen, 1918), 2: 7; for quote of S. B. Jones, see *Christian Recorder*, January 17, 1873, 3.
11. Lillian G. Dabney, *The History of Schools for Negroes in the District of Columbia, 1807-1947* (Washington, D. C.: Catholic University of America Press, 1949), 21-22; Carlton Mabee, *Black Education in New York State* (Syracuse: Syracuse University Press, 1979), 17.
12. Linda M. Perkins, "Quaker Beneficence and Black Control: The Institute for Colored Youth, 1852-1903," in Vincent P. Franklin and James D. Anderson,

eds., *New Perspectives on Black Educational History* (Boston: G. K. Hall, 1978), 22-23; Carlton Mabee, "A List of the First Black Schools in New York State From Colonial Times to 1945," *Afro-Americans in New York Life and History* 2 (July 1978): 9-14; Vincent P. Franklin, "In Pursuit of Freedom: The Educational Activities of Black Social Organizations in Philadelphia, 1900-1930," in Franklin and Anderson, *New Perspectives*, 114; for an example of the Institute for Colored Youth's curriculum, see Linda M. Perkins, *Fanny Jackson Coppin and the Institute for Colored Youth, 1865-1902* (New York: Garland Publishing Co., 1987), 345; Carter G. Woodson, *The Education of Negroes Prior to 1861* (New York: Arno Press, 1968), 135-36, 139-41.

13. Mabee, *Black Education in New York State*, 49-68; Robert J. Swan, "Did Brooklyn (N.Y.) Blacks Have Unusual Control Over Their Schools? Period I: 1815-1845, *Afro-Americans in New York Life and History* 7 (July 1983), 25-46; Vincent P. Franklin, *The Education of Black Philadelphia: The Social and Educational History of a Minority Community, 1900-1950* (Philadelphia: University of Pennsylvania Press, 1979), xvii; Woodson, *Education of Negroes*, 149.

14. Steward, *Gouldtown*, 15; Steward, *From 1864 to 1914*, iv; Steward, "Some Facts," n.d., T. G. Steward Papers; Daniel A. Payne, *Recollections of Seventy Years* (New York: Arno Press, 1968), 114; T. G. Steward, *My First Four Years in the Itineracy of the African Methodist Episcopal Church* (Brooklyn, 1876), 5, 6; Alexander W. Wayman, *Cyclopedia of African Methodism* (Baltimore: Methodist Episcopal Book Depository, 1882), 155; Isiah C. Wears, "Rev. Theophilus Gould Steward," *The AME Church Review* 10 (July 1893): 137-40.

15. Steward, *From 1864 to 1914*, 375, 378.

16. Steward, *Memoirs of Rebecca Steward*, 23.

17. William Steward to Bro, April 4, 1917, T. G. Steward Papers.

18. Steward, *My First Four Years*, xii, 6.

19. Steward, *From 1864 to 1914*, xi.

20. Steward, *My First Four Years*, 7.

21. Steward, *From 1864 to 1914*, 22, 23, 24.

CHAPTER TWO

1. W. T. Richardson to American Missionary Association, January 1865, H5516, H5517, reel 1, South Carolina, American Missionary Association Papers, Schomburg Center (cited hereafter as AMA Papers).

2. Robert Morris, *Reading, 'Riting, and Reconstruction: The Education of Freedmen in the South, 1861-1870* (Chicago: University of Chicago Press, 1981), ix, 13, 14, 115-16, 118; H. Peers Brewe, "The Protestant Episcopal Freedman's Commission, 1865-1870," *Historical Magazine of the Protestant Episcopal Church* 26 (1967): 361-81.

3. Robert Morris, ed., *Freedman's Schools and Textbooks*, 2 vols., *Semi-Annual Report on Schools for Freedmen by John W. Alvord, Numbers 1-10, January 1866-July 1870* (New York: AMS Press, 1980), 1: 1.

4. Ibid.; Alrutheus A. Taylor, *The Negro in South Carolina During the Reconstruction* (Washington, D.C.: Association for the Study of Negro Life and History, 1924), 106; Daniel A. Payne, *History of the African Methodist Episcopal Church* (Philadelphia: AME Sunday School Union, 1891), 469; Josephus R. Coan, *Daniel Alexander Payne: Christian Educator* (Philadelphia: AME Book Concern, 1935), 109; L. L. Berry, *A Century of Missions of the African Methodist Episcopal Church, 1840-1940* (New York: Gutenberg Printing Co., 1942), 65; Clara DeBoer, "The Role of Afro-Americans in the Origin and Work of the American Missionary Association, 1839-1877" (Ph.D. dissertation, Rutgers University, 1973), 3; Daniel A. Payne to Executive Committee, AMA, May 8, 1865, #0874, reel 15, in Black Abolitionist Papers, Schomburg Center; *Quadrennial Address of the Bishops of the AME Church to the General Conference of 1864 presented by W. Paul Quinn, Willis Nazrey, Daniel A. Payne* (n.p., n.d.), 8; *The Twentieth Annual Report of the American Missionary Association and the Proceedings at the Annual Meeting, Held at Galesburg, Illinois, October 31st and November 1st, 1866*, 13, reel 1, American Missionary Association Annual Reports, 1847-1869, copy in Schomburg Center.

5. Steward, *From 1864 to 1914*, 26; Steward, *My First Four Years*, 9; Clarence E. Walker, *A Rock in a Weary Land: The African Methodist Episcopal Church During the Civil War and Reconstruction* (Baton Rouge: Louisiana State University Press, 1982), 50; Benjamin W. Arnett, ed., *Proceedings of the Quarto-centennial Conference of the AME Church of South Carolina at Charleston, May 15, 16, 17, 1889* [1890], 48; Journal of T. G. Steward (strictly private), in T. G. Steward Papers, Schomburg Center; *State Convention of Colored Men Held in Trenton, New Jersey, July 13 & 14, 1865*, #1023-1029, reel 15, Black Abolitionist Papers.

6. Linda M. Perkins, "The Black Female American Missionary Association Teacher in the South, 1861-1870," in Darlene Clark Hine, ed., *Black Women in United States History*, 16 vols. (Brooklyn: Carlson Publishing, Inc., 1990), 3: 1059; Ronald E. Butchart, " 'We Best Can Instruct Our Own People': New York African Americans in the Freedmen's Schools, 1861-1875," *Afro-Americans in New York Life and History* 12 (January 1988): 40.

7. Payne, *History of the AME Church*, 469.

8. Steward, *My First Four Years*, 15; Bernard E. Powers, Jr., "Black Charleston: A Social History, 1822-1885" (Ph.D. dissertation, Northern University, 1982), 85-86.

9. Steward, *My First Four Years*, 16.

10. Powers, "Black Charleston," 179, 197; Eric Foner, *Reconstruction: America's Unfinished Revolution, 1863-1877* (New York: Harper & Row, 1988), 88, 91; John B. Bowles, ed., *Master and Slaves in the House of the Lord: Race and Religion in the American South, 1740-1870* (Lexington: University of Kentucky Press, 1988), 15; Katherine L. Dvorak, "After Apocalypse," ibid., 173, 177, 185,

186. For elaboration on the theme that freedmen left the white churches out of nationalistic sentiments, see Katherine L. Dvorak, *An African-American Exodus: The Segregation of the Southern Churches* (Brooklyn: Carlson Publishing, Inc., 1991).

11. Ralph E. Morrow, *Northern Methodism and Reconstruction* (East Lansing: Michigan State University Press, 1956), 133-39.

12. Foner, *Reconstruction*, 92; Payne, *Recollections of Seventy Years*, 469, 470; Wesley J. Gaines, *African Methodism in the South: Twenty-Five Years of Freedom* (Atlanta: Franklin Publishers, 1890), 6-7; George A. Singleton, *The Romance of African Methodism: A Study of the African Methodist Episcopal Church* (New York: Exposition Press, 1952), 104; James A. Handy, *Scraps of AME Church History* (Philadelphia: AME Book Concern, 1901), 236.

13. Benjamin T. Tanner, *An Apology for African Methodism* (Baltimore: n.p., 1867), 367; Daniel A. Payne, *The African M. E. Church in its Relation to the Freedmen Before the Society for the Promotion of Collegiate and Theological Education of the West Marietta, Ohio, November 7, 1864*, 4.

14. Arnett, *Proceedings of the Quartocentennial Conference*, 50, 51; Charles S. Smith, *A History of the African Methodist Episcopal Church* (Philadelphia: AME Book Concern, 1922), 505.

15. *Christian Recorder*, June 3, 1865, 1; Steward, *My First Four Years*, 19; Smith, *History of the AME Church*, 60.

16. Perkins, "The Black Female Teacher," 1049, 1051, 1053-54; Butchart, "We Can Instruct Our Own," 27, 37. For a historian who believed that northern teachers were meddling abolitionists, see Henry L. Swint, *The Northern Teacher in the South, 1862-1870* (Nashville: Vanderbilt University Press, 1941). Teachers as heroes has been emphasized by many: see, for example, Jacqueline Jones, *Soldiers of Light and Love: Northern Teachers and Georgia Blacks, 1867-1873* (Chapel Hill: University of North Carolina Press, 1980).

17. Steward, *From 1864 to 1914*, 41, 43, 50.

18. Butchart, "We Can Instruct Our Own," 39, 40.

19. Morris, *Third Semi-Annual Report on Schools for Freedmen, January 1, 1867*, 13-14.

20. H. H. Hunter to William E. Whiting, May 6, 1865, H5600, reel 1, South Carolina AMA Papers; W. T. Richardson to George Whipple, March 13, 1865, H5544, reel 1, South Carolina AMA Papers; Mary Still to secretary, AMA, September 25, 1864, #0525, reel 16, Black Abolitionist Papers; Mary Still to M. E. Strieby, November 15, 1864, #0602, reel 15, Black Abolitionist Papers; Mary Still to William E. Whiting, September 11, 1865, #0189, reel 16, Black Abolitionist Papers.

21. Daniel A. Payne to George Whipple, July 6, 1865, #1010, reel 15, Black Abolitionist Papers.

22. Morris, *First Semi-Annual Inspector's Report, January 1, 1866*, 4; *Second Semi-Annual Report, July 1, 1866*, 4; *Nineteenth Annual Report of the American*

Missionary Association, 8, 9; *Twentieth Annual Report of the American Missionary Association*, 11, 26, 28.

23. T. G. Steward to George Whipple, July 1865, H5706, reel 2, South Carolina AMA Papers; Whipple to Steward, July 25, 1865, reel 2, South Carolina AMA Papers; Steward, *From 1864 to 1914*, 40; Clara DeBoer erroneously reported that the AMA paid Steward, see "The Role of Afro-Americans," 297, 418; *Nineteenth Annual Report of the American Missionary Association and the Proceedings at the Annual Meeting, Held at Brooklyn, New York, October 25th and 26th, 1865*, 8, reel 1, American Missionary Association Annual Reports 1847-1869.

24. Mary Still to William E. Whiting, September 11, 1865, #0819, reel 16, Black Abolitionist Papers; Steward, *My First Four Years*, 21-23; Steward, *From 1864 to 1914*, 61; T. G. Steward to George Whipple, August 1, 1865, #77566, reel 1, New Jersey American Missionary Association Papers.

25. Steward, *From 1864 to 1914*, 62.

26. Steward, *My First Four Years*, 23-24.

27. Ibid., 25, 26; Steward, *From 1864 to 1914*, 61-62.

28. *Christian Recorder*, December 30, 1865, 2.

29. Steward, *From 1864 to 1914*, 65; Steward, *My First Four Years*, 27; Steward Family Bible in possession of Gary Steward, Columbus, Ohio.

30. Steward, *From 1864 to 1914*, 64-68; Steward, *My First Four Years*, 28.

31. Morris, *Reading, 'Riting, and Reconstruction*, xi, 115; Taylor, *The Negro in South Carolina*, 110; William Steward to Edwin P. Smith, May 21, 1869, #22518, reel 5, Georgia AMA Papers.

32. Steward, *My First Four Years*, 29; Steward, *From 1864 to 1914*, 69.

33. William Steward to Edwin P. Smith, June 24, 1869, #22647, reel 5, Georgia AMA Papers; William Steward to Edwin P. Smith, May 21, 1869, #22518, reel 5, Georgia AMA Papers.

34. Powers, "Black Charleston," 177.

35. DeBoer, "The Role of Afro-Americans," viii; Perkins, "The Black Female American Missionary Association Teacher," 1054, 1056, 1059.

36. Steward, *From 1864 to 1914*, 69.

37. Morris, *Freedmen's Schools and Textbooks*, 1, 3. William Steward to Edwin P. Smith, August 26, 1869, #77884, reel 1, New Jersey AMA Papers; November 16, 1869, #18932, Florida AMA Papers, reel 1.

38. William Steward to Edwin P. Smith, May 21, 1869, #22518, reel 5, Georgia AMA Papers; Timothy P. Lyman to George Whipple, January 12, 1865, H5495, reel 1, South Carolina AMA Papers; *Christian Recorder*, February 24, 1866, 1.

39. *Christian Recorder*, February 24, 1866, 1; William Steward to Edwin P. Smith, July 20, 1869, #77870, reel 1, New Jersey AMA Papers; William Steward to Edwin P. Smith, November 16, 1869, #18932, reel 1, Florida AMA Papers; Sallie L. Daffin, "The Freedmen," *The Missionary Record of the AME Church* 1 (July 1867): 5.

40. Steward, *My First Four Years*, 22.

41. Ibid., 31-32; Steward, *From 1864 to 1914*, 73, 76, 86; Journal of T. G. Steward; *Christian Recorder*, June 9, 1866, 1; June 23, 1866, 1; Tanner, *An Apology*, 370; Smith, *History of AME Church*, 507-8.
42. T. G. Steward, "Has Our Church a Missionary Society," *Christian Recorder*, September 8, 1866, 1.
43. John M. Brown, "Has Our Church a Missionary Society," ibid., 1. Cain's letter appeared in the June 29, 1867, issue, 1.
44. A. W. Wayman, "A Tour South," *Christian Recorder*, March 9, 1867, 1.
45. Ibid., Steward, *My First Four Years*, 32.
46. T. G. Steward, "A Denial," *Christian Recorder*, August 28, 1869, 2.
47. *Christian Recorder*, September 25, 1869, 4.
48. Ibid., February 16, 1867, 2.
49. Ibid., March 23, 1867, 1-2.
50. A. W. Wayman, *My Recollections of AME Ministers or Forty Years' Experience in the AME Church* (Philadelphia: AME Book Rooms, 1881), 39.
51. Smith, *History of AME Church*, 67-68.
52. Tanner, *An Apology*, 374-75.
53. T. G. Steward to *Christian Recorder*, July 10, 1865, #0005, reel 16, Black Abolitionist Papers; Steward to M. E. Strieby and George Whipple, June 28 [1865] H8728, AMA Papers, in T. G. Steward Papers; T. G. Steward to editor, *The New Republic*, September 29, 1917, 248; *The Crisis* 12 (December 1917): 77.
54. Steward, *From 1864 to 1914*, 86-87; Smith, *History of AME Church*, 515.

CHAPTER THREE

1. Steward, *From 1864 to 1914*, 87.
2. Steward, *First Four Years*, 36. His most controversial theological works were *Genesis Re-read*, an examination of the Creation, and *The End of the World*, a study of how the world's end would not come with fire but with the destruction of Anglo-Saxon control, which would lead to the rise of the Asian-African world.
3. Smith, *History of AME Church*, 504.
4. Steward, *From 1864 to 1914*, 90. Steward, *My First Four Years*, 38, 40. For an overview of Georgia's race relations during Reconstruction, see Russell Duncan, *Freedom's Shore: Tunis Campbell and the Georgia Freedmen* (Athens: University of Georgia Press, 1986).
5. Steward, *My First Four Years*, 40-41, 42; Steward, *From 1864 to 1914*, 90, 91.
6. Steward, *From 1864 to 1914*, 92-94; T. G. Steward Journal, July 21, 24, 28, 30, 31, 1867.
7. Steward, *From 1864 to 1914*, 98-99.
8. T. G. Steward Journal (strictly private), October 12, 13, 20, 1868; Mary E. Sands to E. P. Smith, May 5, 1868, #21487; Sarah H. Champney to E. P. Smith, December 1, 1868, #21787; fragmented letter, unsigned, to E. P. Smith,

October 5, 1868, #21658-21659; Henry Bird, et al. to E. P. Smith, June 29, 1868, #21574 in reel 4, Georgia AMA Papers; William L. Clark to E. P. Smith, March 8, 1869, #22207, reel 5, Georgia AMA Papers.

9. T. G. Steward to J. A. Rockwell, November 6, 1867, #20929, reel 3, Georgia AMA Papers; *Nineteenth Annual Report of the American Missionary Association*, 10-11.

10. T. G. Steward to C. C. Sibley, March 2, 1868, microcopy 798, roll 21, #1050, *Letters Received April-August 1868*, RG 105, *Records of the Assistant Commissioner for the State of Georgia, Bureau of Refugees, Freedmen and Abandoned Lands*, National Archives; see endorsement of Sibley, April 23, 1868, roll 9, target 3, register 12 (46) p. 269; *Indexes and Register, 12, January-June 1868*, RG 105, *Register and Letters Received by the Commissioner of the Bureau of Refugees, Freedmen and Abandoned Lands*, 1865-1872; Steward, *From 1864 to 1914*, 94.

11. Steward, *From 1864 to 1914*, 40, 94; T. G. Steward Journal, September 23, 1867; T. G. Steward Journal (strictly private), June 22, 29, July 6, 13, August 10, 1868; partial letter, no signature, to E. P. Smith, December 1, 1868, #21786, reel 4, Georgia AMA Papers; De Boer, "The Role of Afro-Americans," 495.

12. Undated flyer, #5754, reel 2, South Carolina AMA Papers; J. G. [*sic*] Steward, "Colonization," *Christian Recorder*, August 21, 1870, 4.

13. For an overview of black elites, see William B. Gatewood, *Aristocrats of Color: The Black Elite, 1880-1920* (Bloomington: Indiana University Press, 1990), 69-95.

14. T. G. Steward Journal (strictly private), September 21, 1868, January 23, 1869.

15. T. G. Steward Journal, August 5, 1867; T. G. Steward Journal (strictly private), October 7, 1868.

16. T. G. Steward Journal (strictly private), June 5, 1868.

17. Sarah H. Champney to E. P. Smith, January 30, 1869, #22020, reel 4, Georgia AMA Papers; Champney to Smith, March 29, 1869, #22245, reel 5, Georgia AMA Papers; Mary N. Withington to E. P. Smith, May 30, 1868, #21519, reel 4, Georgia AMA Papers.

18. Edmund L. Drago, *Black Politicians and Reconstruction in Georgia: A Splendid Failure* (Baton Rouge: Louisiana State University Press, 1982), 38.

19. Ibid.

20. Ibid.

21. Steward, *From 1864 to 1914*, 94-95.

22. Drago, *Black Politicians*, 95; Frank N. Schubert, "Theophilus Gould Steward," in Rayford W. Logan and Michael R. Winston, eds., *Dictionary of American Negro Biography* (New York: Norton, 1982), 570.

23. Drago, *Black Politicians*, 166-71; Duncan, *Freedom's Shore*, 46, 100-101.

24. Steward, *From 1864 to 1914*, 29; T. G. Steward Journal (strictly private), September 4, 9, 11, 1868. For biographies of Turner, see M. M. Ponton, *Life and Times of Henry M. Turner* (Atlanta: A. B. Caldwell, 1917); Herbert

Aptheker, *A Documentary History of the Negro People in the United States*, 4 vols. (New York: Citadel, 1968), 2: 568-71.

25. Mary E. Sands to E. P. Smith, May 5, 1868, #21487, reel 4, Georgia AMA Papers; Mary N. Withington to E. P. Smith, April 30, 1868, #21464, reel 4, Georgia AMA Papers.

26. T. G. Steward Journal, October 23, November 3, 4, 5, 9, 1868; fragmented letter to E. P. Smith, October 5, 1868, #21658-21659, reel 4, Georgia AMA Papers.

27. Sarah H. Champney to E. P. Smith, March 29, 1869, #22245, reel 5, Georgia AMA Papers; Champney to Smith, December 1, 1868, #21787, reel 4, Georgia AMA Papers.

28. "Georgia: The Situation," n.d., in Steward, *From 1864 to 1914*, 129-33. For a general study of Georgia politics, see Elizabeth S. Nathans, *Losing the Peace: Georgia Republicans and Reconstruction, 1865-1871* (Baton Rouge: Louisiana State University Press, 1968), v-vi.

29. T. G. Steward Journal (strictly private), June 15, 1868; Foner, *Reconstruction*, 531-32.

30. T. G. Steward Journal (strictly private), June 19, November 24, 1868.

31. Ibid., January 20, February 1, 4, March 16, 19, 22, 1869.

32. T. G. Steward to [Elisha] Weaver, n.d., *Christian Recorder*, November 16, 1867, 1; "Letter from Lumpkin," ibid., December 7, 1867, 2; Steward, *My First Four Years*, 44.

33. *Christian Recorder*, April 4, 1868; Steward, *My First Four Years*, 45; Steward, *From 1868 to 1914*, 105-6.

34. Steward, *From 1894 to 1914*, 80, 106, 108; Smith, *History of AME Church*, 77, 78, 551.

35. T. G. Steward Journal (strictly private), May 27, 29, June 8, 15, July 28, 29, 1868. The boy, whose name was not mentioned, was James. He was christened on April 4, 1869, by Bishop J. M. Brown.

36. Ibid., May 29, 1868. For studies on the property transfer issue, see George Alexander, et al., *A History of the Methodist Church South*, 12 vols. (New York: Christian Literature Company, 1894), 2: 92; C. H. Philipps, *The History of the Colored Methodist Episcopal Church in America* (Jackson, Tennessee: Publishing House, CME Church, 1898), 66-67; Ralph E. Morrow, "The Methodist Episcopal Church, The South, and Reconstruction, 1865-1880" (Ph.D. dissertation, Indiana University, 1954), 185; Tanner, *An Apology*, 367; *Christian Advocate*, August 30, 1871, as quoted in Morrow, *Northern Methodism and Reconstruction*, 134-40.

37. James Lynch, "The Newly Organized Churches of the South," *Christian Recorder*, October 21, 1865, 1; Alexander, *History of the Methodist Church South*, 2: 92; *Western Advocate*, March 20, 1867, as quoted in Morrow, "The Methodist Episcopal Church," 185-86.

38. T. G. Steward Journal (strictly private), July 7, 12, 1868; *Christian Recorder*, May 19, 1866, 1.

39. T. G. Steward Journal (strictly private), July 16, 17, 19, 21, 1868.
40. Ibid., July 31, August 1, 2, 4, 5, 9, 11, 12, 14, 1868; *Christian Recorder*, August 28, 1868, 2; Steward, *From 1864 to 1914*, 117-19.
41. T. G. Steward Journal (strictly private), August 25, 27, 28, 29, 31, 1868.
42. Ibid., September 3, 6, 8, 9, 1868.
43. Ibid., September 20, 1868; Steward, *From 1864 to 1914*, 139.
44. T. G. Steward Journal (strictly private), October 1, 5, 30, 1868.
45. Ibid., January 18, 19, 20, 29, February 11, 1869.
46. Ibid., February 17, 19, 20, 1869.
47. Ibid., February 20, 1869; T. G. Steward, "An Appeal," *Christian Recorder*, May 22, 1869, 1.
48. T. G. Steward Journal (strictly private), February 21, 1869.
49. Ibid., March 25, 27, April 5, 6, 7, 1869; T. G. Steward to the editor, *Christian Recorder*, July 3, 1869, 1.
50. Rev. M. W. Traverse, "Visit to Macon," *Christian Recorder*, July 26, 1883, 2; T. G. Steward, "A Correction," ibid., August 9, 1883, 2.
51. T. G. Steward, "The M.E. Church: Keep it Before the People," *Christian Recorder*, July 3, 1869, 3; Alexander, *History of the Methodist Church South*, 2: 86, 91; Tanner, *An Apology*, 412-13.
52. Editorial, "Methodist Union," *Christian Recorder*, July 31, 1869, 2. It is not known if Steward replied; there are missing pages in later issues.
53. Merger between the AME church and the British Methodist Episcopal church was debated at the 1884 and 1888 General Conferences of the AME church.
54. Philipps, *History of the Colored Methodist Episcopal Church*, 52-53, 66-67; Benjamin T. Tanner, *An Outline of Our History and Government for African Methodist Churchmen Ministerial and Lay* (Philadelphia: Grant, Faires, & Rodgers, 1884), 76-77; "Our Church Property in Georgia," *Christian Recorder*, June 3, 1871, 2.
55. T. G. Steward, "The New Christian Recorder," *Christian Recorder*, August 14, 1869, 2, 3.
56. *Christian Recorder*, February 19, 1871, 3; Smith, *History of AME Church*, 88, 92.
57. *Christian Recorder*, February 10, 1871, 3.
58. The first issue of his essay is no longer extant; see T. G. Steward, "Female Suffrage in Church," *Christian Recorder*, August 20, 1870, 2.
59. Philip S. Foner, *Frederick Douglass* (New York: Citadel Press, 1964), 263; Jualynne Dodson, "Nineteenth-Century AME Preaching Women," in Hine, *Black Women in United States History* 1: 336, 337, 342, 343.
60. *Christian Recorder*, May 20, 1871, 1; Steward, *From 1864 to 1914*, 143; T. G. Steward, "The Appointing Power," *Christian Recorder*, March 23, 1872, 1; May 4, 1872, 4; T. G. Steward, "Episcopacy as it Exists in the Church," ibid., November 21, 1878, 2.
61. *Christian Recorder*, May 31, 1871, 1.

62. Jones, *Soldiers of Light and Love*, 68, argues that the eighteen black New Englanders in Georgia did not develop cordial relationshipos because of their puritanical value system. William Steward is cited as a "tantalizing exception."

63. T. G. Steward Journal (strictly private), lecture notes, n.d.; *Christian Recorder*, July 29, 1871, 2; speech of Jefferson Long, *Congressional Globe, 41st congress, 3rd session*, 881, Aptheker, *Documentary History of Negro People*, 2.

64. T. G. Steward, "The Georgia Conference," *Christian Recorder*, March 4, 1871, 1; Gaines, *African Methodism in the South*, 19.

CHAPTER FOUR

1. *Christian Recorder*, May 13, 1871, 2.
2. Steward, *From 1864 to 1914*, 143-44.
3. Ibid., 144.
4. *Christian Recorder*, July 8, 1871, 3.
5. *Christian Recorder*, October 19, 1872, 1.
6. Levi Coppin, *Unwritten History* (Philadelphia: AME Book Concern, 1919), 189-90, 197-99; "Worshipping," n.d., T. G. Steward Journal (strictly private).
7. T. G. Steward, "The Appointing Powers," *Christian Recorder*, March 23, 1872, 1. His previous discourses are not extant.
8. *Christian Recorder*, March 30, 1872, 2; Theodore Gould, "The Appointing Power, and the Restrictions Limiting Its Exercise," ibid., April 6, 1872, 1; George E. Bowyer, "The Appointing Power," ibid., April 13, 1872, 1; L. Jones, "The Itineracy," ibid., April 27, 1872, 1.
9. T. G. Steward, "The Appointing Power," *Christian Recorder*, May 4, 1872, 4.
10. *Christian Recorder*, May 7, 20, 25, 1872; June 15, 1872, 8; Steward, *From 1864 to 1914*, 142.
11. Coppin, *Unwritten History*, 189-90.
12. Harold B. Hancock, "The Status of the Negro in Delaware After the Civil War," *Delaware History* 13 (April 1968): 57-61.
13. Ibid., 63-64; Ronald L. Lewis, "Reverend T. G. Steward and the Education of Blacks in Reconstruction Delaware," *Delaware History* 19 (spring-summer 1981): 160; Federal Writers' Project, *Delaware: A Guide to the First State* (New York: Hastings House, 1938), 117-18.
14. Hancock, "The Negro in Delaware," 62.
15. Lewis, "Reverend T. G. Steward," 164-65; *Report of the Delaware Association for the Moral Improvement and Education of the Colored People of the State* (Wilmington: Jenkins & Atkinson, 1868) 11-12, 14.
16. Steward gave an Emancipation Day sermon on January 1, 1873. See *Christian Recorder*, January 30, 1873, 1; February 6, 1873, 1, 2; *Proceedings of the Southern State Conventions of Colored Men Held in Columbia, S.C. Commencing October 18th ending October 25th, 1871* (Columbia: Carolina Printing Company, 1871), 10, 11, 48-49, 85; *Proceedings of the Convention of Colored People Held*

in Dover, Delaware, January 9, 1873, 2, 3, 4, 5, 6, 7, in T. G. Steward Papers; *Memorial of the National Convention of Colored Persons Held in Washington, D.C.*, December 19, 1873.

17. *Christian Recorder*, April 3, 1873, 3. Steward was acknowledged by Tanner as the author of the address in the April 17 issue in "Our Swivel" column.

18. *Wilmington Commercial*, May 8, 1873, as quoted in *New National Era and Citizen*, June 12, 1873, 2.

19. "Our Missionary Work," *Christian Recorder*, May 11, 1872, 1-2.

20. T. G. Steward, "The Mission of San Domingo," *Christian Recorder*, May 18, 1872, 2; "Rev. T. G. Steward's 'Adieu,' " ibid., June 12, 1873, 1; Tanner, *An Apology*, 374.

21. T. G. Steward, "The San Domingo Mission," *Christian Recorder*, July 20, 1872, 7; T. S. Malcom, "The Republic of Hayti and Dominica," ibid., August 10, 1872, 1; T. S. Malcom, "Prayer for Hayti," ibid., July 3, 1873, 1.

22. "Our Missionary Work," *Christian Recorder*, May 11, 1872, 1-2; Malcom, "Prayer for Hayti," 1.

23. T. G. Steward, "The San Domingo Mission," *Christian Recorder*, May 8, 1873, 1.

24. Thomas S. Malcom, "The Republic of Hayti," *Christian Recorder*, May 8, 1873, 1.

25. T. G. Steward to editor, *Christian Recorder*, April 26, 1873, 2; May 15, 1873, 2.

26. Thomas S. Malcom, "The San Domingo Mission," *Christian Recorder*, May 15, 1873, 5; Malcom, "Mission to San Domingo," ibid., May 22, 1873, 8; Malcom, "A Self Sustaining Mission," ibid., June 5, 1873, 1.

27. Bishop Payne to Rev. B. T. Tanner, May 25, 1873, 1; June 12, 1873, 1; Berry, *A Century of Missions*, 55; James Redpath to Daniel A. Payne, March 12, 1862, in *Correspondence of James Redpath, Commercial Agent of Hayti for Philadelphia, Joint Plenipotentiary of Hayti to the Govt. of the U.S. and General Agent of Emigration to Hayti for the U.S. & Canada, December 31, 1861 to May 12, 1862*, Schomburg Center.

28. Malcom, "Prayer for Hayti," 1; "Rev. Steward's 'Adieu,' " 4.

29. "Rev. Steward's 'Adieu,' " 4.

30. Holly had supported the Haitian Emigration Bureau efforts to settle African Americans in that republic. See William Seraile, "Afro-American Emigration to Haiti During the American Civil War," *The Americas* 35 (October 1978): 185-200.

31. Journal to Haiti, June 15, 16, 1873.

32. Ibid., June 17, 18, 19, 21, 1873. At no time did he mention meeting any of the approximately 2,500 people who emigrated to the island a decade earlier.

33. Ibid., June 20, 23, July 1, 2, 3, 4, 1873.

34. Ibid., July 5, 6, 8, 1873.

35. T. G. Steward, "How the Black St. Domingo Legion Saved the Patriot Army in the Siege of Savannah, 1779" (Washington, D.C.: American Negro Academy,

1899), 1-15; Steward, *The Haitian Revolution 1791 to 1804; or Sidelights on the French Revolution* (New York: Cromwell, 1914).

36. "Fetishism," T. G. Steward Papers.

37. *Christian Recorder*, August 7, 1873, 4; editorial, "African Methodism in Hayti," ibid., August 14, 1873, 4.

38. *Christian Recorder*, August 28, 1873, 4; September 25, 1873, 4; T. S. Malcom, "The Republic of Hayti," ibid., October 30, 1873, 5.

39. *Christian Recorder*, January 29, 1874, 4; February 19, 1874, 5; March 12, 1874, 2.

40. T. G. Steward, "A Card," *Christian Recorder*, February 26, 1874, 1.

41. "Our Swivel," *Christian Recorder*, February 5, 1874, 4; W. B. Derrick, "Help for St. Domingo," ibid., March 12, 1874, 1; James A. Handy, "Our Missionary Society," ibid., April 30, 1874, 6.

42. John M. Brown to editor, *Christian Recorder*, May 12, 1874, 1; May 21, 1874, 1.

43. Thomas H. Jackson, "Not the Man," *Christian Recorder*, March 26, 1874, 1; T. G. Steward, " 'Not the Man,' " ibid., April 9, 1874, 1.

44. Editorial, "Our Haytian Mission—Again," *Christian Recorder*, October 29, 1874, 4; T. G. Steward to editor, ibid., October 3, 1874, 5; October 29, 1874, 5.

45. *Christian Recorder*, June 24, 1875, 4; editorial, "Who Will Bear It?," ibid., September 9, 1875, 4.

46. Steward, *From 1864 to 1914*, 151-53; Alice, "Delaware," *Christian Recorder*, September 3, 1874, 1.

47. "Philadelphia Items," *Christian Recorder*, February 19, 1874, 5.

48. T. G. Steward, "Death and Life," *Christian Recorder*, August 27, 1874, 1; T. G. Steward, "Covenanting with God," ibid., October 29, 1874, 1.

49. For Steward's sketches, see *Christian Recorder*, March 26, 1874, 1; April 2, 1874, 4; July 30, 1874, 1; August 13, 1874, 2; October 1, 1874, 5; March 30, 1876, 8.

50. T. G. Steward, "Distinguished Women of the Bible—Deborah," *Christian Recorder*, April 27, 1876, 8.

51. *New York Freeman*, January 24, 1885, 3.

52. William Seraile, "Susan McKinney-Steward: New York State's First African American Female Physician," *Afro-Americans in New York Life and History* 9 (July 1985): 27-44.

CHAPTER FIVE

1. Amos Jordan, *Compiled History of the African Wesleyan Methodist Church* (New York, 1973), 7, copy in Schomburg Center; *Centennial Anniversary Celebration of Bridge Street AWME Church, Sunday February 3rd to Sunday, February 10th, 1918*, 17, 33, copy in New York Public Library; *The African Wesleyan Methodist*

Episcopal Church 146th Anniversary Commemorative Journal 1818-1964, 69, Schomburg Center.

2. Steward, *From 1864 to 1914*, 156; T. G. Steward Diary, April 14, 1876, T. G. Steward Papers.

3. *Brooklyn City and Business Directory for the Year 1873/1874*, 5-8, 16-21; *Illustrated New York and Brooklyn Churches* (New York: Nelson & Philipps, 1874), 45, 91; United States Census of Population for the Year 1870, 51; Census of the State of New York for 1875, xiv, xv, 5, 19, 178-79.

4. *Siloam Presbyterian Church, Brooklyn, New York, Semicentennial, May 21st to June 25th, 1899* (Brooklyn: Nolan Brothers, 1899), 8, 11.

5. George W. Hodges, *Early Negro Church Life in New York* (New York: n.p., 1945), 14, 15, 19-20; Joel Schor, *Henry Highland Garnet* (Westport, Conn.: Greenwood Press, 1977).

6. Gatewood, *Aristocrats of Color*, 103, 105; Steward, *From 1864 to 1914*, 156-57; T. G. Steward, "Brooklyn News," *Christian Recorder*, May 31, 1877.

7. Williamson, "Folks in Old New York and Brooklyn," 1, 6-8, lists names of 101 prominent old families that predated 1900; Ralph Foster Weld, *Brooklyn in America* (New York: Columbia University Press, 1950), 164-65; Gail L. Buckley, *The Hornes: An American Family* (New York: Knopf, 1986), 56-66.

8. Maritcha Remond Lyons, "Memories of Yesterdays. All of Which I Saw and Part of Which I Was. An Autobiography," 1928, typescript, reel 1, box 3, page 28, Harry A. Williamson Papers.

9. Census of the State of New York for 1875, 4, 178-79; Steward, *From 1864 to 1914*, 156-57.

10. See inside cover of T. G. Steward, *Journal of the Voyage From New York to Port-au-Prince*, T. G. Steward Papers.

11. Steward, *From 1864 to 1914*, 157.

12. The *Christian Recorder* is no longer available for November 9 and 16, 1876 and "Colored Society" no. 4 did not appear in the November 30 or December 7 issues. T. G. Steward, "Colored Society," no. 3 *Christian Recorder*, November 23, 1876, 1; "Colored Society," no. 5, December 14, 1876, 8; "Colored Society," no. 6, December 28, 1876, 1; "Colored Society," no. 7, January 11, 1877, 8; E. Franklin Frazier, *The Black Bourgeoisie: The Rise of a New Middle Class* (New York: Free Press, 1959).

13. W. E. B. DuBois, *The Souls of Black Folk* (New York: New American Library, 1969), 45.

14. Gatewood, *Aristocrats of Color*, 271-72.

15. *Christian Recorder*, January 18, 1877, 4.

16. "The Dusky Race," *The New York Times*, March 2, 1869, 1.

17. T. G. Steward, "Marriage," *Christian Recorder*, May 13, 27, 1875, 4, 1.

18. *Christian Recorder*, November 2, 1876, 4; November 16, 1876, 4.

19. Steward, *From 1864 to 1914*, 166; T. G. Steward to Benjamin Tanner, June 24, 1873, in *Christian Recorder*, July 17, 1873, 5; *The New York Times*, May 21, 1873, 3.

20. *Christian Recorder*, November 4, 1875, 7; December 30, 1875, 4.
21. See inside cover of Steward, *Voyage from New York to Port-au-Prince*; Steward, *From 1864 to 1914*, 166; T. G. Steward, "Romanism Preferred," *Christian Recorder*, March 15, 1877.
22. *Journal of the Assembly of the State of New York at Their Ninety-six Session* (Albany, 1873), 615; *Journal of the Senate of the State of New York at Their Ninety-six Session* (Albany, 1873), 507; *Proceedings of the Board of Education of . . . Brooklyn*, 1873, 158, 159, 168, 169; *National Monitor*, n.d., as reprinted in the *New National Era*, May 22, July 31, 1873.
23. *The New York Times*, September 3, 1873, September 14, 1875; *Proceedings of the Board of Education of Brooklyn*, 1873, 191, 201-4; *Proceedings of the Board of Education of Brooklyn*, 1874, 22-23. *Nineteenth Annual Report of the Superintendent of Public Instruction of the City of Brooklyn for the Year ending December 31, 1873*, table C, 11. Ironically, the superintendent's reports for 1873, 1874, and 1875 did not mention the school integration controversy.
24. Arthur O. White, "The Black Movement Against Jim Crow Education in Buffalo, New York, 1800-1900," *Phylon* 30 (winter 1969): 378; Steward, *From 1864 to 1914*, 187, 188-89, 261-63; box 80-1, folder 2, Daniel A. Payne Papers; Leroy Graham, *Baltimore: The Nineteenth Century Black Capitol* (Washington, D.C.: University Press of America, 1982), 22; *Thirty-second Annual Report of Education of the City . . . of New York for the Year Ending December 31, 1873*, 33-34; see *Thirty-fourth . . . Report . . . for the Year Ending December 31, 1875*; *New York World*, April 2, May 6, 1884, describes the deal between the black community and Governor Grover Cleveland to maintain two separate black schools despite the board's desire to abolish segregated schools.
25. Steward, *From 1864 to 1914*, 166-67; *Christian Recorder*, March 9, 1876, 4.
26. T. G. Steward Diary, March 13, 1876; Steward, *From 1864 to 1914*, 167-68; Sunday School, Brooklyn, n.d., Address Book, T. G. Steward Papers; *Christian Recorder*, March 23, 1876, 4; August 17, 1876, 4; January 18, 1877, 4; March 22, 1877, 4.
27. T. G. Steward, "Brooklyn News," *Christian Recorder*, May 31, 1877, 1.
28. T. G. Steward Address Book, T. G. Steward Papers.
29. T. G. Steward, "Our View," *Christian Recorder*, August 10, 1876, 2. See October 12, November 30, December 7, 1876, and January 11, 1877, issues for list of ministers who sold the paper to their congregations.
30. Perkins, *Fanny Jackson Coppin*, 180.
31. T. G. Steward, "Odds and Ends after Vacation, etc.," *Christian Recorder*, September 21, 1876, 1; "Sin Punished in This Life Preached at Chester Heights Camp Meeting, August 1876," ibid., July 12, 1877, 1.

CHAPTER SIX

1. Rayford Logan, *Betrayal of the Negro: From Rutherford B. Hayes to Woodrow Wilson* (New York: Collier Books, 1954), 23-47.
2. Steward, *From 1864 to 1914*, 173, 178-79; Steward's Address Book, Zion's Mission AME Church, T. G. Steward Papers.
3. Gatewood, *Aristocrats of Color*, 96-97.
4. "Our Ministry," *Christian Recorder*, June 28, 1877, 2; "Personal Mention," ibid., November 14, 1878, 3; Steward, *From 1864 to 1914*, 179.
5. Gatewood, *Aristocrats of Color*, 8-10; Roger Lane, *Roots of Violence in Black Philadelphia, 1860-1900* (Cambridge: Harvard University Press, 1986), 145; Julie Winch, *Philadelphia's Black Elite: Activism, Accommodation and the Struggle for Autonomy, 1787-1848* (Philadelphia: Temple University Press, 1988); Perkins, *Fanny Jackson Coppin*, 3-5, 173, 192, 195, 199.
6. Steward, *Memoirs of Rebecca Steward*, title page; Steward, *From 1864 to 1914*, 172; Broadstone, *History of Greene County*, 2: 973; N. F. Mossell, *The Work of the Afro-American Woman* (Philadelphia: George F. Ferguson, 1908), 47; *Resolutions From the Women's Parent Mite Missionary Society on Death of Mary Steward Gould, October 4, 1922*, in T. G. Steward Papers.
7. Steward, *From 1864 to 1914*, 172; Broadstone, *History of Greene County*, 2: 973; Mossell, *Work of Afro-American Woman*, 47; Mrs. Rebecca Steward, "The Lord's Prayer," *Christian Recorder*, February 12, 1874, 6.
8. Steward, *Memoirs of Rebecca Steward*, v; *Christian Recorder*, January 17, 1878, 3; the book was sold by subscription for one dollar.
9. Steward, *From 1864 to 1914*, 180, 182; "Our Ministry," *Christian Recorder*, April 4, 1878, 2; *Dollar Weekly News* (Bridgeton, New Jersey), January 18, 1924, 3.
10. Steward, *From 1864 to 1914*, 180.
11. *Christian Recorder*, August 30, 1877, 2; September 6, 1877, 2; October 11, 1877; 2; February 21, 1878, 3; March 7, 1878, 3; April 18, 1878, 3; April 25, 1878, 3; May 2, 1878, 3; March 16, 1878, 2; May 23, 1878, 3; Steward, *From 1864 to 1914*, 183.
12. *Christian Recorder*, May 23, 1878, 3. The other members of the African Emigration Committee were Benjamin Tanner, Theodore Gould, L. C. Chambers, H. H. Lewis, J. S. Thompson, and L. Patterson. Daniel A. Payne Papers, box 80-1, folder 2, journal 1877-78.
13. Box 80-1, folder 2, Daniel A. Payne Papers; Steward, *From 1864 to 1914*, 188-89.
14. Franklin, *Education of Black Philadelphia*, 34; Lane, *Roots of Violence*, 55; Francis J. Grimké, "Colored Men as Professors in Colored Institutions," *AME Church Review* 4 (July 1885): 142-49.
15. T. G. Steward, "Episcopacy as it Exists in the Church," *Christian Recorder*, November 21, 1878, 2; Steward, *From 1864 to 1914*, 184.
16. Steward, *From 1864 to 1914*, 184-86.
17. Ibid.; Daily *Christian Recorder*, May 5, 1880, 16; May 6, 1880, 23.

18. *Christian Recorder*, August 12, 1880, 2; August 19, 1880, 2; August 26, 1880, 2; September 2, 1880, 3; September 9, 1880, 2; September 16, 1880, 3.
19. P. W. Jefferson, "A Rejoinder," *Christian Recorder*, August 26, 1880, 1.
20. Daniel A. Payne, " 'Bishops' of the Church Accused of Dishonesty by Rev. Steward," *Christian Recorder*, October 14, 1880, 2.
21. T. G. Steward, "The General Conference of 1880: Two Questions," *Christian Recorder*, August 12, 1880, 2.
22. "The Bishops Pastoral Letter," *Christian Recorder*, October 28, 1880, 2.
23. Steward, *From 1864 to 1914*, 179.
24. Ibid., 187, 193-95.
25. Proclamation dated June 9, 1880, in T. G. Steward Papers; Daniel R. Goodwin's statement of June 9, 1880, Scrapbook, T. G. Steward Papers.
26. T. G. Steward, "The Richard Allen Professorship," *Christian Recorder*, July 22, 1880, 2.
27. *Christian Recorder*, August 5, 1880, 3; "Bishop Daniel A. Payne to Theophilus Steward," ibid., August 12, 1880, 2; "Notes from the Bishops 'Council,' " ibid., October 21, 1880, 2; for Eddy's will, see ibid., October 12, 1882; J. A. Clark to Steward, April 22, 1881, T. G. Steward Papers; letter of reference from William Bacon Levering, April 27, 1881, Scrapbook, T. G. Steward Papers.
28. *The People's Advocate* (Washington, D.C.), May 21, 1881, 2; T. G. Steward, *The Incarnation of the Son of God. Annual Sermon Preached at Wilberforce University, June 13, 1880* (Philadelphia: AME Book Concern, 1881), 1-22.
29. B. W. Arnett, ed., *The Budget Containing the Annual Reports of the General Officers of the AME Church of the United States of America* (Dayton, Ohio: Christian Pub. House, 1882), 128; *The Scriptural Means of Producing an Immediate Revival of Pure Christianity in the Ministry and Laity of Our Church* (Philadelphia: AME Publishing Dept., 1881), 59-86.
30. Steward, *From 1864 to 1914*, 187; T. G. Steward, "Relish for Preaching," *Christian Recorder*, May 12, 1881, 2.
31. "Personals," *Christian Recorder*, June 2, 1881, 2.
32. A. W. [Wayman], "A Visit," *Christian Recorder*, February 23, 1882, 1.
33. T. G. Steward, "The Doctrine of Prayer," *Christian Recorder*, April 5, 1883, 2.
34. T. G. Steward, "Demand for Trial," *Christian Recorder*, May 25, 1882, 3.
35. T. G. Steward, "The Minutes of 1882," *Christian Recorder*, January 18, 1883, 1.
36. "Personal," *Christian Recorder*, August 3, 1882, 2; T. G. Steward, "The Dedication in Macon, Ga.," ibid., August 10, 1882, 1; August 17, 1882, 1.
37. T. G. Steward, "Other People's Children," *Christian Recorder*, November 2, 1882, 1; "Personal," ibid., November 30, 1882, 1; T. G. Steward, "Hospitality and Ministers," ibid., December 21, 1882, 1; see J. H. A. Johnson, "Hospitality in Religion," ibid., December 28, 1882, 1.
38. *Morning News* (Wilmington), May 4, 1883, as cited in Steward, *From 1864 to 1914*, 193-95; Alice Weld, "Public Schools in Delaware," *Christian Recorder*, December 7, 1882, 1; *The People's Advocate*, April 17, 1880; T. G. Steward, "Gives us a Chapter on Delaware Politics," New York *Globe*, January 20, 1883,

1; Federal Writers Project, *Delaware*, 118; Hancock, "The Status of the Negro in Delaware," 64; Lewis, "Steward and the Education of Blacks in Delaware," 174-75.

39. T. G. Steward, "Delaware People," *Christian Recorder*, February 17, 1883, 1; T. G. Steward, "A National Convention," ibid., March 10, 1883, 1; New York *Globe*, September 29, 1883, 1. It is unknown whether or not Steward attended the convention.

40. T. G. Steward, "The Modification in the Race Idea Suggested by the Necessities of Modern Politics," *Christian Recorder*, April 26, 1883; *The New York Times*, May 15, 1883, 4.

41. Letter from Steward to *Morning News*, May 3, 1883, as quoted in Steward, *From 1864 to 1914*, 195-96; Lewis, "Steward and the Education of Blacks in Delaware," 174-75.

CHAPTER SEVEN

1. Steward, *From 1864 to 1914*, 201-2.

2. Ibid., 203-4.

3. Ibid., 204.

4. Ibid., 204-5; *Christian Recorder*, June 14, 1883, 3.

5. T. G. Steward, "A New Era in the History of the AME Church in Philadelphia," *Christian Recorder*, December 6, 1883, 1; T. G. Steward, "Union AME Church," ibid., March 13, 1884, 1; *The State Journal* (Harrisburg), January 19, 1884, 4 (the correspondent indicated that $2,000 was raised at the January 13 dedicatory service; Steward said that the service raised $3,052.48), see Steward, *From 1864 to 1914*, 207; T. G. Steward, "Important Dedication," *Christian Recorder*, January 10, 1884, 3; T. G. Steward, "How We Raise Our Money," ibid., August 7, 1884, 2; September 11, 1884, 1.

6. *Christian Recorder*, February 7, 1884, 3; February 21, 1884, 3.

7. See personals column in *Christian Recorder*, September 11, 1884, 2; October 9, 1884, 2; October 16, 1884, 2; *The State Journal*, August 30, 1884, 2; September 20, 1884, 2.

8. *The Christian Recorder*, April 10, 1884, 2; Steward, *From 1864 to 1914*, 208-9, 211.

9. Steward, *From 1864 to 1914*, 198-99, 213; New York *Globe*, May 24, 1884, 1; *Christian Recorder*, May 29, 1884, 2; T. G. Steward, "The Communal Service," ibid., September 20, 1883, 1; T. G. Steward, "Confirmation," ibid., April 24, 1884, 1; Smith, *History of AME Church*, 143; T. G. Steward, "Ripeness in the Gospel Ministry," *The AME Church Review* 1 (July 1884): 66-68.

10. Frederick A. McGinnis, *A History and an Interpretation of Wilberforce University* (Blanchester, Ohio: Brown Publishing Co., 1941), 55-56; "Biographical Sketch on President elect S. T. Mitchell," *Christian Recorder*, July 3, 1884, 2.

11. T. G. Steward, "Sunday School Heresies," *Christian Recorder*, November 6, 1884, 1; J. H. Murphy, "Sunday School Heresies," ibid., November 20, 1884, 1; T. G. Steward, "Children in the Church," ibid., December 11, 1884, 1.

12. "Personals," *Christian Recorder*, January 5, 1882, 1; "Local News," ibid., January 19, 1882, 3; January 26, 1882, 3; *The New York Times*, March 4, 1884, 1; "A Colored Weigher," ibid., August 7, 1884, 1; "Colored Men in Business," *New York Freeman*, February 7, 1885, 1; "Progress of the Race," ibid., August 8, 1885, 2; "Quaker City Afro-Americans," Cleveland *Gazette*, November 23, 1889, 1; Perkins, *Fanny Jackson Coppin*, 196.

13. Philip S. Foner, ed., *The Voice of Black America: Major Speeches by Negroes in the United States, 1797-1971* (New York: Simon & Schuster, 1972), 505-7, 398-403; Lane, *Roots of Violence*, 64-67; Lawrence Grossman, *The Democratic Party and the Negro: Northern and National Politics, 1868-1892* (Urbana: University of Illinois Press, 1976), 73-75.

14. New York *Globe*, October 21, 1883, 1; May 2, 1883, 1; *The State Journal*, March 1, 1884, 1; Logan, *Betrayal of the Negro*, 56, 114; Emma Lou Thornbrough, *T. Thomas Fortune: Militant Journalist* (Chicago: University of Chicago Press, 1972), 58; Peter M. Bergman, *The Chronological History of the Negro in America* (New York: Harper & Row, 1969), 293-95.

15. Steward, *From 1864 to 1914*, 218-19; "General City News," *The Philadelphia Press*, November 10, 1884, 3.

16. "Views of prominent Philadelphians on Blaine's Apparent Defeat," *Christian Recorder*, November 13, 1884, 2; "Views on Cleveland's Probable Election," *The State Journal*, November 13, 1884, 1.

17. Steward, *From 1864 to 1914*, 220; William Seraile, "Timothy Thomas Fortune: Father of Black Political Independence," *Afro-Americans in New York Life and History* 2 (July 1978): 15-28; "The Democratic Return to Power—Its Effect?" *AME Church Review* 1 (July 1884), 213-50.

18. *Christian Recorder*, November 22, 1883, 2; Editorial, "Chautauqua and Tawawa," ibid., November 29, 1883, 2; H. M. Turner to T. G. Steward, ibid., January 24, 1884, 3; February 7, 1884, 3.

19. S. H. Coleman, "On to the Florida Conference," *Christian Recorder*, January 1, 1885, 1; "Steward's Reply," ibid., January 15, 1885, 2; fragmentary writing in T. G. Steward Papers, n.d.

20. Scrapbook, Baltimore, T. G. Steward Papers.

21. "Review of *The Bible and Science*," *The Catholic World* 34 (October 1881): 143-44; George M. Searle, "The Supposed Issue Between Religion and Science," ibid. 38 (February 1884): 577-88. T. G. Steward, "The Modern Controversy, Science and Religion: The Question Stated," *Christian Recorder*, January 13, 1881, 2; T. G. Steward, "The Inspiration of the Scriptures," ibid., November 24, 1881, 1.

22. Frank N. Schubert, "Theophilus Gould Steward," in Logan and Winston, *Dictionary of American Negro Biography*, 570-71; David W. Wills, "Aspects of Social Thought in the African Methodist Episcopal Church, 1884-1910" (Ph.D.

dissertation, Harvard University, 1975), 115; Rev. L. J. Coppin, "Two New Books of Rare Merit," *Christian Recorder*, December 10, 1885, 1.

23. Wills, "Aspects of Social Thought," 113-14; Steward, *From 1864 to 1914*, 224; *Christian Recorder*, July 1, 1886, 1; June 2, 1887, 1.

24. "Dr. Steward's New Book," *Christian Recorder*, January 26, 1888, 3.

25. T. G. Steward, *The End of the World; or, Clearing the Way for the Fullness of the Gentiles* (Philadelphia: AME Church Book Rooms, 1888), 2, 74, 76, 83, 120-21, 123-24, 126; Josiah Strong, *Our Country: Its Possible Future and Its Present Crisis* (New York: Home Missionary Society, 1885), v, 134, 161-80.

26. *The End of the World*, ads ran in the *Christian Recorder* from March 29 to May 24, 1888; Sarah C. B. Scarborough to Steward, October 30, 1888, in T. G. Steward Papers.

27. Editorial, "End of the World," *Christian Recorder*, April 12, 1888, 4; *A.M.E. Church Review* 4 (April 1888) 461-66.

28. T. G. Steward, "The Review's Notice of My New Book," *Christian Recorder*, April 19, 1888, 5; fragment writings, n.d., in T. G. Steward Papers.

29. T. G. Steward, "A New Reading of an Old Phase; The End of the World," *AME Church Review* 5 (January 1889): 204-9; T. G. Steward, "The Future of God's People; an Extension of the End of the World," *Christian Recorder*, November 7, 1889, 3.

30. Wills, "Aspects of Social Thought," 2-3, 123; Wills cites Vernon Loggins, *The Negro Author: His Development in America* (New York: Columbia University Press, 1931), 300-301, 330, 403, which finds Steward a pompous writer; Henry M. Turner, "God is a Negro," *Voice of Missions*, February 1, 1898, as reprinted in John Bracey et al., eds., *Black Nationalism in America* (Indianapolis: Bobbs-Merrill, 1970), 154-55.

31. William J. Simmons, *Men of Mark, Eminent, Progressive and Rising* (Chicago: Johnson Publishing Co., 1970), 3.

32. New York *Globe*, April 12, 1884, 3.

33. *Christian Recorder*, November 19, 1885, 2; ibid., November 26, 1885, 2; ibid., December 24, 1885, 1.

34. Steward, *From 1864 to 1914*, 221, 224, 225, 226.

CHAPTER EIGHT

1. "Metropolitan AME Church," Washington *Bee*, May 29, 1886, 2; B. W. Arnett, ed., *The Centennial Budget* (Xenia, Ohio: AME Church, 1888), 100; John T. Jenifer, *Centennial Retrospect: History of the African Methodist Church* (Nashville, 1916), 23.

2. Steward, *From 1864 to 1914*, 229-30; Gatewood, *Aristocrats of Color*, 286-87.

3. Washington *Bee*, May 29, 1886, 2; Steward, *From 1864 to 1914*, 229-29.

4. Union Bethel-Metropolitan AME Church Records, Minutes of the Official Board, July 28, 1884-April 23, 1894, box 70-3, folder 47, 90.

5. T. G. Steward, "The Metropolitan Church," *Christian Recorder*, August 19, 1886, 1-2; see also November 25, 1886, 2; Steward, *From 1864 to 1914*, 227.

6. Steward, "The Metropolitan Church," *Christian Recorder*, September 2, 1886, 1; Boyd, *Directory of the District of Columbia, 1887*, 932-37.

7. New York *Freeman*, November 10, 1886, 2, as cited in *People's Advocate*, n.d.; *Christian Recorder*, November 25, 1886, 2.

8. T. G. Steward, "Metropolitan Notes," *Christian Recorder*, December 9, 1886, 1; February 23, 1887, 2; T. Gould, "A Visit to Washington," February 24, 1887, 1.

9. T. G. Steward, "Something of the People of the Metropolitan Church: A Foul (Fowl) Conspiracy," *Christian Recorder*, January 6, 1887, 1; April 13, 1887, 2; April 27, 1887, 2; May 12, 1887, 2; Steward, *From 1864 to 1914*, 230, 231, 236, 237; Metropolitan Minutes, April 24, 1888, 171; May 1, 1888, 173.

10. Metropolitan Minutes, July 12, 1887, 124; July 20, 1887, 136; August 16, 1887, 141; August 23, 1887, 141; August 30, 1887, 145; October 25, 1887, 152; January 3, 1888, 157; January 10, 1888, 158; January 17, 1888, 159; April 10, 1888, 170.

11. *Christian Recorder*, October 21, 1886, 2; Steward, *From 1864 to 1914*, 237.

12. *Christian Recorder*, January 20, 1887, 2; January 27, 1887, 2; February 10, 1887, 2, 3; Steward, *From 1864 to 1914*, 237.

13. Gatewood, *Aristocrats of Color*, 259, 261.

14. Frederick Douglass to T. G. Steward, July 27, 1886, incomplete letter in Frederick Douglass Papers, reel 9, container 12. For Douglass's complete letter, see Steward, *From 1864 to 1914*, 232-36. John T. Grayson, "Frederick Douglass' Intellectual Development: His Concepts of God, Man, and Nature in Light of American and European Influences" (Ph.D. dissertation, Columbia University, 1981), 108, 179; Foner, *Frederick Douglass*, 268-69; Foner, *Reconstruction*, 28.

15. Foner, *Frederick Douglass*, 337-38.

16. Gatewood, *Aristocrats of Color*, 57; Steward to Douglass, July 14, 1887, reel 4, container 6; Douglass to Steward, July 27, 1887, reel 4, container 6; Douglass to Steward, July 25, 1887, reel 5, container 7, Frederick Douglass Papers; Metropolitan Minutes, September 20, 1887, 148; *Christian Recorder*, September 29, 1887, 5.

17. Steward to Douglass, July 26, 1889, reel 5, container 7, Douglass Papers; Foner, *Frederick Douglass*, 354-61.

18. *Christian Recorder*, November 4, 1886, 2; John W. Cromwell, *History of the Bethel Literary and Historical Association, Being a Paper Read Before the Association on Founder's Day, February 24, 1896* (Washington, D.C.: R. L. Pendleton Press, 1896), 18, 19. Gatewood, *Aristocrats of Color*, 214-15.

19. *Christian Recorder*, September 29, 1887, 6; Arnett, *The Budget, 1887-1888*, 533, 535; The Washington *Bee*, October 29, 1887, 3.

20. T. G. Steward, "Questions for 1888," *Christian Recorder*, May 19, 1887, 1.

21. John M. Collins, "Do We Need More Bishops," *Christian Recorder*, June 30, 1887, 1; J. H. A. Johnson, "More Bishops," ibid., July 14, 1887; August 25,

1887, 1; T. G. Steward, "District Episcopacy or General Superintendency—Which?," ibid., October 13, 1887, 1; Graham, *Baltimore*, 305.

22. T. G. Steward, "General Superintendency," *Christian Recorder*, October 20, 1887, 1; T. G. Steward, "Bishops and the General Conference," ibid., October 27, 1887, 1.

23. T. G. Steward, "Washington Notes," *Christian Recorder*, February 16, 1888, 4-5; "Washington Colored Society," The Washington *Bee*, July 31, 1886, 1; Gatewood, *Aristocrats of Color*, 56, 57, 75, 157; Graham, *Baltimore*, 267.

24. T. G. Steward, "Washington Notes," *Christian Recorder*, February 16, 1888, 4-5; Arnett, *The Budget, 1887-1888*, 101; Steward, *From 1864 to 1914*, 238; "The Pastor Complimented," *Christian Recorder*, April 19, 1888, 3; *Christian Recorder*, May 8, 1890, 6; "Rev. Theo G. Steward," *The Freeman*, April 13, 1889, 1.

25. Steward, *From 1864 to 1914*, 241, 242; *Christian Recorder*, May 24, 1888, 4; May 31, 1888, 3; Cephas C. Bateman, "A Group of Army Authors," *The Californian* 4 (October 1893): 692.

26. Payne, *Recollections of Seventy Years*, 329-30.

27. Smith, *History of AME Church*, 152-54; *Christian Recorder*, May 24, 1888, 2; the vote on Steward's motion was 134 yeas, 64 nays, 83 abstentions, and 6 refusals to vote.

28. Steward, *From 1864 to 1914*, 239, 240; *Christian Recorder*, May 31, 1888, 3; *Indianapolis News*, May 21, 1888, as quoted in Charles Killian, "Daniel A. Payne: Black Spokesman for Reform" (Ph.D. dissertation, Indiana University, 1971), 164; Henry M. Turner, *The Genesis and Theory of Methodist Polity, or the Machinery of Methodism* (Philadelphia: Publication Department, AME Church, 1885), 235-39.

29. A. J. Kershaw, "The AME Church: Its Nineteenth General Conference," *Christian Recorder*, July 19, 1888, 1.

30. I. H. Welch, "Reunion of the Allen Family," *Christian Recorder*, August 23, 1888, 1; T. G. Steward, "Putting One Thing for Another; or, the Fallacy of the Liturgy Argument," ibid., September 6, 1888, 4-5.

31. J. M. Henderson, "Wesley and the Liturgy," *Christian Recorder*, October 4, 1888, 2; J. M. Henderson, "Steward vs Wesley, the AME General Conference, Bishops, et al.," ibid., December 13, 1888, 1; J. M. Henderson, "The Ritual Authorized," ibid., January 3, 1889, 5.

32. T. G. Steward, "The Ritual Argument by Dr. Henderson," *Christian Recorder*, October 25, 1888, 1; T. G. Steward, "Rev. J. M. Henderson's Misstatement," ibid., December 20, 1888, 1; T. G. Steward, "The 'Ritual Argument' or Reasons Why the 'Order of Service' Should Be Entirely Removed From Our Churches," ibid., February 14, 1889, 2; see also "The Ritual Argument Fairly Stated," ibid., January 24, 1889, 4.

33. Editorial, "An Interesting Coincidence," *Christian Recorder*, February 7, 1889, 4.

34. J. M. Henderson, "The End of the Ritual Argument," *Christian Recorder*, February 21, 1889, 2; T. G. Steward, "Conclusion of the 'Ritual Argument'

With Diversion in Logic," ibid., February 21, 1889, 5. Others, however, wrote on the subject; see March 28, 1889, 1, and May 2, 1889, 1.

35. J. C. Embry, "Thanks to Dr. Steward for Aid," *Christian Recorder*, November 1, 1888, 3.
36. Gatewood, *Aristocrats of Color*, 263; Bettye Gardner, "Antebellum Black Education in Baltimore," *Maryland Historical Magazine* 71 (fall 1976): 360, 361, 366.
37. Graham, *Baltimore*, 207-22; Bettye C. Thomas, "Public Education and Black Protest in Baltimore, 1865-1900," *Maryland Historical Magazine* 71 (fall 1976): 383, 384, 389 (see report of Commissioners of Public Schools for 1869).
38. Steward, *From 1864 to 1914*, 261-63.
39. Ibid., 263.
40. Ibid., 257-59; John R. Slattery, "Twenty Years Growth of the Colored People in Baltimore, Md.," *Catholic World* 66 (January 1898): 519; Wm. H. Barnes, "Baltimore Notes," *Christian Recorder*, December 6, 1888, 1.
41. "Colored Industrial Exhibition," *Christian Recorder*, July 26, 1885, 5; "Maryland's Colored Fair," *The New York Times*, October 14, 1888, 20; Graham, *Baltimore*, 205.
42. "Philadelphia Matters," *Christian Recorder*, January 1, 1880, 3; Barnes, "Baltimore Notes," ibid., January 17, 1889, 3; "Dr. Steward Would Have the Negro Race Represented in the Paris Exhibition," ibid., January 24, 1889, 2; "The United States at the Paris Exhibition," *The New York Times*, February 23, 1889, 6.
43. W. R. Arnold, "The First District, Baltimore Conference," *Christian Recorder*, August 23, 1888, 1; Barnes, "Baltimore Notes," ibid., December 6, 1888, 1.
44. Barnes, "Baltimore Notes," *Christian Recorder*, April 11, 1889, 1; August 8, 1889, 4.
45. Steward, *From 1864 to 1914*, 251-57; Steward, "The Composition of the General Conference," *Christian Recorder*, April 18, 1887, 1; see issues of May 9, 1889, 1, and May 30, 1889, 2; J. M. Batten, "Henry M. Turner: Negro Bishop Extraordinary," *Church History* 7 (March 1930): 231-32.
46. T. G. Steward, "To Our Bishops," *Christian Recorder*, September 5, 1889, 6; Editorial, "The Cost is Infinitely Greater Than the Worth of the Goods," ibid., August 15, 1889, 4; "Some Race News," Cleveland *Gazette*, September 21, 1889, 1; T. G. Steward, "How to Save Our Foreign Missions," *Christian Recorder*, December 19, 1889, 2, 4.
47. T. G. Steward, "The South—Its Preachers—Bishop Gaines," *Christian Recorder*, June 13, 1889, 1; I. S. Grant, "Dr. T. G. Steward Is Not In Error—The South—Its Preachers," ibid., August 8, 1889, 3.
48. *Christian Recorder*, November 14, 1889, 5; "The Monumental City," ibid., December 12, 1889, 4; January 22, 1891, 4; T. G. Steward, "Impressions of Philadelphia," ibid., January 29, 1891, 2.
49. Steward, *From 1864 to 1914*, 265.

50. "The Causes of Which Retard the Moral, Material and Education Progress of the Colored People of the United States," [1889-90], T. G. Steward Papers; Edwin S. Redkey, *Black Exodus: Black Nationalist and Back-to-Africa Movements, 1890-1910* (New Haven: Yale University Press, 1969), 47-77, 170-94.
51. Editorial, "Will Editor Cromwell Answer?" Washington *Bee*, October 29, 1887, 2; November 5, 1887, 1.
52. B. T. Washington, "The Colored Ministry: Its Defects and Needs," *Christian Union*, August 14, 1890, 199-200, in Louis R. Harlan, ed., *The Booker T. Washington Papers*, 13 vols. (Urbana: University of Illinois Press, 1972), 3: 71-74.
53. Charles A. Killian, ed., *Sermons and Addresses, 1853-1891 by Daniel A. Payne* (New York: Arno Press, 1972), 2, 195-96; Arthur P. Stokes, "Daniel A. Payne: Churchman and Educator" (Ph.D. dissertation, Ohio State University, 1973); Payne to Washington, November 3, 1890; Harlan, *Booker T. Washington Papers*, 3: 97-98; *Christian Recorder*, December 18, 1890, 2, 5; December 25, 1890, 2, 3, 4.
54. *Christian Recorder*, December 18, 1890, 5.
55. Francis J. Grimké to Washington, December 12, 1890, Harlan, *Booker T. Washington Papers*, 3: 114.
56. T. G. Steward, "The Washington Slander," *Christian Recorder*, January 15, 1891, 2. The Philadelphia Preachers' Meeting of December 25, 1889 adopted a resolution denouncing Washington's action as "mischievous and slanderous," and Payne's support for Washington as not representative of the AME ministry, ibid., January 1, 1891, 3. T. G. Steward, "Now and Then," in Arnett, *Quartocentennial Conference, 1889*, 56-65; T. G. Steward, *Pioneer Echoes, Six Special Sermons: Five of Which Were Preached in South Carolina and Georgia From 1866 to 1871* (Baltimore: Hoffman & Co., 1889), 1-62, copy in Steward Papers.
57. Francis J. Grimké, "The Afro-American Pulpit in Relation to Race Elevation," typescript, 1892, Series D, Sermons, Addresses, Commentaries, Reports, Tributes and Obsequies, A-C, box 40-6, folder 271, Francis J. Grimké Papers, Moorland-Spingarn Research Center; T. G. Steward to Grimké, April 27, 1893, Series B, Correspondence, box 40-5, folder 223; Carter G. Woodson, ed., *The Works of Francis J. Grimké*, 4 vols. (Washington, D.C.: Associated Publishers, 1942), 1: 223-34, 4: 29.
58. *Christian Recorder*, May 11, 1891, 5.
59. Fragmentary notes, n.d., T. G. Steward Papers; T. G. Steward, *From 1864 to 1914*, 256.

CHAPTER NINE

1. Steward, *From 1864 to 1914*, 265; Arlen L. Fowler, *The Black Infantry in the West* (Westport, Conn.: Greenwood Press, 1971), 94-104.
2. Steward, *From 1864 to 1914*, 266.

3. T. G. Steward Military File, ACP, 1891, Adjutant General Office (Washington: National Archives), Record Group 94, box 1330; Steward, *From 1864 to 1914*, 267. Gatewood, *Aristocrats of Color*, 337.

4. J. C. Kelton to Steward, July 25, 1891, Steward Military File; Steward and Steward, *Gouldtown*, 154-55; New York *Age*, August 1, 1891, 1; *Christian Recorder*, August 6, 1891, 5; *The New York Times*, August 17, 1891, 3; *The State Capitol* (Springfield, Illinois), August 22, 1891, 1.

5. Wears, "Rev. Theophilus Gould Steward," 137-40.

6. W. Sherman Savage, *Blacks in the West* (Westport, Conn.: Greenwood Press, 1976), 48-49; Fowler, *Black Infantry*, 92; John H. Nankivell, *History of the Twenty-fifth Regiment United States Army, 1869-1926* (Denver: Smith-Brooks, 1927), 11, 42, 48; "United States Army Chaplains," *The New York Times* magazine, June 12, 1898, 14.

7. Chaplain T. G. Steward, "Camp Life, etc.," *Christian Recorder*, October 8, 1891, 1.

8. Wears, "Rev. Theophilus Gould Steward," 138; *Christian Recorder*, August 27, 1891, 5; September 14, 1893, 1; August 12, 1897, 1; Steward, *From 1894 to 1914*, 274, 278.

9. Monthly Chaplain Report, November, December 1891; "Personals," *Christian Recorder*, December 24, 1891, 4; *Army and Navy Journal*, January 9, 1892, 347.

10. Efficiency report for T. G. Steward prepared by George L. Andrews, January 1892, Steward Military File.

11. T. G. Steward, "The Soldier's Lot Out West," New York *Age*, January 23, 1892, 4.

12. Charles B. Turner, "To Join the Army," New York *Freeman*, December 26, 1885, 4; G. H. Burton, "Hard Times in the Army," New York *Globe*, April 20, 1883, 2; G. H. Burton, "Discontent in the Army," ibid., September 1, 1883, 1; *Army and Navy Journal*, January 16, 1891, 311.

13. Editorial, "Unjust Treatment of Afro-American Soldiers," New York *Age*, February 13, 1892, 2; Indianapolis *Freeman*, July 23, 1904, 6; Letter to editor from Fort Robinson, Nebraska, February 10, 1896, in Cleveland *Gazette*, May 9, 1896, 2.

14. *Army and Navy Journal*, April 23, 1892, 614; T. G. Steward, "Colonel George L. Andrews," *Harper's Weekly* (May 7, 1892): 437.

15. T. G. Steward, "The Canteen in the Army," *Harper's Weekly* (April 9, 1892): 350-51; *Army and Navy Journal*, August 22, 1891, 889; George A. Marshall, "The Army Canteen," *The Arena* 25 (March 1901): 300-307; *The Colored American*, September 14, 1901, 8; Editorial, "The Army Canteen," The Manila (Philippines) *Times*, February 6, 1901, 4; "Alcoholism in the Army," *The New York Times*, October 20, 1894, 3; October 21, 1894, 13.

16. Monthly Chaplain Report, April, June, August, September, October, November 1892, Steward Military File.

17. Monthly Chaplain Report, January, February 1893, Steward Military File.

18. T. G. Steward, "The Doctrine of the Incarnation Stated," *AME Church Review* 10 (January 1893): 214, 222.

19. Steward to Adjutant General, January 25, 1893; Adjutant General to Steward, February 6, 1893, Steward Military File; the Reverend J. H. A. Johnson read his paper, "Ecumenical Conference on Methodism," *Christian Recorder*, October 8, 1891, 4; Jenifer, *Centennial Retrospect*, 331; *Proceedings of the Second Ecumenical Methodist Conference Held in the Metropolitan Methodist Episcopal Church, Washington, October 1891* (New York: Hunt & Eaton, 1892), 573-77; G. A. Collier to Daniel Lamont, May 21, 1895; Lamont to Collier, May 31, 1895; Acting Adjutant General to Commanding Officer, Fort McPherson, Georgia, June 4, 1895; J. Garland Penn to Daniel Lamont, August 21, 1895; Daniel Lamont to J. Garland Penn, August 30, 1895, file #4553, Adjutant General Folder, Record Group 94 (Washington: National Archives).

20. Steward to [M. Barber] Assistant Adjutant General, March 6, 1893, Steward Military File; Steward, *From 1864 to 1914*, 180; undated manuscript [1899?], Monroe Trotter Papers, Boston University.

21. Francis Redmond, "A Tribute to Mrs. Eliza Steward," *Christian Recorder*, November 23, 1893, 1; *Army and Navy Journal*, November 11, 1893, 198; Steward, *From 1864 to 1914*, 280.

22. Monthly Chaplain Report, December 1893, Steward Military File.

23. Ibid., January 1894.

24. Ibid., June 1894.

25. Efficiency report of T. G. Steward, reported by Major C. McKibbin, 25th Infantry, June 30, 1895 for period of May 14, 1895-June 30, 1895; Individual Service report of T. G. Steward reported by himself, June 30, 1895, Steward Military File; Frank L. Mather, ed., *Who's Who of the Colored Race*, vol. 1 (Chicago, 1915), 253; Monthly Chaplain Report, August 1895, February 1896, Steward Military File.

26. Monthly Chaplain Report, June, July, October 1896.

27. For a general study of Susan McKinney Steward, see Seraile, "Susan McKinney-Steward," 27-44.

28. Monthly Chaplain Report, February, June, August, September 1894; entire year 1897; January 1898, Steward Military File.

29. Ibid., December 1894, July, October, 1897, January 1898; T. G. Steward, "A Glimpse of Montana Life," *The Independent*, August 22, 1895, 1150-51; Steward, *From 1864 to 1914*, 283-84, 289; U.S. Census of Population for 1890, 577.

30. Federal Writers Project, *Montana: A State Guidebook* (New York: Hastings House, 1939), 57; James M. Hamilton, *From Wilderness to Statehood: A History of Montana, 1805-1900* (Portland, Oregon: Binfords & Mort, 1957), 352, 356, 498, 499.

31. Monthly Chaplain Report, March 1894, 1896, and 1897, Steward Military File.

32. Steward, *From 1864 to 1914*, 289; T. G. Steward, "The Colored American as a Soldier," *The United States Service* 11 (April 1894): 323-27.

33. T. G. Steward, "Starving Laborers and the 'Hired Soldier,' " *The United States Service* 14 (October 1895): 363-66.

34. T. G. Steward, "Negro Mortality," *Social Economist* 9 (October 1895): 204-7; "Morality Among Negroes in Cities," Proceedings of the Conference for Investigation of City Problems Held at Atlanta University, May 26-27, 1896, in *Atlanta University Publications no. 1* (Atlanta: Atlanta University Press, 1896), 21-22; "Social and Physical Condition of Negroes in Cities," Report of an Investigation Under the Direction of Atlanta University and Proceedings of the Second Conference for the Study of Problems Concerning Negro City Life, held at Atlanta University, May 25-26, 1897, in *Atlanta University Publications no. 2* (Atlanta: Atlanta University Press, 1987).

35. *Christian Recorder*, September 14, 1893, 1; August 26, 1897, 1; untitled typescript [1893], T. G. Steward papers.

36. Steward, *From 1864 to 1914*, 283, 284, 286-89.

37. T. G. Steward to Adjutant General, Washington, D.C., June 1, 1896; *The New York Times*, April 26, 1896, 6; Adjutant General to Steward, March 21, 1896, Steward Military File; for a description of racial insensitivity at West Point, see *The New York Times*, August 28, 1895, 5.

38. John T. Dallas to Steward, March 1898, Monroe Trotter Papers.

39. Alexander Crummell, "The Attitude of the American Mind Toward the Negro Intellect," occasional papers no. 3 (Washington, D.C.: American Negro Academy, 1898), 12-16.

40. T. G. Steward, "Cultured Society and the Negro," *The Independent* (April 16, 1896), 514.

41. T. G. Steward, "The Race Issue, so-called, A Social Matter Only," *The Competitor* 1 (March 1920): 6-7.

42. Alfred A. Moss, Jr., *The American Negro Academy: Voice of the Talented Tenth* (Baton Rouge: Louisiana State University Press, 1981), 38.

43. *The New York Times*, March 30, 1892, 2.

44. Andrew S. Burt, "The Negro as a Soldier," *The Crisis* 1 (February 1911): 23-25; Nankivell, *History of the Twenty-fifth Regiment*, 66.

CHAPTER TEN

1. Howard C. Hill, *Roosevelt and the Caribbean* (Chicago, 1927).

2. William B. Gatewood, ed., *"Smoked Yankees" and the Struggle for Empire: Letters from Negro Soldiers, 1898-1902* (Urbana: University of Illinois Press, 1971), 4, 5, 6; *The Afro-American Sentinel* (Omaha), April 16, 1891, 1.

3. Gatewood, *Smoked Yankees*, 6-7.

4. Ibid., 9-10.

5. *Illinois Record*, April 23, 1898, 2; T. G. Steward, "The First Move in The War," *The Independent* (April 28, 1898): 535-36; Gatewood, *Smoked Yankees*, 21-23.

6. T. G. Steward, "Camp Life at Chickamauga," *The Independent* (May 12, 1898): 614.

7. T. G. Steward, "Going to War," Cleveland *Gazette*, May 28, 1898, 1, reprinted from the *Christian Recorder*, n.d.; Steward, *The End of the World*, 121, 123, 135.

8. John E. Lewis to editor, *Illinois Record*, June 5, 1898, in Gatewood, *Smoked Yankees*, 30; T. G. Steward, "The New Colored Soldier," *The Independent* (June 16, 1898), 781-82; Efficiency Report of T. G. Steward as reported by himself, July 1, 1899, for period of June 30, 1897 to June 30, 1899, Steward Military File.

9. George W. Prioleau to editor, Cleveland *Gazette*, October 22, 1898, in Gatewood, *Smoked Yankees*, 82-84.

10. Ibid., 8-11.

11. Ibid., 29; T. G. Steward to Adjutant General [H. C. Corbin] War Dept., July 5, 1898; special orders no. 180, paragraph 31, August 2, 1898; Steward to Adjutant General, telegram, August 13, 1898; special orders no. 190, paragraph 55, August 13, 1898; Asst. Adjutant General to Steward, telegram, August 13, 1898, Steward Military File.

12. Steward, *The Colored Regulars* (Philadelphia: AME Book Concern, 1904), 227-228; Cleveland *Gazette*, September 24, 1898, 1; Herschel V. Cashin, et al., *Under Fire with the Tenth U.S. Cavalry* (Chicago: American Publishing House, 1899), 140-42.

13. T. G. Steward, "A Plea for Patriotism," *The Independent* (September 29, 1898), 887-88.

14. George W. Prioleau, "America's Hell," Cleveland *Gazette*, October 22, 1898, 1.

15. T. G. Steward to President United States [August 12, 1898], document file #118298-118403, box 815, Record Group 94, Office of the Adjutant General, National Archives; Steward to Adjutant General, August 13, 1898; Steward to Sec. of War, August 13, 1898, document file #1805-9, filed with Frank Rudolph Steward file #118301, box 815, RG 94; Steward to Adjutant General, August 25, 1898; Steward to Sec. of War, September 15, 1898; Sec. of War to Frank R. Steward, September 9, 1899, Frank R. Steward Military File.

16. T. G. Steward, "How to Garrison Cuba," New York *Daily Tribune*, October 31, 1898, 7; T. G. Steward, "The Reign of the Mob," *The Independent* (May 11, 1899): 1296-97.

17. Gatewood, *Smoked Yankees*, 237-314.

18. T. G. Steward, *A Charleston Love Story, or Hortense Vanross* (London: F. Tennyson Neely, 1899); Washington *Bee*, September 28, 1901, 1.

19. M. W. Saddler to editor, July 30, 1898, *The Freeman*, August 27, 1898, as quoted in Gatewood, *Smoked Yankees*, 57; Edward A. Johnson, *History of Negro Soldiers in the Spanish-American War* (Raleigh, N.C.: Capital Printing Co., 1899); see also Johnson, *A School History of the Negro Race in America From 1619 to 1891* (New York: Isaac Goldman Co., 1891).

20. T. G. Steward to Adjutant General, December 17, 1898; special orders no. 122, December 22, 1898; special orders no. 12, January 16, 1899; A. S. Burt to

Adjutant General, January 11, 1899; Burt to Adjutant General, February 13, 1899; Benjamin W. Arnett to McKinley, February 23, 1899; Corbin to Arnett, March 1, 1899; L. J. Coppin to McKinley, March 7, 1899; Nelson W. Miles to Sec. of War, March 8, 1899; Asst. Adjutant Gen. to Commanding General, Dept. Colorado, March 11, 1899 (telegram); Efficiency Report in case of T. G. Steward for period June 30, 1897 to June 30, 1899; Arnett to R. A. Alger, March 12, 1899; special orders no. 63, paragraph 12, March 17, 1899; Steward to Adjutant General, march 28, 1899, Steward Military File; partial letter to Steward, Fort Missoula, unsigned, n.d., T. G. Steward Papers.

21. Special orders no. 63, paragraph 12, March 17, 1899; Steward to Adjutant General, May 2, 1899, May 31, 1899, July 24, 1899, September 14, 1899; see replies to Steward, July 29, 1899, September 22, 28, 1899, Steward Military File; Steward, *From 1864 to 1914*, 307; *Illinois Record*, April 8, 1899, 3.

22. Steward, *The Colored Regulars*, 19; Moss, *The American Negro Academy*, 1; *Christian Recorder*, January 1905 issues contained ads for the book; H. T. Kealing, "The Twenty-fifth as Seen in History," *AME Church Review* 23 (April 1907): 318-26; *AME Church Review* 22 (July 1905): 95-96, 490-91; *Alexander's Magazine* 1 (December 1905): 46-49; John Thomas Simpson, "The Colored Regulars in the U.S. Army," *The Colored American Magazine* 3 (June 1905): 299-303; Judson W. Lyons to Steward, February 7, 1906, T. G. Steward Papers.

23. *New York Age*, December 23, 1899, as cited in Gatewood, *Smoked Yankees*, 7; Emmet J. Scott to Theodore Roosevelt, March 8, 1907, in Harlan, *Booker T. Washington Papers*, 9: 226-29.

24. Special orders no. 232, paragraph 48, October 5, 1899; Adjutant General to commanding general, Dept. California, October 5, 1899, Steward Military File; undated and untitled typescript of T. G. Steward in Monroe Trotter Papers.

25. Gatewood, *Smoked Yankees*, 37-45, 280-81.

26. Steward, *From 1864 to 1914*, 307; Manila *Times*, November 28, 1899, 1; January 27, 1900, 1; March 3, 1900, 1; March 9, 1900, 1; Steward, *From 1864 to 1914*, 312; "The Last of Ninety-nine," T. G. Steward Papers; efficiency report in case of T. G. Steward reported by himself for period June 30, 1900 to JUne 30, 1901, Steward Military File.

27. T. G. Steward, "Two Years in Luzon," *The Colored American Magazine* 4 (November 1901): 8-9.

28. Diary entry, February 12, 1901, T. G. Steward Papers.

29. Steward, "In Luzon," *The Independent*, February 1, 1900, 312-14; Steward, *From 1864 to 1914*, 315, 344, 345, 348, 349; *Christian Recorder*, May 17, 1900, 1, 4; Cleveland *Gazette*, April 21, 1900, as quoted in Gatewood, *Smoked Yankees*, 263-64; Steward to Adjutant 25th Infantry, December 13, 1900; diary entry for December 13, 1900, T. G. Steward Papers.

30. Diary entry for December 13, 1900, T. G. Steward Papers; John W. Galloway to Richmond *Planet*, December 30, 1899, as quoted in Gatewood, *Smoked Yankees*, 251-55.

31. Steward, *From 1864 to 1914*, 332-33.

32. Manila *Times*, January 17, 1900, 1, 8; February 1, 1900, 6; February 14, 1900, 1; March 19, 1900, 4; T. G. Steward to Archbishop Chappelle, February 3, 1901, in Steward, *From 1864 to 1914*, 331, 333-34; "The Last of Ninety-nine," T. G. Steward Papers; Steward, "In Luzon," 312-14.

33. T. G. Steward, "Two Years in Luzon," *The Colored American Magazine* 4 (January/February 1902): 166-67; efficiency report in case of Theophilus Gould Steward reported by himself, April 9, 1902 for period of June 30, 1900 to June 30, 1901, Steward Military File.

34. *Annual Reports of the War Department for the Fiscal Year ended June 30, 1900*, vol. II, *Report of the Military Governor of the Philippine Islands on Civil Affairs* (Washington, D.C.: GPO, 1900).

35. Diary entry, November 21, 23, 24, 1900, T. G. Steward Papers; Steward, *From 1864 to 1914*, 318-21.

36. Steward, *From 1864 to 1914*, 323-25; diary entry November 26, December 1, 3, 5, 1900, T. G. Steward Papers.

37. Steward, *From 1864 to 1914*, 328, 331; diary entry December 7, 14, 165, 20, 1900, T. G. Steward Papers.

38. T. G. Steward, "Two Years in Luzon," *The Colored American Magazine* 5 (August 1902): 244-49.

39. A. S. Burt to Adjutant General, 3rd Dist., Dept. of Northern Luzon, Dagupan, P.I., June 6, 1901, in Nankivell, *History of the Twenty-fifth Regiment*, 109; Rienzi B. Lemus to editor, *The Freeman*, January 15, 1902, March 8, 1902, in Gatewood, *Smoked Yankees*, 310.

40. Appendix D, *Inaugural Address of the Civil Governor* (William H. Taft), July 4, 1901, 281-85, in *Annual Report of the War Department for the Fiscal Year Ending June 30, 1901. Report of the Philippine Commission in Two Parts* (Washington, D.C.: GPO, 1901).

41. Gustavus A. Steward, "Six Months in the Uplift," typed manuscript, July 2, 1933, in possession of his daughter, Anna Steward Bishop, Columbus, Ohio; [T. G. Steward] to Gustavus Adolphus Steward, November 23, 1902, T. G. Steward Papers.

42. Steward, "In Luzon," 312-14; Steward, *From 1864 to 1914*, 329, 335-37.

43. Individual Service Report to Chaplain T. G. Steward, June 30, 1901 to June 30, 1902, Steward Military File; Gatewood, *Smoked Yankees*, 237.

44. Fragmentary writings [1902?], T. G. Steward Papers; Mrs. Jefferson David, "The White Man's Problem: Why We Do Not Want the Philippines," *The Arena* 23 (January 1900): 1-4.

45. T. G. Steward, "Venerable Names in the Philippines," unpublished manuscript, n.d., T. G. Steward Papers.

46. T. G. Steward to Adjutant General, December 16, 1902, Steward Military File; T. Thomas Fortune, "A Social Study of the Filipino," *The Voice of the Negro* 1 (March 1904): 93-99; T. Thomas Fortune, "The Filipino," ibid., 1 (May 1904): 199-203; T. Thomas Fortune, "The Filipino—Across Luzon," ibid., 1 (October

1904): 482-85; For soldiers' praise of the Philippines, see Gatewood, *Smoked Yankees*, 311-12, 316.
47. Philip W. Kennedy, "The Concept of Racial Superiority and United States Imperialism, 1890-1910" (Ph.D. dissertation, St. Louis University, 1962), 96; Stephen Bonsal, "The Negro Soldier in War and Peace," *North American Review* 186 (June 1907): 325, as quoted in Gatewood, *Smoked Yankees*, 243.
48. Steward, *From 1864 to 1914*, 341, 353-54.

CHAPTER ELEVEN

1. Quoted in Emma L. Thornbrough, "Booker T. Washington As Seen By His White Contemporaries," *Journal of Negro History* 53 (April 1968): 172.
2. Steward, *From 1864 to 1914*, 354; Monthly Reports of Chaplains, September 1902-June 1906, Record Group 393 (Washington: National Archives); for a description of Fort Niobrara, see Thomas R. Buecker, "Fort Niobrara, 1800-1906: Guardian of the Rosebud Sioux," *Nebraska History* 65 (fall 1984): 302-25.
3. Monthly chaplain report, September 1902, Steward Military File.
4. Ibid., October, November 1902; September 1903; George A. Marshall, "The Army Canteen," *The Arena* 25 (March 1901): 300-307; *The New York Times*, January 11, 1903, 13; November 28, 1904, 6; September 23, 1905, 9; October 22, 1905, 8; for Taft's view, see *The New York Times*, February 15, 1905, 6.
5. "The Army Canteen," *The New York Times*, December 1, 1905, 8; *Army and Navy Journal*, October 26, 1895, 116; Steward, "The Colored Man as a Soldier," 323-27.
6. Monthly chaplain report, January, March, April, December 1903, Steward Military File.
7. Steward, *From 1864 to 1914*, 356; *Army and Navy Journal*, May 9, 1903, 905.
8. "Negroes Turned Away," New York *Daily Tribune*, November 10, 1903, 6; Michael W. Schuyler, "The Ku Klux Klan in Nebraska," *Nebraska History* 66 (fall 1985): 234-56.
9. Monthly chaplain report, December 1903.
10. Ibid.; I am grateful for information on Walter provided by his niece, Anna Steward Bishop; Steward, *From 1864 to 1914*, 358; "Our Walter," [1904?], T. G. Steward Papers.
11. Monthly chaplain report, February, March, April 1904, Steward Military File.
12. Steward to Adjutant General, U.S.A., January 10, 1903.
13. Steward to the military secretary, War Department, May 30, 1904; Adna R. Chaffee, memorandum for the military secretary, June 16, 1904; Capt. M. D. Cronin to military secretary, June 3, 1904; Frank R. Steward to the President, July 1, 1904; T. G. Steward to the military secretary, July 19, 1904; July 15, 1905, Steward Military File.

14. Monthly chaplain report, July, October, December 1905; January, February 1906; *Army and Navy Journal*, January 6, 1906, 529; March 10, 1906, 785; March 17, 1906, 813.

15. Steward, *From 1864 to 1914*, 359; Steward to Adjutant General, 25th Infantry, June 30, 1906; Col. R. W. Hoyt to military secretary (telegram), July 1, 1906, Senate doc. #701, 61st cong., 3d sess., vol. 6 (Washington, D.C.: GPO, 1911), 1390-91; Ann J. Lane, *The Brownsville Affair: National Crisis and Black Reaction* (Port Washington, N.Y.: Kennikat Press, 1971), 12-15; John D. Weaver, *The Brownsville Raid* (New York: Norton, 1970).

16. Steward, *From 1864 to 1914*, 360; Steward to military secretary, June 11, 1906; military secretary to commanding general, Dept. of Texas, San Antonio, Texas, June 27, 1906, Steward Military File.

17. *The New York Times*, August 21, 1906, 2; T. G. Steward, "New Fort Brown Version," New York *Tribune*, August 26, 1906, 4.

18. *The New York Times*, August 16, 1906, 3; August 17, 1906, 1; August 18, 1906, 1; August 19, 1906, 2; August 21, 1906, 2.

19. Ibid., November 25, 1906, magazine section, 2; Steward, "New Fort Brown Version," 4; monthly chaplain report, August 1906, Steward Military File.

20. Booker T. Washington to Steward, November 10, 1906, microfilm reel 16, Booker T. Washington Papers, Library of Congress; I am grateful to Professor Louis R. Harlan for this information; Steward, "New Fort Brown Version," 4.

21. Steward, *From 1864 to 1914*, 361; Lewis N. Wynee, "Brownsville: The Reaction of the Negro Press," *Phylon* 33 (summer 1972): 153-60; "Reprieve Granted Black Soldiers After 66 Years," *Jet* 43 (October 19, 1972): 20-21.

22. Dr. W. T. Good to whom it may concern, January 10, [19]07; Steward to military secretary, January 12, 1907, January 16, 1907; special orders no. 27, paragraph 1, February 1, 1907; special orders no. 90, paragraph 12, April 17, 1907, Steward Military File; *Army and Navy Journal*, April 27, 1907, 955.

23. T. G. Steward, "Military Education Needed," Indianapolis *Freeman*, August 19, 1905, 1; William S. Scarborough, *The Educated Negro and His Mission*, occasional papers no. 8 (Washington, D.C.: American Negro Academy, 1903); Samuel R. Scottron, "Future of the Colored Man," Brooklyn *Daily Eagle*, January 25, 1901, 15 (Scottron called for business education); "Military Training in Public Schools," *Leslie's Weekly*, February 7, 1895, 82; W. E. B. Du Bois, "The Conservation of Races," occasional papers no. 2 (Washington, D.C.: American Negro Academy, 1897), as quoted in Bracey, *Black Nationalism in America*, 260-61; Booker T. Washington, "Industrial Education for Negroes," in *Negro Problem: A Series of Articles by Representative American Negroes of To-day* (New York: James Potts, 1903), in ibid., 364-66; W. E. B. Du Bois, "The Talented Tenth," ibid., 367-69.

24. T. G. Steward, "Something About Our Flag," *Alexander's Magazine* 1 (February 1906): 53-59.

25. This motto was inscribed in the inside cover of a lesson book dated January 3, 1861, T. G. Steward Papers.

CHAPTER TWELVE

1. Steward, *From 1864 to 1914*, 369-71.
2. Ibid., 365; see photograph of him in *Gouldtown*, 159.
3. *Christian Recorder*, July 18, 1907, 1.
4. Ibid., May 2, 1907, 1.
5. Ibid., June 27, 1907, 1; July 18, 1907, 1; January 2, 1908, 1; B. F. Lee, *AME Handbook* (Nashville: AME Sunday School Union, 1909), 8.
6. Richard R. Wright, "The Negroes of Xenia, Ohio: A Social Study," *Bulletin of the Bureau of Labor 48* (1903): 1006-44.
7. See Raymond Wolters, *The New Negro on Campus: Black College Rebellions of the 1902s* (Princeton: Princeton University Press, 1975).
8. *Christian Recorder*, September 5, 1907, 6; October 24, 1907, 3; *Annual Catalogue*, Wilberforce University, 1909-1910, 1912-1913, 1920-1921, 1921-1922, 1923-1924; Steward, *From 1864 to 1914*, 365, 366, 367; *Cleveland Gazette*, April 3, 1915, 3; April 29, 1922, 1; *Fifty-first Annual Report of the President, Secretary and Treasurer to the Trustees of Wilberforce University, June 16* (for period of June 1, 1913 to June 1, 1914, 3, 15.
9. This issue has been examined in recent years by *The Chronicle of Higher Education* and *Black Issues in Higher Education*. For examples, see Charles Dervarics, "Afrocentric Program Yields Academic Gains," *Black Issues in Higher Education 7* (December 6, 1990): 1, 34.
10. Wolters, *The New Negro on Campus*, 312; Frederick A. McGinnis, *A History and Interpretation of Wilberforce University* (Blanchester, Ohio: Brown Publishing Co., 1941), 170.
11. William Hannibal Thomas, *The American Negro: What He Was, What He Is, And What He May Become* (New York: Macmillan, 1901), 176-77.
12. *Chicago Defender*, May 1, 1920, 1; for restrictions in dress, speech, and travel, see *Wilberforce Bulletin* series 10, June 1925, no. 3, Annual Catalogue Edition, 1924-1925, 23; Aptheker, *Documentary History of Negro*, 3: 493-97, 564-65.
13. Steward, *From 1864 to 1914*, 367; "Debating Clubs," n.d., T. G. Steward Papers.
14. Fragmentary lecture notes, n.d.; "Notes on Teaching," October 7, 1884, T. G. Steward Papers.
15. Untitled, undated notes, T. G. Steward Papers; William A. Joiner, *A Half-Century of Freedom of the Negro in Ohio* (Wilberforce: Smith Advertising Co., [1915]), 101; T. G. Steward to Carter G. Woodson, October 11, 1922, microfilm reel 3, container 6, Carter G. Woodson Papers, Library of Congress; "How the Public Received *The Journal of Negro History*," *The Journal of Negro History* 1 (April 1916): 229.
16. *Fifty-first Annual Report of the President of Wilberforce*, 16.
17. *Wilberforce Bulletin*, June 1925, 25. The scholarship lasted until the mid-1930s.
18. *Wilberforce Annual*, 1922, 42.
19. James R. L. Diggs to W. E. B. DuBois, July 12, 1909; DuBois to Diggs, July 14, 1909, in Herbert Aptheker, ed., *The Correspondence of W. E. B. DuBois*, 3

vols. (Amherst: University of Massachusetts, 1973), 1:150-52. For a biographical sketch of Diggs, see Randall K. Burkett, ed., *Black Redemption: Churchmen Speak for the Garvey Movement* (Philadelphia: Temple University Press, 1978), 99-102; William A. Dunning, *Reconstruction, Political and Economic, 1865-1877* (New York, 1907).

20. Steward, *From 1864 to 1914*, 375, 380, 381, 383. Steward to Adjutant General (Henry P. McCain), June 21, 1909; McCain to Steward, June 23, 1909, T. G. Steward Papers.

21. Steward, *From 1864 to 1914*, 415-16.

22. Ibid., 473. E. Azalia Hackley, "How the Color Question Looks to an American in France," *AME Church Review* 23 (January 1907): 210-15.

23. Steward, *From 1864 to 1914*, 395, 417-18, 424, 430.

24. Ibid., 422, 436, 437.

25. Ibid., 461, 462, 471.

26. Ibid., 471-72, 487, 493, 500, 506; journal trip to Italy, 1909, T. G. Steward Papers.

27. Steward and Steward, *Gouldtown*, 166; Steward, *From 1864 to 1914*, 474.

28. [Theophilus] Bolden [Steward] to Dear father, April 17, 1910; Bolden to father, April 12, 1912, in T. G. Steward Papers.

29. S. M. Steward, "Colored American Women," *The Crisis* 3 (November 1911): 33-34.

30. "The Races in Congress," *The Crisis* 1 (December 1910): 17.

31. Steward, *From 1864 to 1914*, 512; see G. Spiller, ed., *Papers on Interracial Problems Communicated to the First Universal Race Congress Held at the University of London, July 26-29, 1911* (London: P. S. King, 1911).

32. *New York Age*, September 14, 1911, 7; September 28, 1911, 7.

33. Count Meynier to [Steward], November 29, 1911, T. G. Steward Papers.

34. This incident probably occurred shortly after Steward's retirement from the army because he signed the statement Chaplain USA Retired, T. G. Steward Papers.

35. David A. Gerber, *Black Ohio and the Color Line 1860-1915* (Urbana: University of Illinois Press, 1976), 44-59.

36. Ibid., 270; *New York Age*, March 13, 1913; see Tuskegee News Clipping File, reel 2, frame 0075.

37. Du Bois, *Souls of Black Folk*, 45.

38. David W. Blight, "In Search of Learning, Liberty, and Self Definition: James McCune Smith and the Ordeal of the Antebellum Black Intellectual," *Afro-Americans in New York Life and History* 9 (July 1985): 7-25.

39. T. G. Steward, "Some Glimpses of Antebellum Negro Literature," *AME Review* 22 (January 1913): 229-33.

40. "Afro-American Literature," n.d., T. G. Steward Papers; Aptheker, *Documentary History of Negro*, 3: 11, 14, 15.

41. "Gouldtown," *The Crisis* 7 (March 1914): 254; *AME Review* 30 (July 1913): 79-80; Wright, "Economic Conditions of Negroes in the North," 385-86;

Journal of Negro History 1 (April 1916): 221-22; Steward, *From 1864 to 1914*, 368; Garfield W. Steward to author, October 24, 1988.

42. Steward, "The Black St. Domingo Legion," 1-15.

43. Steward, *The Haitian Revolution*, iii-viii.

44. Theodore Lothrop Stoddard, *The French Revolution in San Domingo* (Boston: Houghton Mifflin, 1914), vii, viii-ix.

45. *AME Review* 31 (April 1915): 415-23; *Journal of Negro History* 1 (January 1916): 93.

46. C. L. R. James, *The Black Jacobins: Touissaint L'Ouverture and the San Domingo Revolution*, 2d ed. (New York: Random House, 1963); W. E. B. Du Bois, *The Gift of Black Folk: The Negroes in the Making of America* (Boston: Statford Co., 1924), 93, 154, 303.

47. T. G. Steward, "The Buy a Book Movement," *The Crisis* 11 (February 1915): 184.

48. For Ferris's comments, see Aptheker, *Documentary History of the Negro*, 3: 65-66.

49. Goldsmith, *The Deserted Village*, 24-26.

50. *The Crisis* 12 (April 1916): 303; (May 1916): 22.

51. Arthur E. Barbeau and Florette Henri, *The Unknown Soldiers: Black American Troops in World War I* (Philadelphia: Temple University Press, 1974), 12, 13, chaps. 3-8.

52. Editorial, "The Negro and the Flag," *AME Review* 30 (July 1913): 56-58.

53. B. T. Washington to Robert E. Park, August 5, 1914, August 14, 1914; to Andrew Carnegie, August 6, 1914; to John H. Harris, August 6, 1914, in Harlan, *Booker T. Washington Papers*, 13: 111, 112, 113, 116; B. T. Washington, "Inferior and Superior Races," *The North American Review* 211 (April 1915): 538-42.

54. T. G. Steward to Adjutant General, USA, April 19, 1916, Steward Military File; "How the Colored Man Sees the War," [1915-1918], T. G. Steward Papers.

55. Editorial, "A Philosophy in Time of War," *The Crisis* 16 (August 1918): 164-65.

56. Steward to editor, *The Crisis* 16 (September 1918): 219.

57. W. H. Crogman to F. J. Grimké, September 20, 1917, in Woodson, *Works of Grimké*, vol. 4, 3: 45; Editorial, " 'Fire' Du Bois," *Cleveland Gazette*, August 3, 1918, 2.

58. T. G. Steward, "War-Christmas," *The New Republic* 14 (March 9, 1918): 176.

59. W. E. B. Du Bois, "We Return Fighting," *The Crisis* 18 (May 1919): 14; Barbeau and Henri, *The Unknown Soldiers*, chap. 10.

60. *Address of Welcome Given at a Reception Tendered to the Men Who Have Returned From the Battlefield by the Men's Progressive Club of the Fifteenth Street Presbyterian Church April 24, 1919*, Francis J. Grimké Papers, box 40-6, folder 269, Moorland-Spingarn Collection.

61. T. G. Stewart [sic] to editor, *The Crisis* 19 (January 1920): 125; T. G. Steward, *Our Civilization: A Popular Lecture Delivered by Rev. T. G. Steward* (Wilberforce, 1919), 19, 21, 23-23, 26, 29.

62. "Americanization Day," *The Outlook* 110 (June 30, 1915): 485; *Record of the Proceedings of the First Universal Race Congress Held at the University of London, July 26-29, 1911* (London: P. S. King, 1911), 27.
63. Franklin K. Lane, "How to Make Americans," *The Forum* 61 (April 1919): 399-406; Gustave Miller, "Americanization of Immigrants," *The Outlook* 121 (April 16, 1919): 630-31.
64. *The Competitor* 1 (January 1920). The publication folded in 1921. I am grateful to Robert Swan for bringing this journal to my attention.
65. Steward, "The Race Issue," 6-7; T. G. Steward, "How the Colored Man Sees the War," T. G. Steward Papers.
66. Editorial, "Americanization," *The Crisis* 24 (August 1922): 154. For a representative view of white dissidents, see Sarka B. Hbrkova, " 'Bunk' in Americanization," *The Forum* 63 (April-May 1920): 428-39.
67. T. B. Moroney, "The Americanization of the Negro," *The Catholic World* 113 (August 1921): 577-84.
68. Steward, "How The Colored Man Sees The War."
69. Hallie Q. Brown, ed., *Homespun Heroines and Other Women of Distinction* (Xenia, Ohio: Aldine Publishing Co., 1926), 166-68; *New York Age*, March 16, 1918, 8; *The Crisis* 16 (May 1918): 15; Seraile, "Susan McKinney Steward," 40.

CHAPTER THIRTEEN

1. Bolden to father, December 17, 1912, T. G. Steward Papers.
2. T. G. Steward, "The White World Peril Forecasts and Facts," *AME Review* 37 (July 1920): 34-35.
3. T. G. Steward, "The Coming of the Prince," *AME Review* 37 (October 1920): 84-85.
4. T. G. Steward, "Seeing the Unseen," *AME Review* 38 (July 1921): 6-8; "Angels," ibid. 38 (January 1922): 118-22; "The Spirits of the Just," ibid. 38 (April 1922): 176-79; "Communion with Men, Angels," ibid. 39 (July 1922): 29-32; "The Activities of Departed Spirits," ibid. 39 (October 1922): 89-95.
5. "Notes on the Church," scrapbook 1922, T. G. Steward Papers.
6. T. G. Steward, "Some Vacation Notes," *Christian Recorder* (September 28, 1922), 2.
7. *Christian Recorder*, advertisement (May 11, 1922), 6; Jessie Fauset, "Review of 50 Years in the Gospel Ministry," *The Crisis* 23 (March 1922): 210
8. T. G. Steward, "My Seventy-ninth Birthday," *Christian Recorder*, April 27, 1922, 7; ibid., May 11, 1922, 7; Steward, "Some Vacation Notes," 2.
9. Frank to father, February 10, 1923, T. G. Steward Papers; for the Bruce-Lowell controversy, see *New York Age*, January 10, 1923, 1; *The Crisis* 25 (March 1923): 199, 218, 230-32; "Hamilton Fish Writes Lowell," *Amsterdam News*, January 24, 1923, 12; T. G. Steward to Frank, March 3, 1923, T. G. Steward Papers.

10. Steward to William McDougall, February 23, 1923; undated notes, T. G. Steward Papers; Steward to Frank, March 3, 1923, ibid.; William McDougall, *Is America Safe for Democracy?* (New York: Charles Scribner's Sons, 1921), 7; N. S. Shaler, *The Neighbor* (Boston, 1904), 163.
11. Steward to Frank, March 3, 1923, T. G. Steward Papers.
12. *The Crisis* 25 (March 1923): 211.
13. "The Tuskegee Hospital," *The Crisis* 26 (July 1923): 106-7; T. G. Steward to editor, ibid. 26 (October 1923): 27; see views of John E. Bruce, *Negro World* (July 21, 1923): 4; Isaac Webb to editor, *The Crisis* 26 (August 1923): 166; Wolters, *New Negro on Campus*, chap. 4.
14. "On Being Fourscore," T. G. Steward Papers; Mather, *Who's Who of the Colored Race*, 253.
15. Josephine Washington to Steward, July 8, 1923, T. G. Steward Papers.
16. Charles to Chaplain T. G. Steward, September 27, 1923; Charles to father, Thanksgiving Day [1923?].
17. Will to Theop, January 8, 1924; Frank to father, January 10, 1924, T. G. Steward Papers.
18. P. S. Hill, "A Great Man Has Fallen," *Christian Recorder* (January 24, 1924), 7; January 17, 1924, 4; *The Journal of Negro History* 9 (April 1924): 240.
19. "Manager D. M. Baxter at Chaplain Steward's Funeral," *Christian Recorder* (January 24, 1924): 7.
20. Steward, *From 1864 to 1914*, 372.

Bibliography

Books

Alexander, George. *A History of the Colored Methodist Episcopal Church South*. 12 vols. New York, 1984.

Aptheker, Herbert, ed. *A Documentary History of the Negro People in the United States*. vols. 1-3. New York, 1951-1973.

_____, ed. *The Correspondence of W. E. B. Du Bois*. 3 vols. Amherst, Mass., 1973.

Arnett, B. W., ed. *The Budget Containing the Annual Reports of the General Officers of the AME Church of the United States of America*. Dayton, Ohio, 1882.

_____. *The Centennial Budget*. Xenia, Ohio, 1880.

Barbeau, Arthur E., and Florette Henri. *The Unknown Soldiers: Black American Troops in World War I*. Philadelphia, 1974.

Bergman, Peter M. *The Chronological History of the Negro in America*. New York, 1969.

Berry, L. L. *A Century of Missions of the African Methodist Episcopal Church, 1840-1940*. New York, 1942.

Billington, Ray, ed. *The Journal of Charlotte Forten*. New York, 1953.

Bowles, John B., ed. *Master and Slaves in the House of the Lord: Race and Religion in the American South, 1740-1870*. Lexington, Ky., 1988.

Bracey, John M., August Meier, and Elliott Rudwick, eds. *Black Nationalism in America*. Indianapolis, 1970.

Broadstone, M. A. *History of Greene County, Ohio*. 2 vols. Indianapolis, 1918.

Brown, Hallie Q., ed. *Homespun Heroines and Other Women of Distinction*. Xenia, Ohio, 1926.

Buckley, Gail L. *The Hornes: The American Family*. New York, 1986.

Burkett, Randall K., ed. *Black Redemption: Churchmen Speak for the Garvey Movement*. Philadelphia, 1978.

Cashin, Herschel, et al. *Under Fire with the Tenth U.S. Cavalry*. Chicago, 1899.

Coan, Josephus R. *Daniel Alexander Payne: Christian Educator*. Philadelphia, 1935.

Coppin, Levi J. *Unwritten History*. Philadelphia, 1919.

Cromwell, John W. *The Negro in American History*. Washington, 1914.

Dabney, Lillian G. *The History of Schools for Negroes in the District of Columbia, 1817-1847*. Washington, D.C., 1949.

Drago, Edmund L. *Black Politicians and Reconstruction in Georgia: A Splendid Failure*. Baton Rouge, 1982.

Du Bois, W. E. B. *Darkwater: Voices From Within the Veil*. New York, 1920.

_____. *The Gift of Black Folk: The Negroes in the Making of America*. Boston, 1924.

_____. *The Souls of Black Folk*, New York, 1969.

Dvorak, Katherine L. *An African-American Exodus: The Segregation of the Southern Churches*. Brooklyn, 1991.

Federal Writers Project. *Delaware: A Guide to the First State*. New York, 1938.

_____. *Montana: A State Guidebook*. New York, 1939.

Foner, Eric. *Reconstruction: America's Unfinished Revolution, 1863-1877*. New York, 1988.

Foner, Philip S. *Frederick Douglass*. New York, 1964.

_____, ed. *The Voice of Black America: Major Speeches by Negroes in the United States, 1797-1971*. New York, 1972.

Fowler, Arlen L. *The Black Infantry in the West*. Westport, Conn., 1971.

Franklin, Vincent P. *The Education of Black Philadelphia: The Social and Educational History of a Minority Community, 1900-1950*. Philadelphia, 1979.

Franklin, Vincent P., and James D. Anderson, eds. *New Perspectives on Black Educational History*. Boston, 1978.

Frazier, E. Franklin. *The Black Bourgeoise: The Rise of a New Middle Class*. New York, 1959.

Gaines, Wesley J. *African Methodism in the South: Twenty-five Years of Freedom*. Atlanta, 1890.

Gatewood, William B. *Aristocrats of Color: The Black Elite, 1880-1920*. Bloomington, 1990.

_____, ed. *"Smoked Yankees" and the Struggle for Empire: Letters from Negro Soldiers, 1898-1902*. Urbana, 1971.

Gerber, David A. *Black Ohio and the Color Line, 1860-1915.* Urbana, 1976.

Graham, Leroy. *Baltimore: The Nineteenth-Century Black Capitol.* Washington, D.C., 1982.

Grossman, Lawrence. *The Democratic Party and the Negro: Northern and National Politics, 1868-1892.* Urbana, 1976.

Hamilton, James M. *From Wilderness to Statehood: A History of Montana, 1805-1900.* Portland, Ore., 1957.

Handy, James A. *Scraps of AME Church History.* Philadelphia, 1901.

Harlan, Louis R., ed. *The Booker T. Washington Papers.* 13 vols. Urbana, 1972-84.

Hawkins, Hugh, ed. *Booker T. Washington and His Critics: Black Leadership in Crisis.* 2d ed. Lexington, Mass., 1974.

Hodges, George W. *Early Negro Church Life in New York.* New York, 1945.

James, C. L. R. *The Black Jacobins: Touissaint L'Ouverture and the San Domingo Revolution.* 2d ed. New York, 1963.

Jenifer, John. *A Centennial Retrospect: History of the African Methodist Episcopal Church.* Nashville, 1916.

Johnson, Edward A. *A School History of the Negro Race in America From 1619 to 1891.* New York, 1891.

_____. *History of Negro Soldiers in the Spanish-American War.* Raleigh, 1899.

Joiner, William A. *A Half-Century of Freedom of the Negro in Ohio.* Wilberforce, Ohio, [1915].

Jones, Jacqueline. *Soldiers of Light and Love: Northern Teachers and Georgia Blacks, 1867-1873.* Chapel Hill, 1980.

Jordan, Amos. *Compiled History of the African Wesleyan Methodist Church.* New York, 1973.

Killian, Charles A., ed. *Sermons and Addresses, 1853-1891 by Daniel A. Payne.* New York, 1972.

Lane, Ann J. *The Brownsville Affair: National Crisis and Black Reaction.* Port Washington, N.Y., 1971.

Lane, Roger. *Roots of Violence in Black Philadelphia, 1860-1900.* Cambridge, Mass., 1986.

Lee, B. F. *AME Handbook.* Nashville, 1909.

Logan, Rayford. *Betrayal of the Negro: From Rutherford B. Hayes to Woodrow Wilson.* Rev. ed. New York, 1954.

Loggins, Vernon. *The Negro Author: His Development in America.* New York, 1931.

Lothrop, Theodore. *The French Revolution in San Domingo*. Boston, 1914.

Lynch, John R. *Some Historical Errors of James Ford Rhodes*. Boston, 1923.

Mabee, Carlton. *Black Education in New York State*. Syracuse, 1979.

Mather, Frank L., ed. *Who's Who of the Colored Race*. Vol. 1. Chicago, 1915.

McDougall, William. *Is America Safe for Democracy?* New York, 1921.

McGinnis, Frederick A. *A History and Interpretation of Wilberforce University*. Blanchester, Ohio, 1941.

Moore, John H., ed. *The Juhl Letters to the Charleston Courier: A View of the South, 1865-1871*. Athens, Ga., 1974.

Morris, Robert, ed. *Freedman's Schools and Textbooks*, 2 vols. *Semi-Annual Report on Schools for Freedmen by John W. Alvord, Numbers 1-10, January 1866-July 1870*. New York, 1980.

_____. *Reading, 'Riting, and Reconstruction: The Education of Freedmen in the South, 1861-1870*. Chicago, 1981.

Morrow, Ralph E. *Northern Methodism and Reconstruction*. East Lansing, Mich., 1956.

Moss, Alfred A., Jr. *The American Negro Academy: Voice of the Talented Tenth*. Baton Rouge, 1981.

Mossell, N. F. *The Work of Afro-American Woman*. Philadelphia, 1908.

Nankivell, John H. *History of the Twenty-fifth Regiment United States Army, 1869-1926*. Denver, 1927.

Nathans, Elizabeth S. *Losing the Peace: Georgia Republicans and Reconstruction, 1865-1871*. Baton Rouge, 1968.

Negro Problem: A Series of Articles by Representative American Negroes of Today. New York, 1903.

Payne, Daniel A. *History of the African Methodist Episcopal Church*. Philadelphia, 1891.

_____. *Recollections of Seventy Years*. New York, 1968.

_____. *The African M. E. Church in its Relation to the Freedmen Before the Society for the Promotion of Collegiate and Theological Education of the West Marietta, Ohio, November 7, 1868*.

Perkins, Linda M. *Fanny Jackson Coppin and the Institute for Colored Youth, 1865-1902*. New York, 1987.

Philipps, C. H. *The History of the Colored Methodist Episcopal Church in America*. Jackson, Tenn., 1898.

Ponton, M. M. *Life and Times of Henry M. Turner*. Atlanta, 1917.

Powell, A. Clayton. *Patriotism and the Negro*. New York, 1918.

Price, Clement Alexander, comp. and ed. *Freedom Not Distant: A Documentary History of Afro-Americans in New Jersey.* Newark, 1980.

Redkey, Edwin S. *Black Exodus: Black Nationalist and Back-to-Africa Movements, 1890-1910.* New Haven, 1969.

Richardson, Joe M. *Christian Reconstruction: The American Missionary Association and Southern Blacks, 1861-1890.* Athens, Ga., 1986.

Savage, W. Sherman. *Blacks in the West.* Westport, Conn., 1976.

Schor, Joel. *Henry Highland Garnet.* Westport, Conn., 1977.

The Scriptural Means of Producing an Immediate Revival of Pure Christianity in the Ministry and Laity of Our Church. Philadelphia, 1881.

Simmons, William J. *Men of Mark, Eminent, Progressive and Rising.* Chicago, 1970.

Singleton, George A. *The Romance of African Methodism: A Study of the African Methodist Episcopal Church.* New York, 1952.

Smith, Charles S. *A History of the African Methodist Episcopal Church.* Philadelphia, 1922.

Spiller, G., ed. *Papers on Interracial Problems Communicated to the First Universal Race Congress Held at the University of London, July 26-29, 1911.* London, 1911.

Steward, S. Maria. *Women in Medicine.* Wilberforce, 1914.

Steward, T. G. *A Charleston Love Story, or Hortense Vanross.* London, 1899.

_____. *Death, Hades and the Resurrection.* Philadelphia, 1883.

_____. *From 1864 to 1914: Fifty Years in the Gospel Ministry.* Philadelphia, 1921.

_____. *Genesis Re-read or the Latest Conclusion of Physical Science Viewed in Their Relation to the Mosaic Record.* Philadelphia, 1885.

_____. *Memoirs of Mrs. Rebecca Steward.* Philadelphia, 1877.

_____. *My First Four Years in the Itineracy of the African Methodist Episcopal Church,* Brooklyn, 1876.

_____. *Our Civilization: A Popular Lecture Delivered by Rev. T. G. Steward.* Wilberforce, 1919.

_____. *Pioneer Echoes, Six Special Sermons: Five of Which Were Preached in South Carolina and Georgia From 1866 to 1871.* Baltimore, 1889.

_____. *The Colored Regulars.* Philadelphia, 1904.

_____. *The End of the World; or, Clearing the Way for the Fullness of the Gentiles.* Philadelphia, 1888.

_____. *The Haitian Revolution, 1791 to 1804; or Sidelights on the French Revolution.* New York, 1914.

_____. *The Incarnation of the Son of God. Annual Sermon Preached at Wilberforce University, June 13, 1880.* Philadelphia, 1881.

Steward, William, and T. G. Steward. *Gouldtown, A Very Remarkable Settlement of Ancient Date.* Philadelphia, 1913.

Strong, Josiah. *Our Country: Its Possible Future and Its Present Crisis.* New York, 1885.

Swint, Henry L. *The Northern Teacher in the South, 1862-1870.* Nashville, 1941.

Tanner, Benjamin T. *An Apology for African Methodism.* Baltimore, 1867.

_____. *An Outline of Our History and Government for African Methodist Churchmen Ministerial and Lay.* Philadelphia, 1884.

Taylor, Alrutheus A. *The Negro in South Carolina During the Reconstruction.* Washington, D.C., 1924.

Thomas, William Hannibal. *The American Negro: What He Was, What He Is, and What He May Become.* New York, 1901.

Thornbrough, Emma Lou. *T. Thomas Fortune: Militant Journalist.* Chicago, 1972.

Turner, Henry M. *The Genesis and Theory of Methodist Polity, or the Machinery of Methodism.* Philadelphia, 1885.

Walker, Clarence E. *A Rock in a Weary Land: The African Methodist Episcopal Church During the Civil War and Reconstruction.* Baton Rouge, 1982.

Wayman, Alexander W. *Cyclopedia of African Methodism.* Baltimore, 1882.

_____. *My Recollections of AME Ministers or Forty Years' Experience in the AME Church.* Philadelphia, 1881.

Weaver, John D. *The Brownsville Raid.* New York, 1970.

Winch, Julie. *Philadelphia's Black Elite: Activism, Accommodation and the Struggle for Autonomy, 1787-1848.* Philadelphia, 1988.

Wolters, Raymond. *The New Negro on Campus: Black College Rebellions of the 1920s.* Princeton, 1975.

Woodson, Carter G. *The Education of Negroes Prior to 1861.* New Yori, 1968.

_____, ed. *The Works of Francis J. Grimké.* 4 vols. Washington, D.C., 1942.

Wright, Giles R. *Afro-Americans in New Jersey: Short History.* Trenton, 1980.

Articles

"Americanization." *The Crisis* 24 (August 1922): 154.

"Americanization Day." *The Outlook* 110 (June 30, 1915): 485.

"A Philosophy in Time of War." *The Crisis* 16 (August 1918): 164-65.

Bateman, Cephas C. "A Group of Army Authors." *The Californian* 4 (October 1893): 684-93.

Batten, J. M. "Henry M. Turner: Negro Bishops Extraordinary." *Church History* 7 (March 1930): 231-32.

Blight, David W. "In Search of Learning, Liberty, and Self Definition: James McCune Smith and the Ordeal of the Antebellum Black Intellectual." *Afro-Americans in New York Life and History* 9 (July 1985): 7-25.

Brewe, H. Peers. "The Protestant Episcopal Freedmen's Commission, 1865-1870." *Historical Magazine of the Protestant Episcopal Church* 26 (1967): 361-81.

Brunton, T. Lander. "Review of *The Bible and Science.*" *The Catholic World* 34 (October 1881): 143-44.

Buecker, Thomas R. "Fort Niobrara, 1880-1906: Guardian of the Rosebud Sioux," *Nebraska History* 65 (fall 1984): 302-25.

Burt, Andrew S. "The Negro as a Soldier." *The Crisis* 1 (February 1911): 23-25.

Butchart, Ronald E. " 'We Best Can Instruct Our Own People': New York African Americans in the Freedmen's Schools, 1861-1875." *Afro-Americans in New York Life and History* 12 (January 1988): 27-50.

"The Colored Regulars in the United States." *Alexander's Magazine* 1 (December 1905): 46-49.

Cullen, Countee. "Dad." *The Crisis* 25 (November 1927): 26.

Davis, Mrs. Jefferson. "The White Man's Problem: Why We Do Not Want the Philippines." *The Arena* 23 (January 1900): 1-4.

"The Democratic Return to Power—Its Effect?" *A.M.E. Church Review* 1 (July 1884): 213-50.

Dervarics, Charles. "Afrocentric Program Yields Academic Gains." *Black Issues in Higher Education* 7 (December 6, 1990): 1, 34.

Dodson, Jualynne. "Nineteenth-Century AME Preaching Women." In Darlene C. Hine, *Black Women in United States History.* Brooklyn, 1990, 1: 333-49.

Du Bois, W. E. B. "We Return Fighting." *The Crisis* 18 (May 1919): 14.

Duffin, Sallie L. "The Freedmen." *The Missionary Record of the AME Church* 1 (July 1867): 5.

Fauset, Jessie. "Review of 50 Years in the Gospel Ministry." *The Crisis* 23 (March 1922): 210.

Fortune, T. Thomas. "A Social Study of the Filipino." *The Voice of the Negro* 1 (March 1922): 210.

_____. "The Filipino." *The Voice of the Negro* 1 (May 1904): 199-203.

_____. "The Filipino—Across Luzon." *The Voice of the Negro* 1 (October 1904): 482-85.

Franklin, Vincent P. "In Pursuit of Freedom: The Educational Activities of Black Social Organizations in Philadelphia, 1900-1930." In Franklin and Anderson, *New Perspectives*, 113-28.

Gardner, Bettye. "Antebellum Black Education in Baltimore." *Maryland Historical Magazine* 71 (fall 1976): 360-66.

"Genesis Reread." *A.M.E. Church Review* 2 (April 1886): 235-36.

"Gouldtown." *The Crisis* 7 (March 1914): 254.

Grimké, Francis J. "Colored Men as Professors in Colored Institutions." *A.M.E. Church Review* 4 (July 1885): 142-49.

Hancock, Harold B. "The Status of the Negro in Delaware After the Civil War." *Delaware History* 13 (April 1968): 57-66.

Hbrkova, Sarka B. " 'Bunk' in Americanization." *The Forum* 63 (April-May 1920): 428-39.

"How the Public Received the *Journal of Negro History*." *Journal of Negro History* 1 (April 1916): 229.

Keating, H. T. "The Twenty-fifth As Seen in History." *A.M.E. Church Review* 23 (April 1907): 318-26.

Killian, Charles. "Daniel A. Payne and the AME General Conference of 1888: A Display of Contrasts." *A.M.E. Church Review* 103 (April-June 1888): 9-16.

Lane, Franklin K. "How to Make Americans." *The Forum* 61 (April 1919): 399-406.

"The Lees from Gouldtown." *Negro History Bulletin* 10 (February 1947): 99-100, 108, 119.

Lewis, Ronald L. "Reverend T. G. Steward and the Education of Blacks in Reconstruction Delaware." *Delaware History* 19 (spring-summer 1981): 156-78.

Mabee, Carlton. "A List of the First Black Schools in New York State From Colonial Times to 1945." *Afro-Americans in New York Life and History* 2 (July 1978): 9-14.

Marshall, George A. "The Army Canteen." *The Arena* 25 (March 1901): 300-307.

Meier, August. "Booker T. Washington and the 'Talented Tenth.' " In Hawkins, *Washington and His Critics*, 127-38.

Miller, Gustave. "Americanization of Immigrants." *The Outlook* 121 (April 16, 1919): 630-31.

Moroney, T. B. "The Americanization of the Negro." *The Catholic World* 113 (August 1921): 577-84.

Moton, R. R. "The American Negro and the World War." *The World's Work* 36 (May 1918): 74-77.

"The Negro and the Flag." *A.M.E. Review* 30 (July 1913): 356-58.

"Our Book Talk." *A.M.E. Church Review* 1 (July 1884): 77.

Pace, Harry H. "The Philippine Islands and the American Negro." *The Voice of the Negro* 1 (October 1904): 482-85.

Pamphile, Leon D. "The NAACP and the American Occupation of Haiti." *Phylon* 47 (March 1986): 91-100.

Perkins, Linda M. "Quaker Beneficence and Black Control: The Institute for Colored Youth, 1852-1903." In Franklin and Anderson, *New Perspectives*, 19-43.

_____. "The Black Female American Missionary Association Teacher in the South, 1861-1870." In Hine, *Black Women in United States History*, 3: 1049-63.

Quinn, Edythe A. " 'The Hills' in Mid-Nineteenth Century: The History of a Rural Afro-American Community in Westchester County, New York." *Afro-Americans in New York Life and History* 14 (July 1990): 35-50.

"The Races in Congress." *The Crisis* 1 (December 1910): 17.

"Reprieve Granted Black Soldiers After 66 Years." *Jet* 43 (October 19, 1972): 20-21.

Schubert, Frank N. "Theophilus Gould Steward." In Rayford W. Logan and Michael R. Winston, eds. *Dictionary of American Negro Biography*. New York, 1982, 570-71.

Schuyler, Michael W. "The Ku Klux Klan in Nebraska." *Nebraska History* 66 (fall 1985): 224-56.

Searle, George M. "The Supposed Issue Between Religion and Science." *The Catholic World* 38 (February 1884): 577-88.

Seraile, William. "Henrietta Vinton Davis and the Garvey Movement." *Afro-Americans in New York Life and History* 7 (July 1983): 7-24.

_____. "Afro-American Emigration to Haiti During the American Civil War." *The Americas* 35 (October 1978): 185-200.

_____. "Susan McKinney Steward: New York State's First African American Female Physician." *Afro-Americans in New York Life and History* 9 (July 1985): 27-44.

_____. "Timothy Thomas Fortune: Father of Black Political Independence." *Afro-Americans in New York Life and History* 2 (July 1978): 15-28.

Simpson, John T. "The Colored Regulars in the U.S. Army." *The Colored American Magazine* 3 (June 1905): 299-303.

Slattery, John H. "Twenty Years Growth of the Colored People in Baltimore, Md.," *The Catholic World* 66 (January 1898): 519-27.

Steward, Gustavus A. "The Church of My Fathers." *The Crisis* 39 (July 1932): 220-21, 36.

Steward, S. M. "Colored American Women." *The Crisis* 3 (November 1911): 33-34.

Steward, T. G. "A Glimpse of Montana Life." *The Independent* (August 22, 1895): 1150-51.

_____. "A New Reading of an Old Phase: the End of the World." *A.M.E. Church Review* 5 (January 1889): 204-9.

_____. "A Plea for Patriotism." *The Independent* (September 29, 1898): 887-88.

_____. "Angels." *A.M.E. Review* 38 (January 1922): 118-22.

_____. "Camp Life at Chickamauga." *The Independent* (May 12, 1898): 614.

_____. "Communion With Men, Angels." *A.M.E. Review* 39 (July 1922): 29-32.

_____. "Colonel George L. Andrews." *Harper's Weekly* (May 7, 1892): 437.

_____. "Cultured Society and the Negro." *The Independent* (April 16, 1896): 514.

_____. "In Luzon." *The Independent* (February 1, 1900): 312-14.

_____. "Ira Aldridge: A Great American Negro Orator of the Past Century." *A.M.E. Review* 22 (October 1912): 113-17.

_____. "Negro Mortality." *Social Economist* 9 (October 1895): 204-7.

_____. "Ripeness in the Gospel Ministry." *A.M.E. Church Review* 1 (July 1884): 66-68.

_____. "Seeing the Unseen." *A.M.E. Review* 38 (July 1921): 6-8.

_____. "Some Glimpses of Antebellum Negro Literature." *A.M.E. Review* 22 (January 1913): 229-33.

_____. "Something About Our Flag." *Alexander's Magazine* 1 (February 1906): 53-59.

_____. "The Activities of Departed Spirits." *A.M.E. Review* 39 (October 1922): 89-95.

_____. "The Buy a Book Movement." *The Crisis* 11 (February 1915): 184.

_____. "The Canteen in the Army." *Harper's Weekly* (April 9, 1892): 350-51.

_____. "The Colored American as a Soldier." *The United States Service* 11 (April 1894): 323-27.

_____. "The Coming of the Prince." *A.M.E. Review* 37 (October 1920): 84-85.

_____. "The Doctrine of the Incarnation Stated." *A.M.E. Church Review* 10 (January 1893): 214-23.

_____. "The First Move in the War." *The Independent* (April 28, 1898): 535-36.

_____. "The Morals of the Army." *The Independent* (February 11, 1892): 195.

_____. "The New Colored Soldier." *The Independent* (June 16, 1898): 781-82.

_____. "The Old and New Commandments; or, Brotherhood in Creation and Brotherhood in Christ Compared." *A.M.E. Church Review* 6 (January 1890): 306-8.

_____. "The Race Issue, so-called, A Social Matter Only." *The Competitor* 1 (March 1920: 6-7.

_____. "The Reign of the Mob." *The Independent* (May 11, 1899): 1296-97.

_____. "The Spirits of the Just." *A.M.E. Review* 38 (April 1922): 176-79.

_____. "The White World Peril Forecasts and Facts." *A.M.E. Review* 37 (July 1920): 34-35.

_____. "Two Kinds of 'Fogy.' " *The Independent* (September 16, 1897): 1198-99.

_____. "Two Years in Luzon." *The Colored American Magazine* 4 (November 1901): 4-10; 4 (January/February 1902): 162-67; 5 (August 1902): 244-49.

_____. "War-Christmas." *The New Republic* 14 (March 9, 1918): 176.

Swan, Robert. "Did Brooklyn (N.Y.) Blacks Have Unusual Control Over Their Schools? Period 1: 1815-1845." *Afro-Americans in New York Life and History* 7 (July 1983): 25-46.

Thomas, Bettye C. "Public Education and Black Protest in Baltimore, 1865-1900." *Maryland Historical Magazine* 71 (fall 1976): 381-91.

Thornbrough, Emma L. "Booker T. Washington As Seen By His Contemporaries." *Journal of Negro History* 53 (April 1968): 161-81.

"The Tuskegee Hospital." *The Crisis* 1 (December 1910): 17.

Washington, B. T. "Inferior and Superior Races." *The North American Review* 211 (April 1915): 538-42.

Wears, Isiah C. "Rev. Theophilus Gould Steward." *A.M.E. Church Review* 10 (July 1893): 137-40.

White, Arthur O. "The Black Movement Against Jim Crow Education in Buffalo, New York, 1800-1900." *Phylon* 30 (winter 1969): 375-93.

Wright, Richard. "The Economic Conditions of Negroes in the North, III, Negro Communities in New Jersey." *The Southern Workman* 37 (July 1908): 385-93.

_____. "The Negroes of Xenia, Ohio: A Social Study." *Bulletin of the Bureau of Labor* 48 (1903): 1006-44.

Wynee, Lewis N. "Brownsville: The Reaction of the Negro Press." *Phylon* 33 (summer 1972): 153-60.

Dissertations

DeBoer, Clara. "The Role of Afro-Americans in the Origin and Work of the American Missionary Association, 1839-1877." Rutgers University, 1973.

Grayson, John T. "Frederick Douglass' Intellectual Development: His Concepts of God, Man, and Nature in Light of American and European Influences." Columbia University, 1981.

Kennedy, Philip W. "The Concept of Racial Superiority and United States Imperialism, 1890-1910." St. Louis University, 1962.

Killian, Charles. "Daniel A. Payne: Black Spokesman for Reform." Indiana University, 1971.

Morrow, Ralph E. "The Methodist Episcopal Church, The South, and Reconstruction, 1865-1880." Indiana University, 1954.
Powers, Bernard E., Jr. "Black Charleston: A Social History, 1822-1885." Northwestern University, 1982.
Stokes, Arthur P. "Daniel A. Payne: Churchman and Educator." Ohio State University, 1973.
Wills, David W. "Aspects of Social Thought in the African Methodist Episcopal Church, 1884-1910." Harvard University, 1975.

Manuscript Collections

American Missionary Association Papers, Schomburg Center for Research in Black Culture, New York Public Library, New York City.
Black Abolitionist Papers, Schomburg Center.
Correspondence of James Redpath, Commercial Agent of Hayti for Philadelphia, Joint Plenipotentiary of Hayti to the Government of the U.S. and Gen. Agent of Emigration to Hayti for the U.S. and Canada December 31, 1861 to May 12, 1862, Schomburg Center.
Frederick Douglass Papers, Library of Congress, Washington, D.C.
Francis J. Grimké Papers, Moorland-Spingarn Research Center.
Gustavus A. Steward Papers, in possession of his daughter, Anna Steward Bishop, Columbus, Ohio.
Theophilus G. Steward Papers, Schomburg Center.
Monroe Trotter/Guardian Papers, Boston University, Boston, Massachusetts.
Booker T. Washington Papers, Library of Congress.
Harry A. Williamson Papers, Schomburg Center.
Carter G. Woodson Papers, Library of Congress.

Published Papers

Crummell, Alexander. *"The Attitude of the American Mind Toward the Negro Intellect." American Negro Academy occasional papers no. 3.* Washington, D.C., 1898.
Du Bois, W. E. B. *"The Conservation of Races." American Negro Academy occasional papers no. 2.* Washington, D.C., 1897.

Scarborough, William S. *"The Educated Negro and His Mission." American Negro Academy occasional papers no. 8.* Washington, D.C., 1903.
Steward, T. G. *"How the Black St. Domingo Legion Saved the Patriot Army in the Siege of Savannah, 1779." American Negro Academy occasional papers no. 5.* Washington, D.C., 1899.

Unpublished Papers

"Afro-American Literature," n.d. T. G. Steward Papers.
"Debating Club." n.d. T. G. Steward papers
Diary of T. G. Steward, 1876, 1895, 1900, 1901. T. G. Steward Papers.
"How the Colored Man Sees the War." n.d. T. G. Steward Papers.
Journal of T. G. Steward, 1867-1868. T. G. Steward Papers.
Journal of T. G. Steward (strictly private), 1868-69. T. G. Steward Papers.
Journal of the Voyage From New York to Port-au-Prince, June 5-July 19, 1873. T. G. Steward Papers.
"Notes on Teaching," n.d. T. G. Steward Papers.
"On Being Fourscore," n.d. T. G. Steward Papers.
Steward, G. A. "Why I was Not Ordained by a Theological Derelict," n.d. G. A. Steward Papers.
_____. "Six Months in the Uplift," n.d. G. A. Steward Papers.
Steward, T. G. "The Last of Ninety-nine," [1899]. T. G. Steward Papers.

Proceedings

Arnett, B. W., ed. *Proceedings of the Quartocentennial Conference of the African Methodist Episcopal Church of South Carolina at Charleston, May 15, 16, 17, 1889* [1890].
"Mortality Among Negroes in Cities." *Proceedings of the Conference for Investigation of City Problems Held at Atlanta University.* No. 1, 21-22.
Proceedings of the Second Ecumenical Methodist Conference Held in the Metropolitan Methodist Episcopal Church, Washington, October 1891.
Proceedings of the Southern State Convention of Colored Men Held in Columbia, S.C., Commencing October 18th—Ending October 25th, 1871.
Records of the Proceedings of the First Race Universal Congress Held at the University of London, July 26-29, 1911.

Reports

Annual Report of the War Department for the Fiscal Year Ending June 30, 1900, vol. II. Report of the Military Governor of the Philippine Islands on Civil Affairs. Washington, D.C.: GPO, 1900.

Annual Report for the War Department for the Fiscal Year Ending June 30, 1901. Report of the Philippine Commission in Two Parts. Washington, D.C.: GPO, 1901.

Fifty-first Annual Report of the President, Secretary and Treasurer to the Trustees of Wilberforce University, June 16, 1914 (for the period of June 1, 1913 to June 1, 1914.

Nineteenth Annual Report of the Superintendent of Public Instruction of the City of Brooklyn for the year Ending December 31, 1873.

Report of the Delaware Association for the Moral Improvement and Education of the Colored People of the State. Wilmington: Jenkins & Atkinson, 1868.

"Social and Physical Conditions of Negroes in Cities." Report of an Investigation Under the Direction of Atlanta University and Proceedings of the Second Conference for the Study of Problems Concerning Negro City life at Atlanta University, May 25-26, 1897. Atlanta University Publication no. 2, 1897.

Thirty-second Annual Report of Education of the City . . . of New York for the Year Ending December 31, 1873.

Thirty-fourth Annual Report of Education of the City . . . of New York for the Year Ending December 31, 1875.

Government Documents

Census of the State of New York for 1875.

Indexes and Register, 12, January-June 1868. Register and Letters Received by the Commissioner of the Bureau of Refugees, Freedmen and Abandoned Land, 1865-1872. Record Group 105, National Archives.

Letters Received April-August 1868. Records of the Assistant Commissioner for the State of Georgia Bureau of Refugees, Freedmen and Abandoned Land. Record Group 105, National Archives.

Military File of Frank Rudolph Steward. Adjutant General Office, Record Group 94, National Archives.

Military File of Theophilus Gould Steward. Adjutant General Office, Record Group 94, National Archives.
Pension Record of Frank Rudolph Steward, Office of the Veterans Administration.
Record of Deeds, vols. 185, 202. Cumberland County Court House, Bridgeton, N.J.
United States Census of Population for the Year 1870.
United States Census of Population for the Year 1890.

Newspapers

Afro-American Sentinel (Omaha, Nebraska)
Amsterdam News
Army and Navy Journal (Washington, D.C.)
Broad Ax (Chicago)
Brooklyn (N.Y.) *Daily Eagle*
Chicago Defender
Christian Recorder (Philadelphia)
Cleveland Gazette
Colored American (Washington, D.C.)
Dollar Weekly News (Bridgeton, N.J.)
The Freeman (Indianapolis)
Illinois Record
Indianapolis News
Indianapolis Sentinel
Leslie's Weekly (New York)
Manila Times (Philippines)
Memphis Scimitar
Morning News (Wilmington, Delaware)
National Leader (Washington, D.C.)
Negro World (New York)
New National Era and Citizen (Washington, D.C.)
New York Age
New York Freeman
New York Globe
The New York Times
New York Tribune

New York World
Ohio Standard and Observer
People's Advocate (Washington, D.C.)
Philadelphia Press
State Capitol (Springfield, Illinois)
State Journal (Harrisburg, Pennsylvania)
Valentine Democrat (Nebraska)
Washington Bee
Washington Republican
Wilmington Commercial (Delaware)

Church Records

The African Wesleyan Methodist Episcopal Church 146th Anniversary Commemorative Journal 1818-1964. Brooklyn, 1964.
Illustrated New York and Brooklyn Churches. New York, 1874.
Journal of the Twenty-seventh Quadrennial Session of the General Conference of the AME Church Held in Louisville, Kentucky May 5th-21st, 1924. Philadelphia, 1924.
Siloam Presbyterian Church. Brooklyn, N.Y., Semicentennial, May 21st to July 25th, 1899. Brooklyn, 1899.
Union Bethel-Metropolitan AME Church Record. Minutes of the Official Board, November 21, 1894-November 12, 1901. Moorland-Spingarn Research Center, Howard University.

Directories

Brooklyn City and Business Directory for the Year 1873/1874.
Directory of the District of Columbia, 1887.
Gopsill's Philadelphia City Directory for 1878, 1879, 1880.

Bulletins and Catalogs

Alumni List. *The Bulletin of the Divinity School of the Protestant Episcopal Church in Philadelphia*. Vol. 9, March 1923.

Annual Catalogue, Wilberforce University, 1909-1910, 1912-1913, 1920-1921, 1921-1922, 1923-1924.

Wilberforce Bulletin. Series 10, June 1925, no. 3. *Annual Catalogue Edition 1924-1925.*

Memorial

Memorial of the National Convention of Colored Persons Held in Washington, D.C., December 19, 1873.

Index

Abolition, 7
Adams, E. J., 28
Adams, Elizabeth, 1
The African Abroad (William H. Ferris), 167
African-Americans
    and Americanization, 170, 172-73
    and black colleges, 159, 159-60
    in Brooklyn, N.Y., 59-62, 65, 196n
    career opportunities denied to, 7
    class conflict among, 60-62
    class differences in relations with whites,
        125-26
    condemn Theodore Roosevelt for
        discharging black soldiers, 153
    in Delaware, 46-48, 55-56, 57, 79-80
    denied dormitory space at Harvard
        University, 177
    disfranchised in Delaware, 47
    dissatisfaction with Republican Party, 69,
        85-87
    dual identity of, 164
    education of, 4-5, 46-48, 55, 64-65, 71,
        73, 75, 79-80, 102-4
    and emigration to Haiti, 193n
    and emigration to the Philippines, 134,
        136-44
    and end of Reconstruction, 69
    establish black-controlled hospital, 105
    and freedmen, 11, 13-19
    as future world leaders, 90-91
    in Georgia, 27-28, 30-32, 37, 41
    health of, 123
    and housing discrimination in Brooklyn,
        N.Y., 59
    industrial exhibitions of, 104

leave white churches in Charleston, S.C.,
    11-12
literary associations of, 98
literature of, 164-65, 166-67
    and lynching, 167
    and migration to Africa, 28, 73, 107
    and military education, 154-55
    in Montana, 111-13, 116-20, 122-27, 152
    music of, 57
    in New Jersey, 1-2
    in North, 144
    as police officers in Philadelphia, 86
    and race riots of 1919, 169-70
    reform activity of, 70-71
    religious practices of, 23
    and school segregation in Brooklyn, N.Y.,
        65
    self-labeling of, 173
    sexuality stereotypes of, 159
    skin color and social tensions among, 18,
        22, 29
    in South, 106, 125, 134
    and Spanish-American War, 126, 129,
        131, 134
    Theophilus Gould Steward on status of,
        61-62
    Theophilus Gould Steward urges more
        support for black authors from, 166-67
    in U.S. Army, 112-13, 116-20, 122-38,
        147-55, 167-69, 170
    and U.S. government segregation, 179
    urged to support World War I, 167-69
    See also Freedmen; Integration; Segrega-
        tion
African Methodist Episcopal Church

237

Annual Conference of (1882), 78
and Baptist Church, 25
bishops disagree over missions secretary,
105-6
bishop selection process of, 98-99
bishops' powers attacked, 73-74
and British Methodist Episcopal Church,
100, 191n
criticism of poor education of Southern
clergy, 107-9
denounces Booker T. Washington, 205n
and disputed church ownership, 34-39
educational activities of, 63-64
and financing for Washington Metropolitan African Methodist Episcopal
Church, 93-95, 100
foreign missionary work of, 73, 148
and freedmen's aid, 9-24
General Conference of (1868), 34, 74-75,
100, 105
in Georgia, 33, 35-38, 39, 41, 78
in Haiti, 49-51, 53-55
leading ministers rated by A. J. Kershaw,
101
and Methodist Episcopal Church, 55-56,
64
and Methodist Episcopal Church, North,
35
and Methodist Episcopal Church, South,
12
ministerial transfers within, 41, 45-46
missionary activities of, xiii
money allocation of, 75
opposes school segregation, 73
ordination of ministers in, 7
in Philadelphia, 67, 69-75, 80-83, 92
proposed restructuring of services in,
43-44
and racism, 106
ritualism in services of, 100-102
in South, 106
in South Carolina, 10-24
Sunday School changes in, 84-85
tensions in, 35-37
theological training of ministers, 40
theology of, 25, 176
Theophilus Gould Steward and, 83,
157-58, 163

and Theophilus Gould Steward's theology,
88, 88-91
urges blacks to fight in World War I, 168
women's rights debated in, 40
Aged Minister Association, 105
Aguinaldo, Emilo, 142
Alger, Russell, 135
Allen, Richard, 57, 63-64, 102, 164
Allensworth, Allen, 113, 130
"The AME Church and Its Relationship to
the Elevation of the Race" (Theophilus
Gould Steward), 98
American Anti-Slavery Society, 96
American Colonization Society, 28
American Equal Rights Association, 40
American Freedmen's Union Commission, 14
Americanization, 170, 172-73
American Missionary Association, 23
elitism of freedmen's teachers from, 29-30
and freedmen's aid, 9-11
and freedmen's schools in Georgia, 27-28
teachers, 13-19
American Negro Academy, xiii, 126, 136,
155, 166, 169
Americus, Ga., 17-19, 29, 31
Anderson, Matilda C., 14
Andrews, Colonel, 113, 116
Armstrong, Esther, 43
Army, U.S.
black troops in, 112-13, 116, 126, 153
complies with anticanteen laws on military
bases, 148
conducts inquiry into Brownsville, Texas,
race riot, 153
denies promotion to Theophilus Gould
Steward, 150-51
racism in, 124-25, 131, 132-33, 137-38,
168, 170
troops used as strikebreakers, 123
See also Colored Infantry, U.S.
"The Army as a Trained Force" (Theophilus
Gould Steward), 151
Arnett, Benjamin W., 53, 88, 100, 135
Arthur, Chester A., 86
Association for the Study of Negro Life and
History, 160-61
Augusta, Ga., 29

Bainbridge, Ga., 27
Baldwin's Readers, 141
Baltimore, Md.
  Bethel African Methodist Episcopal Church in, 99, 102, 104, 106-7
  black education in, 102-4
  Democrats rampage in, 87
  Industrial Exhibition (1888), 104
  Providence Hospital in, 105
  race relations in, 99
  Waters Chapel in, 109
Baltimore Association for the Moral and Educational Improvement of the Colored People, 103
Banneker, Benjamin, 164
Baptist Church, 12, 25
Barnes, William H., 104
Baxter, D. M., 181
Baxter, Richard, 2, 6
Beckett, J. W., 81
Beecher, Henry Ward, 60, 179
Bethel Literary and Historical Association, 98
Bishop, Anna Steward, xiv, 212n
Bishop, William H., 102-3
The Black Bourgeoisie (E. Franklin Frazier), 61
The Black Jacobins (C. L. R. James), 166
Black Reconstruction, 161
Blaine, James G., 86, 87
Blyden, Edward, 107
Bradwell, Charles L., 25
British Methodist Episcopal Church, 39, 100, 191n
Brooklyn, N.Y.
  black religious activities in, 59-60
  Bridge Street Church in, 57, 59-67, 92, 132
  class conflict among blacks in, 60-62
  housing discrimination in, 59
  school segregation in, 65, 196n
Brown, Andrew, 41
Brown, Hallie Q., 173
Brown, H. J., 103
Brown, J. M., 36, 37, 53-55, 75, 190n
Brown, John, 62, 96
Brown, John M., 20-21
Brown, William Wells, 165
Brownsville, Texas, 152-53, 155
Bruce, Blanche Kelso, 111

Bruce, Roscoe Conklin, 177
Brunswick, Ga., 27
Burke, Mr., 34-35
Burns, Robert, 2
Burt, Andrew W., 141
Burt, A. S., 124-25, 134-35
Burton, G. H., 116
Butchart, Ronald, 13
Butler, Benjamin F., 37, 96
Butler, Matthew, 107

Cain, Richard H., 11, 17, 28, 33
  as African Methodist Episcopal Church bishop, 34, 74-75
  dispute with Theophilus Gould Steward, 20-24
  on education of freedmen, 19
  funeral of, 96
  on lack of funding for Southern missionaries, 21
  on white Methodist recruitment efforts in Georgia, 35
Camden, Del., 48-49
Camilla, Ga., 29, 31-32
Campbell, Jabez P., 9, 35, 39, 77, 88, 100
Campbell, Tunis, 31
Campbell, William, 35-37
Cardoza, Francis L., 96
Cardoza, Thomas, 15
Carleton, Mont., 122
Carroll, Lewis, 86
Catholic Church, 64-65, 139
"The Causes Which Retard the Moral, Material and Educational Progress of the Colored People of the United States" (Theophilus Gould Steward), 107
Chambers, Sergeant, 119
Champney, Sarah H., 27, 29-30, 32
Chappelle, Archbishop, 138
Charleston, S.C., 11, 23, 28
Charleston Love Story (Theophilus Gould Steward), 134
Chase, W. Calvin, 99, 108
Chattanooga, Tenn., 130
Civil and Political Rights Association, 31
Civil War, 9
Clark, Peter, 86
Cleveland, Grover, 87, 196n

Coker, Daniel, 99
Colfax, Schuyler, 31
"The Colored American as a Soldier" (Theophilus Gould Steward), 122
"Colored American Women" (Susan Smith McKinney-Steward), 163
Colored Infantry, U.S. (25th Division), xiii, 1
  at Fort Niobrara, 147-55
  at Fort Reno, 153
  mobilized for Spanish-American War, 126
  in Philippines, 134, 136-44
  and racism in South, 130, 131-32
  in Texas, 151-52
  Theophilus Gould Steward as chaplain of, 111-13, 116-20, 122-34
Colored Methodist Episcopal Church, 12, 39, 41
Colored National Labor Union, 104
The Colored Regulars (Theophilus Gould Steward), 135-36, 158, 166
"Colored Society" (Theophilus Gould Steward), 61
"The Coming of the Prince" (Theophilus Gould Steward), 175
The Competitor, 170, 172
Condol, Nathan T., 11
"Confirmation" (Theophilus Gould Steward), 83
Coppin, Fanny Jackson, 4, 66, 70-71, 104
Coppin, Levi Jenkins, 44, 46, 71, 92, 135, 148
Cornish, Samuel E., 60
Cotton States and International Exposition Company, 118
Cousin, Robert, 59
"Covenanting With God" (Theophilus Gould Steward), 56
Crayton, Thomas, 26
Crogman, William H., 169
Cromwell, John W., 94, 99, 108
Cromwell, Oliver, 1
Crummell, Alexander, 7, 92, 125, 126
Cuthbert, Ga., 27
Cutler, Annie, 92

Daffin, Sallie, 19
Dallas, John T., 125

Darwin, Charles, 88
Davis, Jefferson, 143
Davis, Varina, 143
Davis, W. H., 81
Day, William Howard, 179
Death, Hades and Resurrection (Theophilus Gould Steward), 88
"Death and Life" (Theophilus Gould Steward), 56
De Boer, Clara, 10, 18, 187n
Delaware
  black education in, 46-48, 55, 79-80
  disfranchises blacks, 47
  racism in, 56
  Republican Party in, 47, 55, 57
  status of blacks in, 55-56
  white violence toward blacks in, 47
Delaware Association for the Moral Improvement and Education of Colored People, 47
Democratic Party
  attacked by Theophilus Gould Steward, 87
  fails to attract black voters, 86-87
  and school segregation in Delaware, 79
  wins black support in Philadelphia, 85-86
Derrick, W. B., 54
Dickerson, W. F., 75
Diggs, James R. L., 161
Divine Attributes (Theophilus Gould Steward), 88
"The Doctrine of Prayer" (Theophilus Gould Steward), 77-78
Dodge, Grace, 149
Dorsey, Charles H., 60, 65
Douglass, Frederick, 92, 93-94, 164, 179
  on attendance at Washington's Metropolitan African Methodist Episcopal Church, 96-97
  endorses Theophilus Gould Steward for chaplaincy of Colored Infantry division, 111
  marriage to Helen Pitts criticized, 97
  as minister to Haiti, 98, 166
  My Bondage and Freedom, 165
  on race relations in Delaware, 48
  secular reform style criticized, 96-97
  supports Grover Cleveland, 87
  and woman suffrage, 40
Douglass, Lewis, 129

Downing, George T., 86
Du Bois, W. E. B., 62, 161, 165, 167
  on Americanization, 164, 172-73
  denounces American racism, 170
  on education, 154
  eulogizes Susan Smith McKinney-Steward,
    173
  on First Universal Race Conference, 163
  The Gift of Black Folk, 166
  and segregation, 126
  supports black staff for Tuskegee veterans
    hospital, 179
  urges blacks to support World War I,
    168-69
Dunbar, Paul Laurence, 170
Dunbar-Nelson, Alice, 170
Duncan, Clara, 11, 18
Dunning, William A., 161

Eddy, Hiram, 28
Eddy, Joshua P. B., 76
Education
  at black colleges, 159
  of blacks, 4-5, 46-48, 55, 64, 65, 71, 73,
    75, 79-80, 102-4, 122
  of freedmen, 13-15, 17-19, 27-28, 29-30
  industrial, 154-55
  military, 154-55
  in the Philippines, 139, 141-42
Embry, J. C., 90, 102
*The End of the World; or, Clearing the Way
  for the Fullness of Gentiles* (Theophilus
  Gould Steward), 90-91, 131, 138, 169,
  175, 188n
England, 161
Evolution, 88-89

Fauset, Jessie, 166
Felts, C. C., 82, 83
Fenwick, Lord John, 1
Ferris, William H., 167
Finch, Professor, 160
First Universal Race Conference, 163
Fort Brown, Texas, 152-53, 155
Fort Missoula, Mont., 111-13, 116-20,
  122-27
Fort Niobrara, Neb., 145, 147-52

Fort Riley, Kans., 149, 152
Fortune, Timothy Thomas, 79, 92
  on politics, 86, 87
  on racism at West Point, 125
  supports black migration to the
    Philippines, 144
  urges recruitment of blacks by U.S. Army,
    136
France, 162, 168
Frankfort, Penn., 75-77
Franklin, Vincent P., 5
Frazier, E. Franklin, 61
Freedmen
  aid for during Reconstruction, 9-11
  character of, 23
  and colonization efforts, 28
  denied jury service, 30-31
  denominational conflicts over, 25, 35-36,
    38-39
  education of, 13-15, 17-19, 27-28, 29-30,
    48
  inadequate food supplies for, 14, 16
  Independence Day celebrations of, 26
  missionary work for, 9-24
  morality of, 52
  political activities of, 28
  protest compulsory labor contracts, 31
  and religion, 12, 26, 30, 186n
  respond positively to black northerners, 41
  support Ulysses S. Grant, 32
  Theophilus Gould Steward on morality of,
    52
  violence against, 29, 31-32
  See also African-Americans; Integration;
    Reconstruction; Segregation
Freedmen's Savings Bank, 32-33
Free Love, 62-63
Freeman, A. N., 60
The French Revolution in San Domingo
  (Theodore Lothrop Stoddard), 166
*From 1864 to 1914: Fifty Years in the Gospel
  Ministry* (Theophilus Gould Steward), xiv,
  6, 176

Gadsden, Elizabeth
  See Steward, Elizabeth Gadsden
Gadsden, Martha, 95
Galloway, John W., 138

Garlington, E. A., 153
Garnet, Henry Highland, 7, 60, 64, 65, 92, 179
Garnet, Sarah, 65, 149, 163
Garrison, William Lloyd, 179
Garvey, Marcus, 167, 177
Genesis Re-read (Theophilus Gould Steward), 89-90, 188n
Georgia
    African Methodist Episcopal Church successes in, 41
    black political participation in, 30-32
    election fraud in, 31-32
    freedmen's schools in, 27-28
    Ku Klux Klan violence in, 31
    legislature refuses to seat black representatives, 31
    Reconstruction violence in, 29, 31-32, 37
    Redemption in, 31-32
"Georgia: The Situation," 32
Gibbs, J. C., 28
Gibson, Malachi, 104
The Gift of Black Folk (W. E. B. Du Bois), 166
Good, W. T., 154
Goodwin, Daniel R., 76
Gould, Abijah, 6
Gould, Benjamin, 1, 3
Gould, Elijah, 3
Gould, Mary Steward, 163
Gould, Phoebe Bowen, 3
Gould, Theodore, 45, 46, 83, 95
Gouldtown, A Very Remarkable Settlement of Ancient Date (Theophilus Gould Steward and William Steward), 165, 166
Gouldtown, N.J., 1-2, 4, 5, 165
Gouldtown Literary and Moral Improvement Society, 5
Grant, I. S., 106
Grant, Ulysses S., 9, 31, 32, 47, 96, 180
Gregg, John A., 180
Grimké, Archibald H., 170
Grimké, Francis J., 73, 108-9, 111, 165, 169, 170

Haiti
    African Methodist Episcopal Church in, 49-51, 53-55

blacks urged to immigrate to, 193n
    as centerpiece of black civilization, 63-64
    Frederick Douglass as minister to, 98, 166
    Theophilus Gould Steward on, 51-52, 165-66
    U.S. government distrust of blacks in, 179
The Haitian Revolution (Theophilus Gould Steward), 165-66
Hall, John, 10
Hall, Thomas I., 104
Hand Book of Theology Designed for Young Ministers of the African Methodist Episcopal Church Who Have Not Had the Benefit of a Theological Training and as a Pocket Manual for all Ministers (Theophilus Gould Steward), 40
Handy, James A., 10, 54
Harding, Warren G., 179
Harris, John Hobbs, 168
Harrison, Benjamin, 98, 111
Harvard University, 177
Hawkinsville, Ga., 29
Hayes, Rutherford B., 69
Hearst, William Randolph, 129
Henderson, J. M., 101-2
Henry, Thomas T., 85
Highgate, Edmonia G., 14
Hill, Washington, 49
Hilles, William, 47
History of Negro Soldiers in the Spanish-American War (Edward A. Johnson), 134
Holly, James Theodore, 51, 52, 54, 63-64, 193n
Hose, Sam, 134
"How the Colored Man Sees the War" (Theophilus Gould Steward), 168
Hoyt, R. W., 151
Hunter, Hazikiah, 14
Hunter, H. H., 14
Hunter, W. H., 43

The Incarnation of the Son of God (Theophilus Gould Steward), 77
Independence Day, 26
Indians, 124
Inskip, John, 72
"The Inspiration of the Scriptures" (Theophilus Gould Steward), 89

Institute for Colored Youth, 4, 71, 73
Integration, 61-62, 64, 80, 126, 172-73
    See also Racism; Segregation
Is America Safe For Democracy? (William
    McDougall), 177
Italy, 162

Jackson, Robert, 59
Jackson, Thomas H., 54, 88, 161
James, C. L. R., 166
Jefferson, P. W., 75
Jenifer, J. T., 84, 158
Johnson, Andrew, 41
Johnson, Edward A., 134
Johnson, Jack, 164
Johnson, James H. A., 10, 12, 99, 102
Johnson, James W., 170
Johnson, William, 64
Jones, Ellen, 59
Jones, Eugene K., 170
Jones, S. B., 72
Jones, Willis, 59
The Journal of Negro History, 160-61
July 4th, 26

Kershaw, A. J., 101
King, Samuel G., 85-86
Ku Klux Klan, 30-31, 41, 149, 177

Langston, John Mercer, 166
Lassen, Helen S., 173
Latimer, Lewis H., 60
Laws, William J., 158
Lecciones de Lenguajie, 141
Le Conte, Joseph, 77
Lee, Benjamin F., 84, 95, 100, 102, 151, 180
    on finances of African Methodist Episco-
        pal Church, 94
    oratorical style of, 101
    reviews The End of the World; or, Clearing
        the Way for the Fullness of Gentiles, 91
    on Theophilus Gould Steward's Baltimore
        preaching, 106-7
    urges public financial support for Mt.
        Pisgah Church, 107
Leigh, C. C., 10

Letters From a Selfmade Merchant To His
    Sons, 149
Lewis, John E., 131
Lincoln, Abraham, 32, 62, 96, 180
Logan, John, 87
Long, Jefferson, 31, 41
"The Lord's Day" (Theophilus Gould
    Steward), 118
Lovering, Lt. Colonel, 153
Lowe, Ramona, xiv
Lowell, A. Laurence, 177
Lumpkin, Ga., 26, 29, 33
Lynch, James, 10, 21, 35
Lynch, John R., 111, 161
Lynching, 167
Lyons, Judson W., 136
Lyons, Maritcha R., 65

McCleary, J. B., 134
McDougall, William, 177
McIntosh County, Ga., 31
McKibbin, Major, 119
McKinley, William, 129, 133, 135, 136
McKinney, Susan Smith, 57, 60, 64
    marriage to Theophilus Gould Steward,
        120
    See also McKinney-Steward, Susan Smith
McKinney, William, 120
McKinney-Steward, Susan Smith, xiii, 127,
    132, 136, 145, 149, 153, 155
    attends First Universal Race Conference,
        163
    death of, 173-74
    discrimination against in Xenia, Ohio, 164
    Fort Niobrara work of, 148
    photograph of, 121
    travels in Europe, 161-63
    work at Wilberforce University, 135
    See also McKinney, Susan Smith
Macon, Ga.
    African Methodist Episcopal Church in,
        35-37, 37-38, 78
    black community in, 29
    church ownership disputed in, 34-39
    Freedmen's Savings Bank in, 32-33
    freedmen's schools in, 28, 29
    Independence Day celebrations in, 26
    Reconstruction in, 31, 37

Turner Lyceum in, 28
Malcolm, Thomas S., 49-50, 53
Marietta, Ga., 41
Marion, S.C., 17-20
Marriage, 62-63
Masten, Sallie, 43
The Memoirs of Mrs. Steward (Theophilus Gould Steward), 71-72
Merritt, Wesley, 123
Methodist Episcopal Church, 12, 55-56, 64
Methodist Episcopal Church, North, 35, 38-39
Methodist Episcopal Church, South, 12, 34-39
Meynier, Count, 164
Miles, W. H., 39
Milford, Del., 56
Miller, Kelly, 172
Milton, John, 2, 4
Minneapolis, Minn., 136
Miscegenation
  among Flathead Indians, 124
  in Haiti, 52
  in New Jersey, 1-2
  in Ohio, 164
  in the Philippines, 143
Mississippi, 30
Missoula, Mont., 122, 124, 126-27, 150
Mitchell, John G., 84
Mitchell, Samuel, 84
"The Modern Controversy Science and Religion" (Theophilus Gould Steward), 89
Montana
  blacks in, 122
  black soldiers at Fort Missoula, 111-13, 116-20, 122-27
  educational system in, 122
  miscegenation among Flathead Indians in, 124
  race relations in, 152
Moore, William, 7, 34
Moorland, Jesse E., 170, 172
Morris, A. E., 161
Mossell, Charles W., 55
Moton, Robert R., 172
My Bondage and Freedom (Frederick Douglass), 165
Myers, Isaac, 102-3, 104, 105

My First Four Years in the Itineracy of the African Methodist Episcopal Church (Theophilus Gould Steward), 6, 63

National Association for the Advancement of Colored People (NAACP), 167, 175
National Christian Home Guard, 105
National Freedmen Aid Association, 10
National Freedmen's Aid and Southern Educational Society, 149
Native Americans, 124
Nebraska, 145, 147-52
The Negro in Our History (Carter G. Woodson), 160-61
The Neighbor (N. S. Shaler), 177
New Jersey, 1-2, 30
New Jersey Equal Rights League, 10
"A New Reading of an Old Phrase: The End of the World" (Theophilus Gould Steward), 91
Newton, Ga., 29-30
Nicholson, W. R., 91
Northrup, Solomon, 164

"The Ocean Paths" (Theophilus Gould Steward), 159
Ohio, 164
"On Being Fourscore" (Theophilus Gould Steward), 179
Origin of the Species (Charles Darwin), 88
"Other People's Children" (Theophilus Gould Steward), 78
Ottenheimer, Mr., 30
Our Country (Josiah Strong), 90
Overton, Stephen, 59
Owens, Chandler, 167-68

Parent Home and Foreign Missionary Society, 20, 54
Park, Robert Ezra, 168
Paterno, Pedro A., 142
Payne, Daniel A., 7, 71, 92
  on 1888 African Methodist Episcopal General Conference delegates, 100

criticizes women's rights activism in African Methodist Episcopal churches, 40
and denunciation of Southern clergy, 108-9
encourages financial support for Wilberforce University, 76
and missionary work, 9-11, 15-16
opposes African Methodist Episcopal merger with British Methodist Episcopal Church, 100
opposes African Methodist Episcopal missions secretary, 106
supports Booker T. Washington, 205n
supports ritualism in African Methodist Episcopal Church services, 101
and Tawawa Theological, Scientific, and Literary Association, 88
and Theophilus Gould Steward, 19-20, 50, 75, 89
Payne Theological Seminary, 159, 161, 180
Payton, James H., 78
Penn, J. Garland, 118
Pennsylvania, 92
See also Philadelphia
Penrose, C. W., 152
Perkins, Linda, 13, 18
Perry, Rufus, 65
Philadelphia
African Methodist Episcopal Church camp meetings in, 82-83
African Methodist Episcopal Zion mission in, 67, 69-75
black community in, 70-71
black education in, 71, 73
black police officers appointed in, 86
blacks challenge Republican Party in, 85-86
racism in, 85
Union African Methodist Episcopal Church in, 80-83, 92
Philippines
American occupation of, 129, 134, 136-44
American racism in, 137-38, 147
education in, 139, 141-42
independence movement in, 142-43
miscegenation in, 143
religion in, 138-39
status of women in, 137, 138, 141

Theophilus Gould Steward's ministry in, 137-44
Phillips, Wendell, 96
Pierce, John, 1
Pierce, Peter, 1
Piercetown, N.J., 1
Pilgrim's Progress (John Bunyan), 2
Pitts, Helen, 97
"A Plea for Patriotism" (Theophilus Gould Steward), 132
Prioleau, George W., 130, 131, 132, 133
Proctor, Redford, 111
"The Proper Attitude of the Colored People in the Next National Election" (Theophilus Gould Steward), 64
Prostitution, 120, 148, 151
Protestant Episcopal Church Divinity School, 40, 72
Purvis, Robert, 85

Quarles, John F., 86
"Questions for 1888" (Theophilus Gould Steward), 98

Racism
and African Methodist Episcopal Church, 106
of Americans in the Philippines, 137-38
among white book critics, 166
at Harvard University, 177
at West Point, 124-25
Booker T. Washington on, 165
in Delaware, 47, 56
denounced by W. E. B. Du Bois, 170
during 1890s, 122, 125
in education, 4-5
in employment, 7
and freedmen's school teachers, 18
in North, 144
in Ohio, 164
in Philadelphia, 85
and race riots of 1919, 169-70
and Southern lynchings, 167
as subject of interracial national convention, 80
in Texas, 152-53, 155
in the Philippines, 147

toward black soldiers in South, 130, 131-32
in United States, 147
in U.S. Army, 112-13, 116, 168, 170
in U.S. government, 179
of white Christians, 56, 64-65
See also Integration; Segregation
Rainey, Joseph H., 87
Ramson, R. C., 158
Randolph, A. Philip, 167-68
Randolph, B. F., 28
Ray, Peter W., 60
Reason, Charles L., 60, 65
Reconstruction
   aid for freedmen during, 9-11
   black church ownership disputed during, 34-39
   black political activities during, 30-32
   black school funding during, 48
   and Compromise of 1877, 69
   disfranchisement of whites during, 30
   food scarcities during, 26
   historians of, 161
   hostility to northerners during, 27
   Independence Day celebrations during, 26
   intimidation of freedmen's school teachers during, 18
   jury service denied blacks during, 30-31
   presidential policies aid Ku Klux Klan during, 41
   violence in Georgia during, 29, 31-32, 37
Redpath, James, 50
Religion
   in Gouldtown, N.J., 2, 4
   Rebecca Gould Steward on, 4, 6
   theory of evolution challenges, 88-89
Religion and Science (Joseph Le Conte), 77
Republican Party
   appoints black officeholders, 85-86
   black dissatisfaction with, 69, 85-87
   in Delaware, 47, 55, 57, 79-80
Richardson, W. T., 14
"Ripeness in the Gospel Ministry" (Theophilus Gould Steward), 83
The Rising Tide of Color (Theodore Lothrop Stoddard), 175
Ritner, J. Newton, 124
Robinson, A. A., 78
Robinson Crusoe (Daniel Defoe), 2

Rockwell, John A., 27
Roosevelt, Franklin D., 69
Roosevelt, Theodore, 136, 147, 150-51, 153
Russwurm, John, 60

The Saints' Everlasting Rest (Richard Baxter), 2, 6
Salter, Moses B., 25
Saulsbury, Gove, 46
Savannah, Ga., 29
Scarborough, Sarah C. Bierce, 90
Scarborough, William S., 158-59, 161, 164, 172, 173
Scott, Emmett J., 136, 170
Scott, R. K., 14
Scottron, Samuel, 60
Searle, George M., 89
Seaton, Jacob A., 104
Segregation
   of freedmen's school teachers, 18
   of schools, 48-49, 65, 73, 79-80, 99, 196n
   of trains, 130
   of U.S. Army, 170
   in U.S. government, 179
   See also Integration; Racism
Shakespeare, William, 2, 4
Shaler, N. S., 177
Shorter, James A., 57
Shorter Charles H., 100
Sibley, C. C., 28
"The Sling and the Stone," 39-40
Smalls, Robert, 26, 93-94, 161
Smith, C. S., 84
Smith, Joseph H., 6
Smith, T. Clay, 144
Smith, William, 86
"Some Glimpses of Antebellum Negro Literature" (Theophilus Gould Steward), 164
South Carolina
   African Methodist Episcopal Church in, 10-24
   black political participation in, 30
   black religious practices in, 23
   church membership in, 11-12
   Unitarian Church establishes libraries in, 17

Spanish-American War, 126, 129, 131, 151, 169
Spenser, Alvin, 59
Springtown, N.J., 2
Stanford, A. L., 16
Stanton, Edwin C., 12
Stevens, Thaddeus, 96
Steward, Adah
  photograph of, 178
Steward, Alice, 3
Steward, Austin, 164
Steward, Benjamin, 124, 149
  photograph of, 178
Steward, Charles, 96, 124, 125, 180
  photograph of, 178
Steward, Elizabeth Gadsden, 21, 24, 25, 26, 27, 33, 37, 50, 53, 77, 81, 112, 155
  death of, 118
  and death of mother, 95
  death of son, 65
  marriage to Theophilus Gould Steward, 17
  photograph of, 115
  pregnancy of, 34
  supports family move to Montana, 111
Steward, Frank, 96, 124, 125, 133, 150-51, 177, 179, 180
  photograph of, 178
Steward, Garfield W., 165
Steward, Gustavus, 125, 127, 142, 155, 177, 178
Steward, James, 3, 6, 73, 118, 190n
Steward, Margaret, 3
Steward, Mary, 3
Steward, Rebecca Gould, 16, 176
  biography of, 3-4
  death of, 71
  influence on Theophilus Gould Steward, 71-72, 88, 118
  religious skepticism of, 4
Steward, Stephen, 3, 5, 65, 154
Steward, Susan Smith McKinney
  See McKinney, Susan Smith; McKinney-Steward, Susan Smith
Steward, Theophilus Bolden, 124-25, 163, 170, 173, 175
  photograph of, 178

Steward, Theophilus Gould
  on advantages for blacks in U.S. Army, 154-55
  and African Methodist Episcopal Church, 35-41, 43-46, 49-51, 64, 73-75, 78, 83-85, 98-102, 106, 151, 157-58
  and Aged Minister Association, 105
  on all-white juries, 30-31
  on Americanization, 170, 172-73
  on Andrew Johnson's Reconstruction policies, 41
  and Annie Cutler, 92
  applies for position at West Point, 124-25
  and attacks on Southern clergy, 107-9, 109
  attends First Universal Race Conference, 163
  in Baltimore, 99, 102, 104, 106-7, 109
  belief in capitalism of, 162
  biography of, xiii-xiv
  as bishopric candidate, 100
  black attitudes toward, 29, 41
  on black education, 64-65
  on black emigration to Africa, 28, 73, 107
  on black equality, 164
  and black industrial exhibitions, 104
  on black literature, 164-65
  on black music, 57
  on blacks as world leaders, 90, 138
  on black self-labeling, 173
  on black sexuality, 159-60
  on blacks in South, 106
  on blacks in World War I, 167-69
  on blacks' status in America, 61-62
  and Booker T. Washington, 154
  and Bridge Street Church, 60-61, 132
  and Brownsville, Texas, race riot, 153-54
  and "Buy a Book Movement," 166-67
  on Catholic Church, 64-65, 139
  challenges Anglo-Saxon superiority, 90
  as chaplain to 25th U.S. Colored Infantry, 111-13, 116-20, 122-34
  on character of freedmen, 23
  childhood of, 3-6
  on children's rights, 84-85
  class pretensions of, 29, 74-75, 81
  on Grover Cleveland and Democratic Party, 87
  criticism of, 19-20, 78

Steward, Theophilus Gould (cont.)

criticizes African Methodist Episcopal Church, 176
criticizes Booker T. Washington, 165
criticizes Henry M. Turner, 105
on dark-skinned blacks, 177
death of, 180-81
and death of Elizabeth Gadsden Steward, 118
and death of James Steward, 118
and death of son, 65
and death of Susan Smith McKinney-Steward, 173-74
and death of Walter Steward, 149-50
Delaware ministry of, 43-50, 55-57, 77-80
dependence on white benefactors, 111, 125
disapproves of church ostentation, 66, 70
and Frederick Douglass, 96-98
education of, 5, 7, 43, 62, 63, 72, 75
establishes lecture series in Brooklyn, N.Y., 63
establishes Turner Lyceum, 28
in Europe, 161-63
on European race relations, 161-62
family history of, 1-2
financial difficulties of, 15-16, 20-22, 24, 27-28, 33, 53-54, 69, 75, 95, 112, 158-59
and Freedmen's Savings Bank, 32-33
fundraising activities of, 82, 93-95, 105
on God and man, 45
on Haitian revolution, 165-66
on Haitians, 51-52
on Harvard University's denial of dormitory space to blacks, 177
health of, 15-16, 107, 108, 119, 151, 152, 154, 157, 163, 173, 177, 180
on health of black Americans, 123
on incarnation, 117
on industrial education, 154-55
on integration, 61-62, 64, 80, 126, 172-73
on John Wesley's contribution to African Methodism, 102
joins American Negro Academy, 126
leaves itineracy, 109-10

lectures on Philippines to American audiences, 143
on liberty, 166
lobbies for black presence at Chicago World's Fair of 1893, 117-18
on lynching, 167
on marriage, 62-63
marries Elizabeth Gadsden, 17
marries Susan Smith McKinney, 120
and Methodist Episcopal Church, North, 38-39
military career of, 155
millennial views of, 91
as minister, 6-7, 22-23, 59-67, 67, 69-75, 75-77, 80-83, 92-100, 107, 145, 147-52
on ministerial hospitality, 78-79
on miscegenation among Flathead Indians, 124
and missionary work, 10-24, 25-51, 73
on morality of freedmen, 52
on National Association for the Advancement of Colored People, 175
and National Christian Home Guard, 105
in Nebraska, 147-49
on need for government welfare jobs, 123
oratorical style of, 101
as parent, 103, 142, 180
patriotism of, 132-36, 147, 154-55, 164, 167
on Philippines as haven for American blacks, 144
Philippine service of, 137-44
photographs of, 114, 140, 171, 178
physical activity of, 149
political activities of, 30-32, 47-48, 79-80, 87
on prayer, 77-78
preaching style of, 44-45
prohibited from attending Atlanta Exposition, 118
"race first" philosophy of, 177, 179
and race relations, 28
and racial uplift, 119
racial views of, 124
on racism, 56, 64-65, 80, 130, 144-45, 170, 172-73
Rebecca Gould Steward's influence on, 4, 6, 71-72, 88, 118
on redemption in Georgia, 32

refused dining service in Missoula, Mont., 124
removed from active military duty, 154
requests U.S. Army promotion, 150-51
resigns as missionary to Haiti, 53-55
and Richard H. Cain, 20-24
and schools in the Philippines, 139, 141-42
on science and religion, 89
seeks information on French Army, 163-64
seeks U.S. Army commission for Frank Steward, 133
on segregation, 65, 73
sermons of, 13, 25, 36-38, 41, 50-51, 56, 67, 73, 77, 87, 92
and Spanish-American War, 127-36
on Benjamin T. Tanner, 66
temperance work of, 82, 99, 113, 116-17, 119, 137, 148, 151
in Texas, 152-54
theology of, 25, 40, 72, 88-91, 175-76
on true womanhood, 56-57
and Tuskegee veterans hospital, 179
on use of federal troops as strikebreakers, 123
vacations, 66-67
on violent social change, 172
on war, 131, 169
wears military uniform, 157
white attitudes toward, 17-18, 29
on white Methodists, 176
and white Montanans, 122
white reviewers snub writings of, 166
on white superiority, 122-23
and Wilberforce University, 76-78, 83-84, 155, 157-61, 163
on wine drinking in France, 162
on woman suffrage, 40
on women, 160
on Carter G. Woodson, 160-61
writings of, 39-40, 56, 61-63, 71-72, 77, 78, 88-91, 122, 130, 134-35, 143, 164, 165-67, 175-76

Steward, Walter, 117, 127, 145, 149-50, 212n

Steward, William, 3, 6, 17, 18, 19, 154, 165, 180, 192n
Stewart, T. McCants, 86
Still, Mary, 14, 15
Still, William, 85, 87, 92
Stoddard, Theodore Lothrop, 166, 175
The Story of the Gospel, 117
Strong, Josiah, 90
Summerville, S.C., 16
Sumner, Charles, 62, 96, 179
Sunday Schools, 4
Supreme Court, U.S., 86
Sussex County, Del., 55-56

Taft, William Howard, 142, 143, 144, 148
Tanner, Benjamin T.
and African Methodist Episcopal Church, 12, 45, 49-51, 53-55, 64, 74
on need for Methodist unity, 38-39
opposes Spanish-American War, 129
theology of, 88
and Theophilus Gould Steward, 23, 39, 56, 62-63, 70, 72, 73, 91, 92
Theophilus Gould Steward on, 66
Tate, Mr., 152
Tawawa Theological, Scientific, and Literary Association, 88
Temperance, 82, 99, 113, 116-17, 119, 137, 148, 151
Terrell, Mary Church, 98, 172
Terrell, Robert H., 172
Texas, 152-55
Thomas, William Hannibal, 159, 160
Tilden, Samuel, 69
Townsend, J.M., 99
Trotter, Monroe, 86, 165
Tucker, Miles, 85
Turner, Henry M., 28, 66, 75
and African Methodist Episcopal Church, 34, 101, 105
on education for freedmen, 30
and Freedmen's Savings Bank, 33
in Georgia legislature, 31
ordains female preacher, 40
praises Theophilus Gould Steward's theology, 88
religious nationalism of, 91

selected to write history of African
    Methodism, 158
Turner Lyceum, 28, 32
Tuskegee, Ala., 179
Twain, Mark, 54

Underground Railroad, 2, 60
Unitarian Church, 17
Universal Negro Improvement Association,
    177
Up From Slavery (Booker T. Washington),
    165

Valentine, Neb., 148, 149, 151-52
Vanderhorst, Richard H., 39, 41
Vann, Robert L., 170
"Venerable names in the Philippines"
    (Theophilus Gould Steward), 143
Vesey, Denmark, 10
"The Virility of the American Negro"
    (Theophilus Gould Steward), 159

Walter Hall Steward Memorial Fund, 161
Wanamaker, John, 111
Ward, T. M. D., 39
Warren, Joseph, 104
Washington, Booker T., 92, 98, 118, 136,
    170, 173
    on black intellectuals, 165
    and Brownsville, Texas, race riot, 153
    denounced by African Methodist Episcopal
        Church, 205n
    on industrial education, 154
    on poorly educated Southern clergy, 107-9
    and Theophilus Gould Steward, 126, 165
    visits White House, 147
    on World War I, 168
Washington, D.C.
    Bethel Literary and Historical Association
        in, 98
    black community in, 93, 99
    church competition in, 94
    Metropolitan African Methodist Episcopal
        Church in, 92-98, 99-100
    Mt. Pisgah Church in, 107
    school system in, 96

segregation in, 99
Wayman, Alexander W., 13, 21, 23, 77, 78
Wears, Isaiah C., 112
Welch, I. H., 101
Wells-Barnett, Ida B., 167
Wesley, John, 102
Westchester County, N.Y., 2
Wheatley, Phillis, 164
Whipple, George, 9, 14, 15-16
White, George H., 167
Whittenmore, B. F., 17
Wilberforce University, xiii, 53, 90, 95, 100,
    101, 109, 131, 135, 166, 172, 176,
    180, 181
    African Methodist Episcopal Church raises
        money for, 76-77
    bestows honorary doctorate on Theophilus
        Gould Steward, 78
    history of, 158
    presidential search at, 83-84
    salary difficulties at, 158-59
    student unrest at, 158, 159-60
    Theophilus Gould Steward as faculty
        member of, 155, 157-61, 163
Williams, Bert, 172
Williams, George W., 165
Wills, David, 89, 91
Wilmington, Del., 43, 46, 50, 77-80
Wilson, Woodrow, 169, 179
Winder, William H. W., 59
Withington, Mary N., 30
Women
    in African Methodist Episcopal churches,
        40
    denied participation on debating team at
        Wilberforce University, 160
    in Haiti, 52
    Theophilus Gould Steward on, 56-57,
        62-63
    in the Philippines, 137, 138, 141
Women's Christian Temperance Union, 148
    See also Temperance
Women's Mite Society, 55
Woodson, Carter G., 160-61
World War I, 167-69, 175
Wright, Richard R., Jr., 172
Wright, Theodore, 60

Xenia, Ohio, 164

YMCA, 147-49
Young, Charles A., 131, 172
Young, Henry J., 43
Young, Samuel E., 104
Young Men's Christian Association, 147-49